UNIX System
Programming

UNIX System Programming

A programmer's guide to software development

Second edition
Revised and Updated
by Keith Haviland and Dina Gray

Keith Haviland
Andersen Consulting

Dina Gray
at AIT Limited

Ben Salama

An imprint of Pearson Education
Harlow, England • Reading, Massachusetts • Menlo Park, California
New York • Don Mills, Ontario • Amsterdam • Bonn • Sydney • Singapore
Tokyo • Madrid • San Juan • Milan • Mexico City • Seoul • Taipei

PEARSON EDUCATION LIMITED

Head Office:
Edinburgh Gate
Harlow CM20 2JE
Tel: +44 (0)1279 623623
Fax: +44 (0)1279 431059

London Office:
128 Long Acre
London WC2E 9AN
Tel: +44 (0)20 7447 2000
Fax: +44 (0)20 7240 5771

Website: *www.awl.com/cseng*

Second edition first published in Great Britain 1998
First edition published 1987

© Pearson Education Limited 1998

The rights of Keith Haviland, Dina Gray and Ben Salama to be identified as authors of
this work have been asserted by them in accordance with the Copyright, Designs and
Patents Act 1988.

ISBN 0-201-87758-9

British Library Cataloguing in Publication Data
A catalogue record for this book is available from the British Library

Library of Congress Cataloging in Publication Data
Haviland, Keith, 1958-
    UNIX system programming : a programmer's guide to software
    development / Keith Haviland, Dina Gray, Ben Salama. -- 2nd ed. /
    rev. and updated by Keith Haviland and Dina Gray.
        p.   cm.
    Includes bibliographical references and index.
    ISBN 0-201-87758-9
    1. UNIX (Computer file)   2. Operating systems (Computers)
I. Gray, Dina.   II. Salama, Ben, 1954-   . 'III. Title.
QA76.76.063H383   1999
005.4'32--dc21   98-39273
                                                              CIP

10 9 8 7 6 5 4 3

Cover designed by Senate.
Typeset by CRB Associates, Reepham, Norfolk.
Printed and bound in Great Britain by Henry Ling Ltd.

The publishers' policy is to use paper manufactured from sustainable forests.

Preface

The purpose of this book

Since its humble beginnings at Bell Laboratories in 1969, the UNIX Operating System has become increasingly popular, finding favour first in the academic world and then as a de facto standard operating system for a new generation of multi-user micro- and minicomputers in the 1980s. At the time of writing this growth seems set to continue.

So began the first edition of this book in 1987. More than a decade later, UNIX has lived up to its promise and is a key part of the technology landscape as we move into the 21st century. Always strong in the scientific and technical community, there are now many large-scale data management and transaction processing systems built on UNIX platforms, and UNIX of course is at the core of the server backbone of the Internet.

UNIX Systems Programming has also done well, and the first edition has been printed once or twice a year since its first publication. The book has been remarkably resilient, reflecting the standard and enduring nature of the UNIX operating system. However, there now have been sufficient changes to justify a second edition, and we also wanted to cover topics relevant to the more distributed environments typical of IT solutions at the close of the 1990s.

However, our aim with the second edition remains the same as before. We will again concentrate on the programming interface that exists between the UNIX kernel (that part of UNIX which qualifies as an operating system proper) and application software that runs in the UNIX environment. This interface is often called the UNIX system call interface (although the difference between such calls and normal library routines is not as clear as it used to be). As we shall see, such calls are the primitives upon which all UNIX programs – whether supplied along with the operating system or independently developed – are ultimately built. Our target audience consists of programmers with some basic UNIX experience who will be developing UNIX software in the C language. The text will be relevant to developers of systems level software, and applications and business programs – anyone in fact with a serious interest in developing UNIX programs.

Aside from system calls, we shall also consider some of the more important subroutine libraries provided with a UNIX system. These library routines are, obviously, written using system calls and in many cases perform the same action as a system call, but at a higher level or perhaps in a more programmer friendly manner. By exploring both system calls and subroutine libraries we hope that you will get an appreciation of when not to re-invent the wheel, as well as a better understanding of the internal workings of this still elegant operating system.

The X/Open Specification

UNIX has a long history, and there have been many formal and *de facto* standards, and commercial and academic variants. The core of the UNIX system, however – the main focus of this book – has been remarkably stable.

The first edition of *UNIX System Programming* was based on Issue 2 of the AT&T *System V Interface Definition* (SVID), System V being one of the most influential actual software implementations of UNIX. For the second edition, we have largely based the text and examples on the *X/Open Issue 4 Version 2* documents *System Interface Definitions* and *System Interfaces and Headers*, and certain parts of the related *Networking Services* document – all from 1994. For convenience, we will refer to this documentation set as the *XSI* through the book – shorthand for *X/Open System Interfaces*. You should note that we will discuss features related to actual implementations where necessary.

A small amount of background is worthwhile here. X/Open began as a consortium of hardware suppliers with a strong interest in open systems and UNIX as a platform, although membership broadened considerably over time. One of the consortium's major roles was practical UNIX standardization, and its base portability guide (called the *XPG*) was used as the starting point for an initiative by several major vendors (including Sun, IBM, Hewlett-Packard, Novell and the Open Software Foundation), usually known as the **Spec 1170 Initiative**. (The 1170 refers to the number of calls, headers, commands and utilities covered in the exercise!) Its aim was to produce a single, unified specification for UNIX system services, including the system calls that are the heart of this text. The result was a generally practical set of specifications, pulling together many of the conflicting UNIX standard streams, of which the key documents mentioned above are a major part. Other documents produced cover UNIX commands and screen handling.

From a system programming perspective, the *XSI* documents form a pragmatic starting point, and the vast majority of examples in this book should run on the vast majority of current UNIX platforms. This X/Open standard draws together a number of highly relevant and complimentary standards and actual practice. It is derived from ANSI/ISO C standards, the important base *POSIX* standard (IEEE Std 1003.1-1990), the SVID, elements from Open Software Foundation specifications and commonly used routines from the very influential Berkeley UNIX.

Of course standardization is an ongoing process. X/Open and the OSF (Open Software Foundation) merged in 1996 to become **The Open Group**. Recent developments (at the time of writing) from *POSIX* and the field have found their expression in what The Open Group refer to as Version 2 of the *Single UNIX Specification*, which in turn contains Issue 5 of the *System Interface Definitions, System Interfaces and Headers* and *Networking Services*. The important, but generally specialized, extensions here cover areas such as threads, real-time extensions and dynamic linking.

As a final word on a dry subject, note that:

1. Any standard is very broad, covering alternative methods of doing things and rarely used, but still important, functionality. We have concentrated on what we think will give you an excellent grounding in UNIX programming, but have not attempted to be exhaustive from a standards perspective.

2. If formal standards compliance is important to you, then you will need to consider setting (and testing) relevant flags such as _XOPEN_SOURCE or _POSIX_SOURCE in your programs.

Organization of the text

This book is organized as follows:

●   Chapter 1 is a review of some fundamental concepts and basic terminology. The two most important terms discussed are **file** and **process**. We hope that most readers of the book will be familiar with at least some of the material presented here (see the following subsection on prerequisites).

●   Chapter 2 describes the system call primitives for handling files. It covers opening and creating files, reading and writing data to and from files, and random access. We also introduce ways of handling the errors that can be generated by system calls.

●   Chapter 3 is a study of the file in context. Here we look at the issues of file ownership, how file system privileges are managed under UNIX, and how these attributes can be manipulated with system calls.

●   Chapter 4 looks primarily at the UNIX **directory** concept from a programming viewpoint. We also include a short discussion on the underlying structure of the UNIX file store, covering **file systems** and the **special files** used to represent devices.

●   Chapter 5 deals with the fundamental nature and control of UNIX processes. The important system calls fork and exec are introduced, and explained at length. Among the examples is a small **shell** or command processor.

●   Chapter 6 is the first of three on inter-process communication. This chapter covers **signals** and **signal handling**, useful for trapping and communicating abnormal conditions.

●   Chapter 7 looks at that most useful of UNIX inter-process communication techniques, the **pipe**, whereby the output of one program can be coupled to the input of another. We examine creating, reading and writing with pipes, and selection across multiple pipes.

- Chapter 8 deals with inter-process communication techniques that were introduced into UNIX with System V. **Record locking**, **message passing**, **semaphores** and **shared memory** are described here.

- Chapter 9 deals with the terminal at system call level. It includes a major example using **pseudo terminals**.

- Chapter 10 gives a brief discussion of UNIX networking and looks at how **sockets** can be used to send messages from one machine to another.

- Chapter 11 is where we turn away from system calls and start an examination of major library packages. This chapter contains a systematic study of the important **Standard I/O Library**, which offers many more file handling facilities than the system call primitives introduced in Chapter 2.

- Finally, Chapter 12 is a review of miscellaneous system calls and library routines, although many of them are very important to creating real programs. String handling, time functions and memory management are among the topics discussed.

What you need to know

This book is not intended as a general introduction to UNIX or the C language, but as a detailed study of the UNIX system call interface. To make best use of it you should be familiar with the following topics:

- logging into your UNIX system;

- creating files using one of the standard editors provided on your system;

- the tree-like directory structure presented by UNIX;

- basic commands for manipulating files and directories;

- creating and compiling simple C programs (including programs with code held in several source files);

- making simple use of the I/O routines `printf` and `getchar` from within a C program;

- using command line arguments, that is, `argc` and `argv`, within a C program;

- using your system's manual. (Unhappily, it is no longer possible to give absolutely specific advice in this area since the once-standard format of the manual has been rearranged by several manufacturers. The traditional arrangement divides the manual into eight sections, where each section is arranged alphabetically. The first three are of most relevance to us: *Section 1* describes commands; *Section 2* describes system calls; and *Section 3* covers subroutines.)

Those of you who are unhappy with any of these points should limber up with the exercises listed below. If you need more help, the Bibliography at the end of this book should direct you to a suitable text.

One final point: computing is *not* a spectator sport and throughout this book there is a strong emphasis on exercises and examples. Before starting, you should ensure you have access to a suitable UNIX machine.

Exercise P.1   Explain the purpose of the following UNIX commands:

```
ls cat rm cp mv mkdir cc
```

Exercise P.2   Using your favourite editor, create a small text file. Use `cat` to create another file consisting of five repetitions of this.

Using `wc` count the number of characters and words in both. Explain the result. Create a subdirectory and move the two files into this.

Exercise P.3   Create a file containing a directory listing of both your home directory and the directory `/bin`.

Exercise P.4   Devise a single command line which displays the number of users currently logged onto your system.

Exercise P.5   Write, compile and execute a C program that prints a welcoming message of your choice.

Exercise P.6   Write, compile and run a C program that prints its arguments.

Exercise P.7   Using `getchar()` and `printf()`, write a program that counts the number of words, lines and characters in its input.

Exercise P.8   Create a file containing a C subroutine which prints the message 'hello, world'. Create a separate file containing the main program which calls this routine. Compile and execute the resulting program, calling it `hw`.

Exercise P.9   Look up the entries for the following topics in your system's manual: the `cat` command, the `printf` subroutine and the `write` system call.

Changes from the first edition

For those who know the first edition, this section describes specific changes. If this is your first reading, you can safely move on.

The major changes can be summarized as follows:

- We have used the usual ANSI C function prototype technique (with some occasional concessions to readability) to describe the parameters and return values associated with system calls and other functions. For example, the initial definition of `open` in the first edition was:

```
#include <fcntl.h>

int filedes, flags;
char *pathname;
 .
 .
 .
filedes = open (pathname, flags);
```

In the second edition, we have used:

```
#include <sys/types.h>
#include <sys/stat.h>
#include <fcntl.h>

int open (const char *pathname, int flags, [mode_t mode]);
```

- We have used the additional types introduced by UNIX standards activity over the last decade, including:

  ssize_t   to hold size information for files
  mode_t   to hold file mode/permission information
  off_t   to hold offset information for files during random access
  uid_t   to hold a user-id number
  gid_t   to hold a group-id number
  pid_t   to hold the process-id number for a UNIX process

  In older versions of UNIX, and the first edition, various types of integers were typically used instead of the types above, which will usually reduce to integers in actual implementations. The types above do offer higher portability, although maybe at the cost of simplicity and readability.

In terms of changes to chapters:

- Chapter 1 *Basic Concepts and Terminology* is little changed.

- Chapter 2 *The File* is substantially the same, although we have emphasized the use of open over creat, and introduced remove as an alternative to unlink.

- Chapter 3 *The File in Context*. Changes include: introduction of symbolic constants to represent permission values, a brief description of rename and a discussion of symbolic links.

- Chapter 4 *Directories, File Systems and Special Files* has been updated to include a discussion of mkdir, and new routines to access directories. Calls to control file and directory limits have also been introduced.

- Chapter 5 *The Process* has an extended treatment of wait and waitpid, and now covers process groups, sessions and session-ids.

- Chapter 6 *Signals and Signal Handling* has been extensively changed. Instead of signal, the safer sigaction call has been introduced, with an extended treatment of handling signal sets.

- Chapter 7 *Inter-Process Communication Using Pipes*. This was part of Chapter 6 in the first edition, but has been split out for readability. Much of the material has changed little, but a major section on using select to handle multiple pipes has been added.

- Chapter 8 *Advanced Inter-Process Communications* (originally Chapter 7 in the first edition) has had the section on record locking brought up to date. The sections on shared memory, semaphores and messaging have been subject to minor updates.

- Chapter 9 *The Terminal* (originally Chapter 8) has undergone significant change and includes more material on internal kernel structure, and the replacement of the use of ioctl with the more programmer friendly use of termios structures. The major file transfer example has been replaced – for these days of networked machines – with an example based around pseudo terminals.

- Chapter 10 *Sockets* is wholly new, and centres on using sockets across UNIX networks.

- Chapter 11 *The Standard I/O Library* (originally Chapter 9) has had minor updates.

- Chapter 12 *Miscellaneous System Calls and Library Routines* (originally Chapter 11) now includes a section on memory mapped I/O.

- Finally note that the original Chapter 10 from the first edition – which focused on the curses screen handling library – has been gracefully retired in these days of graphical user interfaces.

Acknowledgements

We would like to thank Steve Pate, Nigel Barnes, Andris Nestors, Jason Reed, Phil Tomkins, Colin White, Jo Cowley and Victoria Cave. We would also like to thank Dylan Reisenberger, Steve Temblett and Karen Mosman for their help during the production of the second edition.

We should also thank those who helped with the first edition: Steve Ratcliffe, for reading the many versions of each chapter in the first edition and checking all the *original* program examples; and Jonathan Leffler, Greg Brougham, Dominic Dunlop, Nigel Martin, Bill Fraser-Campbell, Dave Lukes and Floyd Williams for their comments, suggestions and assistance during the preparation of the text.

Contents

CHAPTER 1

Basic concepts and terminology

In this chapter we will briefly review some basic ideas and terminology that we shall make use of throughout this book. We will start by examining the notion of the UNIX **file**.

1.1 The file

Information on a UNIX system is stored in files. Typical UNIX commands that manipulate files include:

   $ *vi my_test.c*

which will invoke the `vi` editor in order to create or edit the file `my_test.c`,

   $ *cat my_test.c*

which will display the contents of `my_test.c` on the terminal, and:

   $ *cc -o my_test my_test.c*

which will invoke the C compiler to generate the program file my_test from the source file my_test.c, assuming, of course, that my_test.c contains no syntactical errors.

Most files will be given some sort of logical structure by the user who created them. A document, for example, will consist of words, lines, paragraphs and pages. To the system, however, all UNIX files actually appear as simple, unstructured sequences of bytes or characters. The file access primitives provided by the system allow individual bytes to be accessed either sequentially or randomly. There are no record or file terminator characters embedded into files and no multiple record types to negotiate.

This simplicity is entirely deliberate and typical of the UNIX philosophy. The UNIX file is a clean, general concept from which more complex and specific structures (such as an indexed file organization) can be developed. Premature detail and special cases have been ruthlessly eliminated. For example, within ordinary text files the newline character (actually ASCII line-feed) that indicates the end of a line of text is, as far as UNIX is concerned, just another character, to be read or written by system utilities and user programs. Only programs that expect their input to be made up of lines need concern themselves with the semantics of the newline character.

Nor does UNIX distinguish between different types of file. A file can contain readable text (such as a shopping list or the paragraph you are reading now) or it can contain 'binary' data (such as the compiled form of a program). In either case the same primitive operations or utilities can be used to manipulate the file. As a corollary of this, you will find none of the formal naming schemes encountered under other operating systems (saying that, however, some programs, such as cc, do follow certain simple naming conventions). UNIX file names are entirely arbitrary, and in SVR4 (System V Release 4) can be 255 characters in length. However, to be truly portable the *XSI* specifies that they should not exceed 14 characters in length – a limit found in early versions of UNIX.

1.1.1 Directories and pathnames

An important concept allied to the file is the **directory**. Directories are collections of files, allowing some logical organization of the information contained on a system. For example, each user normally has his or her own 'home' directory to work in, while commands, system libraries and administrative programs are generally located in their own specific directories. As well as containing files, directories can also contain any number of subdirectories. These in turn can contain their own subdirectories and so on. In fact, directories can be nested to any depth. UNIX files are therefore organized into a hierarchical, tree-like structure where each non-terminal node corresponds to a directory. The top of this tree is a single directory, conventionally called the **root directory**.

We will study the UNIX directory structure in detail in Chapter 4. However, because we will use UNIX files throughout the text, it is worth noting that the full names of UNIX files – called **pathnames** – reflect this tree structure. Each

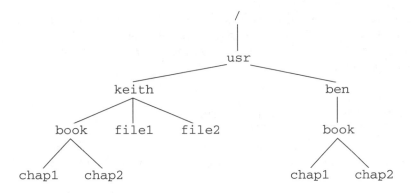

Figure 1.1 *An example directory tree.*

pathname gives the sequence of directories that lead to the file. For example, the pathname:

```
/usr/keith/book/chap1
```

can be dissected as follows: the first '/' character means that the pathname starts at the root directory; that is, this pathname gives the *absolute* location of the file within the file store. Next comes usr, which is a subdirectory within the root directory. The directory keith is another step down and is therefore a subdirectory of /usr. Likewise the directory book is a subdirectory of /usr/keith. The final component, chap1 could equally well be a directory instead of a regular file since directories are identified by the same naming scheme as files. An example directory tree containing this pathname is shown in Figure 1.1.

A pathname that does not begin with a '/' character is called a **relative pathname** and gives the route to the file relative to a user's **current working directory**. For example, the pathname:

```
chap1/intro.txt
```

describes a file intro.txt which is contained in the subdirectory chap1 of the current directory. In the limiting case, a name such as:

```
intro.txt
```

simply identifies the file intro.txt within the current working directory. Again note, that for a program to be *truly* portable, each individual component of a pathname should be limited to 14 characters in length.

1.1.2 Ownerships and permissions

A file is not characterized just by the data it contains: there are a number of other primitive attributes associated with any UNIX file. For example, each file is **owned** by a particular user. Ownership bestows certain rights, one of which is the ability to change another type of file attribute, namely **permissions**. As we shall see in Chapter 3, permissions determine which users can read or write a file, or execute it if it contains a program.

1.1.3 Generalization of the file concept

UNIX extends the file concept to cover not only normal files (**regular files** in UNIX terminology) but also peripheral devices and inter-process communication channels. This means that the same primitive operations can be used to read and write text files, binary files, terminals, magnetic tape units and even main memory. This scheme allows programs to be thought of as general tools, capable of using any type of device. For example:

```
$ cat file > /dev/rmt0
```

is a crude way of writing a file to a tape (the pathname /dev/rmt0 being a common mnemonic for a magnetic tape drive).

1.2 The process

A **process** in UNIX terminology is simply an instance of an executing program. The easiest way to create a process is to give a command to the UNIX command processor or **shell**. For example if a user types:

```
$ ls
```

the shell process that accepts the command will create another process specifically to run the directory listing program ls. Since UNIX is a multitasking system, more than one process can run concurrently. In fact there will be at least one, usually more, for each current user of a UNIX system.

1.2.1 Inter-process communication

UNIX allows concurrent processes to cooperate by using a variety of inter-process communication (IPC) methods.

One such method is the **pipe**. Pipes are normally used to couple the output of one program to the input of another without having to store data in an intermediate file. Again, users can take advantage of this general facility through the shell. The command line:

```
$ ls | wc -l
```

causes the shell to create two processes to run ls and the word count program wc concurrently. It also connects the output of ls to the input of wc. The result is to produce a count of the number of files in the current directory.

Other UNIX inter-process communication facilities include **signals**, which offer an interrupt-based communications model. More advanced facilities include **shared memory** and **semaphores**. In addition **sockets**, normally used for cooperating processes across a network, can also be used for simple IPC between processes on the same machine.

1.3 System calls and library subroutines

In the Preface we said that the primary focus of this book is on the **system call interface**. For some readers of this book, the term **system call** is one that will need further definition.

System calls are in fact the software developer's passport into the UNIX **kernel**. The kernel, which we first met in the Preface, is a single piece of software which is permanently memory-resident and deals with a UNIX system's process scheduling and I/O control. In essence, the kernel is that part of UNIX which qualifies as an operating system proper. All user processes, and all file system accesses, will be resourced, monitored and controlled by the kernel.

System calls are invoked in the same way a programmer would call an ordinary C subroutine or function. For example, data could be read from a file by using the C library subroutine fread as follows:

```
nread = fread(inputbuf, OBJSIZE, numberobjs, fileptr);
```

or the data could be read using the lower-level read system call as follows:

```
nread = read(filedes, inputbuf, BUFSIZE);
```

The essential difference between a subroutine and a system call is that when a program calls a subroutine the code executed is always part of the final object program, even if it was linked in from a library; with a system call the major part of the code executed is actually part of the kernel itself and not the calling program. In other words the calling program is making direct use of the facilities provided by the kernel. The switch between user process and kernel is usually achieved via a software interrupt mechanism.

You should not be surprised to learn that the majority of system calls perform operations on either files or processes. In fact, system calls constitute the fundamental primitive operations associated with both types of object.

In the case of a file these operations may include transferring data to and from the file, randomly seeking through the file or changing the access permissions associated with the file.

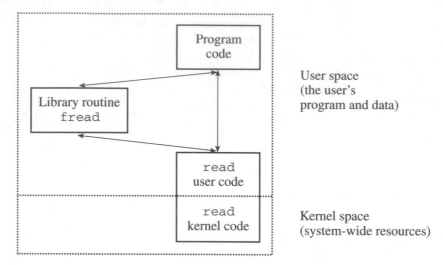

Figure 1.2 *Relationship between program code, a library routine and a system call.*

In the case of processes, the system call operations may create a new process, terminate an existing one, obtain information about the state of a process or establish a communications channel between two processes.

A small number of system calls have nothing to do with either files or processes. Typically, system calls in this category are concerned with system-wide information or control. For example, one system call allows a program to interrogate the kernel to find out its idea of the current date and time; another allows a program to reset these.

As well as the system call interface, UNIX systems also provide extensive libraries of standard subroutines. One very important example is the **Standard I/O Library**. The subroutines contained in this library provide facilities not directly offered by the file access system calls, including formatted conversions and automatic buffering. Although the Standard I/O Library subroutines guarantee efficiency, they ultimately use the system call interface themselves. They should be seen as presenting an extra layer of file access facilities based on system call primitives, not a separate subsystem. The real point here is that any process that interacts with its environment, in however small a way, must make use of system calls at some point.

Figure 1.2 shows the relationship between program code and a library routine, and the relationship between a library routine and a system call. It shows that the library routine `fread` ultimately is an interface to the underlying `read` system call.

Exercise 1.1 Explain the meaning of the following terms:

kernel   system call   C subroutine   process   directory   pathname

---

CHAPTER 2

The file

2.1 UNIX file access primitives

2.1.1 Introduction

In this chapter we will look at the fundamental primitives UNIX provides for handling files from within programs. These primitives consist of a small set of system calls that give direct access to the I/O facilities provided by the UNIX kernel. They form the building blocks for all UNIX I/O, and any other file access mechanism will ultimately be based around them. Their names are listed in Table 2.1. The duplication in functions performed by the various calls represents the evolution of UNIX over the past decade or so.

A typical UNIX program will call `open` (or `creat`) to initialize a file, then use `read`, `write` and `lseek` to manipulate data within that file. If the file is no longer needed by the program, it can call `close` to indicate that it has finished with the file. Finally, if the file is no longer needed by the user then it can be eliminated completely from the operating system by a call to `unlink` or `remove`.

The following trivial program, which simply reads the first part of a file, shows this general structure more clearly. Since it is only an introductory example, we have omitted some normally essential refinements such as error handling. Be warned, for in production programs this kind of omission is bad practice.

Table 2.1 *UNIX primitives*

Name	Meaning
open	Opens a file for reading or writing, or creates an empty file
creat	Creates an empty file
close	Closes a previously opened file
read	Extracts information from a file
write	Places information into a file
lseek	Moves to a specified byte in a file
unlink	Removes a file
remove	Alternative method to remove a file
fcntl	Controls attributes associated with a file

```
/* a rudimentary example program */

/* these header files are discussed below */
#include <fcntl.h>
#include <unistd.h>

main()
{
    int fd;
    ssize_t nread;
    char buf[1024];

    /* open file "data" for reading */
    fd = open("data", O_RDONLY);

    /* read in the data */
    nread = read(fd, buf, 1024);

    /* close the file */
    close(fd);
}
```

The first statement in the example to make use of one of the system call primitives is:

```
fd = open("data", O_RDONLY);
```

This causes the file data, in the current working directory, to be opened for use by the program. The second argument in the call, O_RDONLY, is an integer constant defined in the header file <fcntl.h>, that tells the system to open the file **read only**. In other words, the program will only be able to read the contents of the file, it will not be able to alter the file by writing to it.

The return value from the open call, which is placed into the integer variable fd, is extremely important. If open is successful, fd will contain something called a

file descriptor. A file descriptor is a non-negative integer, whose value is determined by the system. It identifies the open file and is passed as a parameter to the other file access primitives, such as read, write, lseek and close. If the open call fails, it will instead return −1, which is the number returned by almost all system calls to indicate an error. In a real program we would test specially for this value, and take appropriate action if it arose.

Once the file is opened, our example program uses the read system call:

```
nread = read(fd, buf, 1024);
```

This means: take 1024 characters, if possible, from the file identified by fd and place them into the character array buf. The return value nread gives the number of characters actually read, which will normally be 1024, but would be less if the file is smaller than 1024 bytes in length. Like open, if something goes wrong, read will return −1.

The variable nread is of type ssize_t as defined in <sys/types.h>. If you are wondering why this header file was not included in the example it is because some basic types – such as ssize_t – are also defined in <unistd.h>. ssize_t is our first example of various special types defined for making safe use of system calls. It will normally reduce to a base integer type (and indeed in the first edition of this book nread was of type int – an older and somewhat simpler world).

This statement demonstrates another important point: the file access primitives deal in simple, linear sequences of characters or bytes. The read call will not, for example, perform any useful conversions such as translating the character representation of an integer into the form used internally by a computer. Both read (and write for that matter) should not be confused with higher level namesakes in languages such as Fortran or Pascal. read is typical of the philosophy that underlies the system call interface; it performs a single, simple function and provides a building block on which other facilities can be built.

At the end of the example the file is closed with:

```
close(fd);
```

This tells the system that the program has finished with the file associated with fd. It is easy to see that the close call is the inverse of open. Actually, since the program is just about to terminate anyway, the call to close is not really necessary, all open files being automatically closed when a process exits. It is good discipline to use close, however.

This brief example should give you a flavour of the UNIX file access primitives. We will now discuss each of them in greater detail.

2.1.2 The open **system call**

Before an existing file can be read or written it must be opened with the open system call. The text below shows how it is to be used. For clarity and consistency with system documentation, all of our usage sections will use the ANSI C function prototype structure. They will specify the header files in which the actual prototype appears, and in which any useful constants are defined.

Usage
| ```
#include <sys/types.h>
#include <sys/stat.h>
#include <fcntl.h>

int open(const char *pathname, int flags, [mode_t mode]);
``` |

The first argument, `pathname`, is a pointer to a string that contains the pathname of the file to be opened. The value indicated by `pathname` can be an absolute pathname, such as:

```
/usr/keith/junk
```

which gives the location of the file in relation to the root directory. It can also be a relative pathname giving the file's location in relation to the current working directory; for example:

```
keith/junk
```

or simply:

```
junk
```

In the last case, of course, the program would open the file `junk` in the current working directory. In general, whenever a system call or library subroutine takes a filename argument, it will accept any valid UNIX pathname.

The second argument of `open`, called `flags` in our usage description, is of integer type and specifies the access method. The value of `flags` is taken from constants defined in the system include file `<fcntl.h>` by means of the pre-processor directive `#define` (the term `fcntl`, by the way, stands for **file control**). Like most standard include files, `<fcntl.h>` normally resides in the directory `/usr/include` and can be incorporated into a program with the directive:

```
#include <fcntl.h>
```

There are three constants defined in `<fcntl.h>` that are of immediate interest to us:

`O_RDONLY`	open file for reading only
`O_WRONLY`	open file for writing only
`O_RDWR`	open file for both reading and writing
```

If the open call succeeds and the file is successfully opened, the return value from open will contain a non-negative integer, the file descriptor. The value of the file descriptor will actually be the smallest non-negative integer that is not already being used as a file descriptor by the process making the call; a fact you will not often need to know. As we saw in the introduction, if an error occurs, open will instead return −1. This can happen, for example, if the file does not already exist. To create a new file the programmer can use the open call with the flags set to O_CREAT, which is described in the next section.

The optional third parameter, mode, is only used with the O_CREAT flag and again will be discussed in the next section – it is concerned with file security permissions. Notice the use of the square brackets in our usage description to denote the *optional* nature of mode. You do not always need to use it.

The following skeleton program opens a file junk for reading and writing, and also checks to see if an error has occurred during opening. This last point is an important one; it makes good sense to build error checking into all programs that use system calls, since things will sometimes go wrong, however straightforward the application. The example makes use of the library routines printf, for displaying a message, and exit, which terminates the calling process. Both of these are provided as standard with any UNIX system.

```
#include <stdlib.h>              /* for the exit call */
#include <fcntl.h>

char *workfile="junk";          /* define workfile name */

main()
{
 int filedes;

 /* Open using O_RDWR from <fcntl.h> */
 /* File to be opened for read/write */

 if((filedes = open(workfile, O_RDWR)) == -1)
 {
      printf("Couldn't open %s\n", workfile);
      exit(1);                  /* error so exit */
 }

 /* rest of program follows */

 exit(0);                       /* normal exit */

}
```

Notice how we use exit with an argument of 1 when an error occurs, and 0 on successful completion. This conforms to UNIX conventions and is good programming practice. As we shall see in later chapters, the argument passed to exit (the program's **exit status**) can be accessed after execution has finished. Also notice the use of the header file <stdlib.h> which contains the function prototype for the exit call.

Caveats

There are a number of caveats we can add to this discussion. First, note that there is a limit on the number of files that may be left open simultaneously by an executing program. POSIX (and therefore the *XSI*) specifies a minimum of 20. To work around this the close system call can be used to tell the system you have finished with a file. We will look at close in Section 2.1.5. There is also a system-wide limit on the number of files that can be opened by all processes taken together, determined by the size of a table inside the kernel.

Second, a word of warning: in early versions of UNIX the include file <fcntl.h> did not exist and actual numeric values were used to form the flags parameter. It is still common, though not wholly satisfactory, practice to use these numeric values rather than the constant names defined in <fcntl.h>. So you may see a statement like:

```
filedes = open(filename, 0);
```

which under normal circumstances opens a file for read-only access and is equivalent to:

```
filedes = open(filename, O_RDONLY);
```

Exercise 2.1   Create the small skeleton program described above. Test it when the file junk does not exist. Then create junk with your favourite editor and rerun the program. The contents of junk are entirely arbitrary.

2.1.3 Creating a file with open

The open call can also be used to create a file from scratch, as follows:

```
filedes = open("/tmp/newfile", O_WRONLY | O_CREAT, 0644);
```

Here, a new flag O_CREAT is combined with O_WRONLY to instruct open to create /tmp/newfile. If /tmp/newfile does not already exist, it will be created as a file of zero length, and opened for writing only.

This example introduces open's third parameter, mode. This is only needed for file creation. Without going into too much detail at this stage, the mode contains a number which gives the file **access permissions**. These determine which users of the system can read, write or execute the file. The example above uses octal value 0644. This will allow the user who created the file to read and write to it. Other users will only be allowed read access. We will explain how this value is constructed in the next chapter. For simplicity we shall use it in examples throughout the rest of the current chapter.

The following skeleton program creates a file newfile in the current working directory.

```
#include <stdlib.h>
#include <fcntl.h>

#define PERMS 0644        /* Permission for open with O_CREAT */

char *filename="newfile";

main()
{
 int filedes;

 if((filedes = open(filename, O_RDWR|O_CREAT, PERMS)) == -1)
 {
       printf("Couldn't create %s\n",filename);
       exit(1);              /* error, so exit */
 }

 /* rest of program follows */

 exit(0);
}
```

What happens if newfile already exists? If its access permissions allow, it will be opened for writing as if O_CREAT was not specified. In this case the mode parameter has no effect. Alternatively, combining the O_CREAT flag with the O_EXCL (exclusive) flag will cause an open call to fail if the file already exists. For example:

```
fd = open("lock", O_WRONLY|O_CREAT|O_EXCL, 0644);
```

means: if file lock does not exist, then create it with permissions 0644. If it does exist, then fail, returning −1 in fd.

Another useful flag here is O_TRUNC. When used with O_CREAT it will force a file to be truncated to zero bytes if it exists and its access permissions allow. For example:

```
fd = open("file", O_WRONLY|O_CREAT|O_TRUNC, 0644);
```

This is needed if you do not want output from a particular program to be prefaced with data from past runs of that program.

Exercise 2.2 Interestingly enough O_TRUNC can be used on its own without O_CREAT. Predict its results, then try it with an example program for the cases where the target does, and does not, exist.

2.1.4 The `creat` system call

The `creat` system call can be used as an alternative way to create a file. In fact, it is the *original* way, but is now somewhat redundant and offers less control than `open`. We include it here for completeness. Like `open`, it returns either a non-negative file descriptor or −1 on error. If the return value is a valid file descriptor, then the file will be open for writing. `creat` is called as follows:

Usage

`#include <sys/types.h>`
`#include <sys/stat.h>`
`#include <fcntl.h>`
 	
`int creat(const char *pathname, mode_t mode);`

The first parameter, `pathname`, points to a UNIX pathname. This gives the desired name and location of a new file. As with `open` the `mode` parameter gives the required access permissions. Again as with `open`, if the file already exists then the second argument is ignored. However, unlike `open`, `creat` will always truncate an existing file before returning its file descriptor. An example use of `creat` is:

```
filedes = creat("/tmp/newfile", 0644);
```

which is equivalent to:

```
fildes = open("/tmp/newfile", O_WRONLY|O_CREAT|O_TRUNC, 0644);
```

It should be stressed that `creat` always opens a file for writing only. A program cannot, for example, create a file with `creat`, write data to it, then move backwards and attempt to read from it, unless it closes the file and reopens it with `open`.

Exercise 2.3 Write a short program that first creates a file using `creat`, then without calling `close`, immediately opens it with the `open` system call for reading and writing. In both cases make the program indicate success or failure by using `printf` to display a message.

2.1.5 The `close` system call

The `close` system call is the inverse of `open`. It tells the system that the calling process has finished with a file. It is useful because of the limit to the number of files a running program may keep open at the same time.

Usage
`#include <unistd.h>`
`int close(int filedes);`

     The `close` system call takes just one argument, the file descriptor to be closed. This file descriptor will normally come from a previous call to either `open` or `creat`. The following program fragment illustrates the simple relationship between `open` and `close`:

```
filedes = open("file", O_RDONLY);
    .
    .
    .
close(filedes);
```

The `close` system call returns 0 if successful, −1 on error (which can happen if the integer argument is not a valid file descriptor).
     Note that, to prevent total chaos, all open files are automatically closed when a program completes execution.

2.1.6 The `read` system call

The `read` system call is used to copy an arbitrary number of characters or bytes from a file into a buffer under the control of the calling program. The buffer is formally declared as a pointer to `void`, which means that it may hold items of any type. Although the buffer is normally an array of `char`, it can also quite easily be an array of user-defined `struct`s.
     Note that C programmers tend to use the terms 'characters' and 'bytes' interchangeably. A byte is the unit of storage required to hold a character, and it is eight bits in length on most machines. The term 'character' usually describes a member of the ASCII character set, which consists of a pattern of just seven bits. A byte therefore can typically hold more values than there are ASCII characters, a situation you will find with binary data. The C `char` type represents the more general notion of byte, and its name is a bit of a misnomer.

Usage

```
#include <unistd.h>

ssize_t read(int filedes, void *buffer, size_t n);
```

The first parameter `filedes` is a file descriptor which has been obtained from a previous call to either `open` or `creat`. The second, `buffer`, is a pointer to an array or structure into which data will be copied. In many cases, this will simply be the name of the array itself. For example:

```
int fd;
ssize_t nread;
char buffer[SOMEVALUE];

/* fd obtained from call to open */
.
.
.
nread = read(fd, buffer, SOMEVALUE);
```

As you might guess from this example, `read`'s third parameter is a positive number (defined as the special type `size_t`) which gives the number of bytes to be read from the file.

The number returned by `read` (assigned to `nread` above) records the number of bytes actually read. Usually, this will be the number of characters requested by the program, but as we shall see, this is not always the case, and `nread` can take smaller values. In addition, when an error occurs `read` will return −1. This happens, for example, when `read` is passed an invalid file descriptor.

The read–write pointer

Naturally enough, a program can call `read` successively in order to scan sequentially through a file. For example, if we assume the file `foo` contains at least 1024 characters, the following fragment should place the first 512 characters from `foo` into `buf1`, and the second 512 characters into `buf2`:

```
int fd;
ssize_t n1,n2;
char buf1[512], buf2[512];
.
.
.
if(( fd = open("foo", O_RDONLY)) == -1)
    return (-1);

n1 = read(fd, buf1, 512);
n2 = read(fd, buf2, 512);
```

The system keeps track of a process' position in a file with an entity called the **read–write pointer**, sometimes referred to as the **file pointer**. Essentially, this records the position of the next byte in the file to be read (or written) through a specific file descriptor, and can be thought of as a kind of bookmark. Its value is maintained internally by the system and the programmer does not have to explicitly allocate a variable to contain it. Random access, where the position of the read–write pointer is explicitly changed, can be performed with the lseek system call, which is described in Section 2.1.10. In the case of read, the system simply advances the read–write pointer by thc number of bytes read after each call.

Since read can be used to scan through a file from beginning to end, a program must be able to detect the end of a file. This is where the return value from read becomes important. When the number of characters requested in a read call is greater than the number of characters left in the file, the system will transfer only the characters remaining, setting the return value appropriately. Any further calls to read will return a value of 0. There is, after all, no data remaining to be read. Checking for a return value of 0 from read is, in fact, the normal way of testing for end of file within a program, or at least a program which uses read.

The next example program count puts some of these points together:

```
/* count -- counts the characters in a file */

#include <stdlib.h>
#include <fcntl.h>
#include <unistd.h>

#define BUFSIZE 512

main()
{
    char buffer[BUFSIZE];
    int filedes;
    ssize_t nread;
    long total = 0;

    /* open "anotherfile" read only */
    if(( filedes = open("anotherfile", O_RDONLY)) == -1)
    {
      printf("error in opening anotherfile\n");
      exit(1);
    }

    /* loop until EOF, shown by return value of 0 */
    while( (nread = read(filedes, buffer, BUFSIZE)) >0)
      total += nread;            /* increment total */

    printf("total chars in anotherfile: %ld\n", total);
    exit(0);
}
```

This program will read through the file anotherfile in chunks of 512 characters. After each call to read, it increments the total variable by the number of characters actually copied into the array buffer. (Why do you think total is declared as a long integer?)

We used the value 512 for the number of characters to be read because a UNIX system is configured to work most efficiently when moving data in blocks that are multiples of the disk block size; in this case 512. (The actual block size is system dependent and can be as great as 8K or more.) However, we could have given read any number we might have thought of, including 1. There is no functional benefit in using the particular figure appropriate to your system, just a useful efficiency gain, but as we shall see in Section 2.1.9 this gain can be considerable.

To make use of the true disk blocking factor for your system, you can utilize the definition of BUFSIZ in the file /usr/include/stdio.h (which is actually related to the well-known Standard I/O Library). For example:

```
#include <stdio.h>

    .
    .
    .
nread = read(filedes, buffer, BUFSIZ);
```

Exercise 2.4   If you know how, make count accept a command line argument instead of using a fixed file name. Test it on a small file, with several lines.

Exercise 2.5   Make count also display the number of words and lines in the file. Define a word as being either a punctuation mark or any alphanumeric string not containing 'white space' characters such as space, tab or newline. A line, of course, is any sequence of characters terminated by newline.

2.1.7 The write system call

The write system call is the natural inverse of read. It copies data from a program buffer, again normally declared as an array, to an external file.

Usage
#include <unistd.h>
ssize_t write(int filedes, const void *buffer, size_t n);

Like read, write takes three arguments: filedes, which is a file descriptor, buffer, which is a pointer to the data to be written, and n, a positive number giving the number of bytes to be written. The value returned is either the number of characters write managed to output, or the error code -1. Actually, if it is not -1, then the returned value will almost always be equal to n. If it is any less something has gone badly wrong. This can occur, for example, when the write call fills up the output medium before it has completed. (If the medium is already full before the write call is made, then -1 will be returned.)

The write call is often used with a file descriptor that has been obtained from a newly created file. In this case it is easy to see what happens. The file is initially zero bytes long (it has either been freshly created or truncated), and each call to write simply adds data to the end of the file, with the read−write pointer being advanced to the position immediately after the last byte written. For example, all being well, the fragment:

```
int fd;
ssize_t w1, w2;
char header1[512], header2[1024];
    .
    .
    .
if( ( fd = open("newfile", O_WRONLY|O_CREAT|O_EXCL, 0644)) == -1)
    return (-1);

w1 = write(fd, header1, 512);
w2 = write(fd, header2, 1024);
```

results in a file of 1536 bytes containing the contents of header1 and header2 in succession.

What happens if a program opens an existing file for writing and then immediately writes to that file? The answer is equally simple: the old data in the file will be overwritten by the new, character by character. For example, suppose the file oldhat is 500 characters in length. If a program opens oldhat in the usual manner for writing, then outputs 10 characters, the first 10 characters of oldhat will be replaced by the contents of the program's write buffer. The next such write will replace the next 10 characters and so on. Once the end of the original file is reached, the file, now containing all new data, will be extended with each successive call to write. To get around this a file can be opened with the O_APPEND flag. For example:

```
filedes = open(filename, O_WRONLY|O_APPEND);
```

If the open succeeds the read−write pointer will be placed just after the last byte in the file and any write will add data at the file's end. This is explained more fully in Section 2.1.12.

2.1.8 The copyfile **example**

We are now in the position to tackle our first practical example. The task is to write a function copyfile which will copy the contents of one file to another. The return value should either be zero indicating success, or a negative number to indicate an error.

The basic logic is clear: open the first file, then create the second; read from the first and write to the second until the end of the first is reached. Finally close both.

The finished solution might look something like:

```
/* copyfile -- copy name1 to name2 */

#include <unistd.h>
#include <fcntl.h>

#define BUFSIZE    512    /* size of chunk to be read */
#define PERM       0644   /* file permission for new file */

/* copy name1 to name2 */
int copyfile( const char *name1, const char *name2)
{
    int infile, outfile;
    ssize_t nread;
    char buffer[BUFSIZE];

    if( ( infile = open(name1, O_RDONLY ) ) == -1)
      return (-1);

    if((outfile = open(name2,O_WRONLY|O_CREAT|O_TRUNC,PERM)) == -1)
    {
      close(infile);
      return (-2);
    }

    /* now read from name1 BUFSIZE chars at a time */
    while( (nread = read(infile, buffer, BUFSIZE) ) > 0)
    {
      /* write buffer to output file */
      if( write(outfile, buffer, nread) < nread )
      {
          close(infile);
          close(outfile);
          return (-3);              /* write error */
      }
    }

    close(infile);
    close(outfile);

    if( nread == -1)
      return (-4);                  /* error on last read */
```

```
    else
        return (0);                    /* all is well */
}
```

`copyfile` can now be used with a call like:

```
retcode = copyfile("squarepeg", "roundhole");
```

Exercise 2.6 Adapt `copyfile` so that it accepts two file descriptors rather than two filenames as parameters. Test this new version.

Exercise 2.7 If you are familiar with command line arguments, use one of the `copyfile` routines to create a program `mycp` that copies one filename argument to another.

2.1.9 `read, write` and efficiency

The `copyfile` routine provides a way of gauging the efficiency of the file access primitives in relation to buffer size. One technique is to simply compile `copyfile` with different values for `BUFSIZE`, then time the resulting program with the UNIX `time` command. We did this using the following `main` function:

```
/* main function to test "copyfile" */

main()
{
  copyfile("test.in", "test.out");
}
```

and obtained the results shown in Table 2.2 by copying the same large file (68 307 bytes) on a computer running SVR4 UNIX with a natural disk blocking factor of 512. Here the format of the table reflects the output from the `time` command. The first column gives the value of `BUFSIZE`. The second column gives the real, or actual, elapsed time the process took to run in minutes, seconds and tenths of a second. The

Table 2.2 *Results of* `copyfile` *test*

BUFSIZE	Real time	User time	System time
1	0:24.49	0:3.13	0:21.16
64	0:0.46	0:0.12	0:0.33
512	0:0.12	0:0.02	0:0.08
4096	0:0.07	0:0.00	0:0.05
8192	0:0.07	0:0.01	0:0.05

third column gives the 'user' time, which is the amount of time taken up by those parts of a program that are not system calls. Because of the granularity of the clock used by time, one entry in this column is misleadingly reported as being zero. The fourth and final column is the amount of time the kernel spent servicing system calls. As you can see, columns three and four do not add up to give the real elapsed time. This is because a UNIX system runs several, maybe many, processes simultaneously. It will not spend all its time running your programs!

Our results are pretty conclusive; reading and writing one byte at a time gives appalling performance, while increasing the buffer size improves performance greatly. The best performance of all is achieved when BUFSIZE is a multiple of the system's natural disk blocking factor, as shown by the results for BUFSIZE values of 512, 4096 and 8192 bytes.

We should also stress that a large part (but not all) of any efficiency gain comes simply from reducing the number of system calls. Switching mode between program and kernel when a system call is made can be relatively expensive. In general, you should ideally minimize the number of system calls made by a program where you need very high performance.

2.1.10 lseek and random access

The lseek system call enables the user to change the position of the read–write pointer; that is, change the number of the byte that will be read or written next. lseek therefore enables random access into a file.

Usage

```
#include <sys/types.h>
#include <unistd.h>

off_t lseek(int filedes, off_t offset, int start_flag);
```

The first parameter filedes is an open file descriptor. The second parameter, offset, actually determines the new position of the read–write pointer. It gives the number of bytes to add to a starting position. What the starting position will be is determined by the third argument, the integer start_flag. This specifies where in the file the offset is to be measured from. start_flag can take a number of symbolic values (from <unistd.h>) as shown below:

SEEK_SET   The offset is measured from the beginning of the file; usual actual integer value = 0

SEEK_CUR   The offset is measured from the current position of the file pointer; usual value = 1

SEEK_END   The offset is measured from the end of the file; usual value = 2

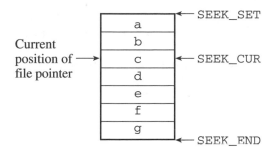

Figure 2.1 *Symbolic values of* `start_flag`.

These are shown more graphically in Figure 2.1, which represents a 7-byte file.
An example of using `lseek` is:

```
off_t newpos;
   .
   .
   .
newpos = lseek(fd, (off_t)-16, SEEK_END);
```

which gives a position 16 bytes *before* the end of the file. Notice the cast of −16 bytes to type (`off_t`).

In all cases the return value (contained in `newpos` in the example) will give the new position in the file. If an error occurs then it will contain the usual error code of −1.

There are a number of points worth noting here. Firstly, both `newpos` and `offset` are of type `off_t`, as defined in `<sys/types.h>`, which will be a type large enough to cope with movement through any file on the system. Secondly, `offset` can be negative, as shown in the example. In other words it is possible to move backwards from the starting point indicated by `start_flag`. An error will only result if you try to move to a position before the start of the file. Thirdly, it is possible to specify a position beyond the end of a file. If this is done there is obviously no data waiting to be read – UNIX does not yet support time travel – but a subsequent `write` is perfectly meaningful and will cause the file to be extended. Any empty space between the old end of file and the starting position of the new data may not actually be physically allocated but it will appear to future `read` calls to be filled with the ASCII null character.

As a simple example we can construct a program fragment that will append to the end of an existing file by opening the file, moving to the file end with `lseek`, and starting to write:

```
filedes = open(filename, O_RDWR);
lseek(filedes, (off_t)0, SEEK_END);
write(filedes, outbuf, OBSIZE);
```

Here the direction parameter for lseek is set to SEEK_END to move the read–write pointer to the end of the file. Since we want to move no further, the offset is given as zero.

lseek can also be called in the same way to give the size of the file, since it returns the new position in the file.

```
off_t filesize;
int filedes;
    .
    .
    .
filesize = lseek(filedes, (off_t)0, SEEK_END);
```

Exercise 2.8 Write a function that uses lseek to get the size of an open file, but appears not to have changed the value of the read–write pointer.

2.1.11 The hotel example

As a highly contrived, but possibly illuminating, example, suppose we have a file residents for recording the names of the residents of a hotel. Line 1 contains the name of the occupant of room 1, line 2 the name of the occupant of room 2 and so on (as you can see this is a hotel with a peculiarly well-behaved room-numbering system). Each line is exactly 41 characters in length, the first 40 characters containing the occupant's name while the 41st is a newline character which makes the file displayable with the UNIX cat command.

The following getoccupier function will, given an integer room number, calculate the location of the first byte of the occupier's name, then move to that position and read the data contained there. It returns either a pointer to a string containing the occupier's name, or a null pointer on error (we will use the value for NULL as defined in <stdio.h> for this). Note how we give the file descriptor variable infile an initial value of −1. By testing for this we can ensure the file is opened just once.

```
/* getoccupier -- get occupier's name from residents file */

#include <stdio.h>
#include <fcntl.h>
#include <unistd.h>

#define NAMELENGTH 41

char namebuf[NAMELENGTH];       /* buffer to hold name */
int infile = -1;                /* will hold file descriptor */
```

```
char *getoccupier(int roomno)
{
 off_t offset;
 ssize_t nread;

 /* open the file first time around */
 if( infile == -1 &&
    (infile = open("residents", O_RDONLY)) == -1)
 {
      return (NULL);     /* couldn't open file */
 }

 offset = (roomno - 1) * NAMELENGTH;

 /* find room slot and read occupier's name */
 if(lseek(infile, offset, SEEK_SET) == -1)
      return (NULL);

 if( (nread = read(infile, namebuf, NAMELENGTH)) <= 0)
      return (NULL);

 /* create a string by replacing the newline character
    with the null terminator */
 namebuf[nread - 1] = '\0';
 return (namebuf);
}
```

Assuming that the hotel contains 10 rooms, the following program will successively call getoccupier to scan through the file, using the printf routine from the Standard I/O Library to display each name it finds:

```
/* listoc -- list all occupants' names */

#define NROOMS    10

main()
{
 int j;
 char *getoccupier(int), *p;

 for( j = 1; j <= NROOMS; j++)
 {
      if(p = getoccupier(j))
            printf("Room %2d, %s\n", j, p);
      else
            printf("Error on room %d\n", j);
 }
}
```

Exercise 2.9 Invent a mechanism for deciding whether a room is empty. Modify getoccupier, and the data file if necessary, to reflect this. Now write a routine called findfree to locate the lowest numbered free room.

Exercise 2.10 Write a routine `freeroom` to remove a guest from his or her room. Then write `addguest` to place a new guest into a room, checking first whether it is empty.

Exercise 2.11 Incorporate `getoccupier`, `freeroom`, `addguest` and `findfree` into a simple utility program `frontdesk` which maintains the data file. Either use command line arguments or write an interactive program that calls `printf` and `getchar`. In either case you will need a way of converting strings to integers in order to calculate room numbers. You can use the library routine `atoi` as follows:

```
i = atoi(string);
```

where `string` is a character pointer and `i` an integer.

Exercise 2.12 As a more general exercise write a program around `lseek` that copies the bytes of one file to another in reverse order. Is your solution efficient?

Exercise 2.13 Using `lseek`, write routines to copy the last 10 characters, the last 10 words and the last 10 lines of one file to another.

2.1.12 Appending data to a file

As should be clear from Section 2.1.10, the following code could be used to append data to the end of a file:

```
/* seek to file end */
lseek(filedes, (off_t)0, SEEK_END);
write(filedes, appbuf, BUFSIZE);
```

However, a neater way would be to use one of the additional flags to `open`, `O_APPEND`. If set, `O_APPEND` causes the file pointer to be positioned at the end of a file whenever a write takes place. This is useful if the programmer wants to just add data to the end of a file and protect the original contents against accidental corruption.

`O_APPEND` can be used as follows:

```
filedes = open("yetanother", O_WRONLY | O_APPEND);
```

Each subsequent use of `write`, such as:

```
write(filedes, appbuf, BUFSIZE);
```

will append data to the end of the file.

Exercise 2.14 Write a routine `fileopen` which takes two arguments; the first is a string containing the filename, the second a string which can take the following values:

r   open a file read only
w   open a file write only
rw   open a file read and write
a   open a file for appending data

`fileopen` should return a file descriptor or the error code −1.

2.1.13 Deleting a file

There are two methods of eliminating a file from the system. These are the `unlink` and `remove` calls.

Usage

```
#include <unistd.h>
int unlink(const char *pathname);

#include <stdio.h>
int remove(const char *pathname);
```

Both calls take one argument: a string containing the name of the file to be deleted. For example:

```
unlink ("/tmp/usedfile");
remove("/tmp/tmpfile");
```

Both calls return either 0, indicating success, or −1 to indicate failure.

Why have two calls? In the beginning there was only `unlink`. The `remove` call, specified in the ANSI C standard, is a recent addition to the *XSI* for removing regular files, `remove` is identical to `unlink`. For removing empty directories, `remove(path)` is equivalent to `rmdir(path)` – another system call which should always be used instead of `unlink` for directories. We will meet it again in Chapter 4.

2.1.14 The `fcntl` system call

The `fcntl` system call was introduced to provide a degree of control over already-open files. It is a rather strange beast that performs a variety of functions instead of having a single, well-defined role.

<table>
<tr><td>

Usage

</td></tr>
<tr><td>

```
#include <sys/types.h>
#include <unistd.h>
#include <fcntl.h>

/* NB: the type of the last parameter can vary
   as indicated by the ellipsis "..." */

int fcntl(int filedes, int cmd, ...);
```

</td></tr>
</table>

The fcntl system call acts on the open file identified by the file descriptor filedes. The programmer selects a particular function by choosing a value for the integer cmd parameter from the header file <fcntl.h>. The type of the third parameter depends upon the value of the cmd parameter. For example, if fcntl is used to set file status flags then the third parameter is an integer, or, as will be seen later, if fcntl is used to lock a file then the third parameter is a pointer to a struct flock. In some cases the third parameter is not used at all.

Some of these functions are concerned with the interaction of files and processes and we will not look at them here; however, there are two functions that are of immediate interest, identified by the cmd values F_GETFL and F_SETFL.

F_GETFL instructs fcntl to return the current file status flags as set by open. The following function filestatus uses fcntl in this way to display the current state of an open file.

```
/* filestatus -- describe the current state of file */

#include <fcntl.h>

int filestatus(int filedes)
{
 int arg1;

 if(( arg1 = fcntl(filedes, F_GETFL)) == -1)
 {
      printf("filestatus failed\n");
      return (-1);
 }

 printf("File descriptor %d: ",filedes);

 /* test the argument against the open flags */
 switch( arg1 & O_ACCMODE){
 case O_WRONLY:
            printf("write-only");
            break;
 case O_RDWR:
            printf("read-write");
            break;
 case O_RDONLY:
            printf("read-only");
            break;
```

```
default:
            printf("No such mode");
}

if(arg1 & O_APPEND)
        printf(" - append flag set");

printf("\n");
return (0);
}
```

Notice how we test whether a particular bit is set in the file status flags held in arg1 by using the bitwise AND operator, denoted by the single & symbol. The bit is tested against O_ACCMODE, a mask defined in <fcntl.h> specifically for this purpose.

F_SETFL is used to reset the file status flags associated with a file. The new flags are given in the third argument for fcntl. Only certain flags can be set in this way; you cannot for example suddenly turn a file open for reading only into a file open for both reading and writing (why?). However, you can ensure that all future writes will append to the end of file with a call of the following form:

```
if( fcntl(filedes, F_SETFL, O_APPEND) == -1)
    printf("fcntl error \n");
```

2.2 Standard input, standard output and standard error

2.2.1 Basic concepts

A UNIX system automatically opens three files for any executing program. These are **standard input, standard output** and **standard error**. These are always identified by the file descriptors 0, 1 and 2, respectively. Because of the similar sounding names, do not confuse them with the Standard I/O Library.

By default, a read from standard input will cause a program to accept data from the keyboard. Similarly, writing to either standard output or standard error will, by default, cause a message to be displayed on the terminal screen. This, in fact, provides our first example of the way the file access primitives can be used for all types of I/O and not just that involving ordinary disk files.

A program that uses these standard file descriptors is by no means committed to using the terminal, however. Each can be separately reassigned when the program is invoked using the redirection features provided by a standard UNIX shell (a UNIX command processor). For example the command:

```
$ prog_name < infile
```

will cause the program to accept data from infile when it reads from file descriptor 0, rather than the terminal, the normal source for standard input.

Any data written to standard output can similarly be redirected to an output file. For example:

$ *prog_name > outfile*

Most useful of all perhaps, the standard output of one program can be made the standard input of another using the UNIX pipe facility. The following shell command means that anything written by prog_1 on its standard output becomes the standard input of prog_2:

$ *prog_1 | prog_2*

These standard input and output file descriptors offer the chance to build flexible, consistent programs. A program can be developed as a general tool that is able, for example, to accept input direct from the user, from a file or even the output of another program as required. In each case the program simply reads from standard input using file descriptor 0 and the final decision of the source of input is left until runtime.

2.2.2 The io example

As an extremely simple example of the use of the standard file descriptors, the program io uses the system calls read and write and the file descriptors 0 and 1 to copy its standard input to its standard output. It is in essence a cut-down version of the UNIX cat program. Notice the absence of any calls to open or creat.

```
/* io -- copy std input to std output */

#include <stdlib.h>
#include <unistd.h>

#define SIZE 512

main()
{
    ssize_t nread;
    char buf[SIZE];

    while( (nread = read(0, buf, SIZE)) > 0)
        write(1, buf, nread);
    exit(0);
}
```

Suppose this program is contained in the source file io.c and is compiled to give the executable binary io:

$ *cc -o io io.c*

If io is now invoked simply by typing its name, it will wait for input from the terminal. If the user types a line of data and then presses the *Return* or *Enter* key, io will simply redisplay the line typed; that is, it writes the input line to standard output. The actual dialogue might look something like:

```
$ io              (user types io, followed by Return)
This is line 1    (user types this, followed by Return)
This is line 1    (io redisplays line)
.
.
.
```

After redisplaying the line, io will be waiting for more input. The user can keep on typing indefinitely. io will obediently redisplay each line as *Return* or *Enter* is typed.

To terminate the program, the user can type the system's end of file character on a line by itself. This is typically ^D; that is, *Ctrl-D*, sent by pressing the *Ctrl* and *D* keys simultaneously. This action will cause read to return 0, indicating that the end of the data has been reached. The complete dialogue might therefore look like:

```
$ io
This is line 1
This is line 1
This is line 2
This is line 2
< Ctrl-D >        (user types Ctrl-D)
$
```

The more perceptive of you might have noticed that io is not behaving as we might immediately expect. Instead of reading in a full 512 characters before printing them, as the program logic seems to suggest, it prints each line as the *Return* key is pressed. This is because read, when used to accept data from a terminal, usually returns after each newline character – clearly an aid to meaningful interaction. To be even more precise, this is true only for a common terminal setting. Terminals can also be set into other modes, allowing, for example, single character input. More about this can be found in Chapter 9.

Since io does use the standard file descriptors, it can be used in conjunction with the shell's redirection and piping facilities. For example, the command:

```
$ io < /etc/motd > message
```

will cause io to copy the contents of the message of the day file /etc/motd to the file message, while the command line:

```
$ io < /etc/motd | wc
```

will cause the standard output of io to be piped into the UNIX word-count utility wc. Since the standard output of io will in fact be identical to the contents of /etc/motd, this is a cumbersome way of counting the words, lines and characters in the file.

Exercise 2.15 Write a version of io that checks to see if there are any command line arguments. If any exist, the program should treat each argument as a filename and copy the contents of each file to its standard output. If there are no command line arguments, input should be taken from standard input. How should the new io program deal with files it cannot open?

Exercise 2.16 Sometimes data in a file will accumulate slowly over a lengthy period. Write a version of io called watch that will read up to the end of file on standard input, echoing the data on standard output. When it reaches the end of its input, watch should pause for five seconds. It should then restart reading its standard input to see if any more data has arrived, without reopening the file or adjusting the read–write pointer. To put the process to rest for a set time, you can use the standard library subroutine sleep which takes a single argument, an integer giving the number of seconds to wait. For example:

```
sleep(5);
```

tells a process to sleep for five seconds. watch is similar to a program called readslow that is found in some versions of UNIX. Also, see your manual entry for the -f option of the tail command.

2.2.3 Using standard error

Standard error is a rather special output file descriptor, which is by convention reserved for error and warning messages, and enables a program to separate error messages from normal output. For example, the use of standard error allows a program to display error messages on the terminal while standard output is being written to a file. However, if required, standard error can also be redirected in a manner similar to standard output. For example, the standard shell command:

$ *make > log.out 2> log.err*

causes error messages from the make command to be sent to the file log.err. Standard output is sent to log.out.

A programmer could make use of standard error in a program by using the write system call and file descriptor 2:

```
char msg[6]="boob\n";
     .
     .
write(2, msg, 5);
```

This however is rather crude and cumbersome. We will provide a better solution at the end of this chapter.

2.3 The Standard I/O Library: a look ahead

The file access system calls ultimately provide the basis for all input and output by UNIX programs. However, these calls are true primitives and handle data only in the form of simple sequences of bytes, leaving everything else up to the programmer. Efficiency considerations also fall into the lap of the developer.

   To make life a little easier, UNIX offers the ANSI C Standard I/O Library, which offers many more facilities than the system calls we have so far described. Since this book is mostly concerned with the system call interface to the kernel we have delayed a full treatment of the Standard I/O Library until Chapter 11. However, for comparative purposes it is worth briefly investigating Standard I/O here.

   Perhaps the most obvious difference between Standard I/O and the system call primitives lies in the way files are described. Instead of integer file descriptors, the Standard I/O routines work, implicitly or explicitly, with a structure called FILE. The next example shows how to open a file with the fopen routine:

```
#include <stdio.h>
#include <stdlib.h>

main()
{
    FILE *stream;

    if( ( stream = fopen("junk", "r")) == NULL)
    {
      printf("Could not open file junk\n");
      exit(1);
    }
}
```

   The first line of the example:

```
#include <stdio.h>
```

includes the Standard I/O library header file <stdio.h>. This file contains, among many other things, the definition of FILE, NULL and extern declarations for functions such as fopen. These days NULL is also defined in <unistd.h>.

The real meat of the example is contained in the statement:

```
if( ( stream = fopen("junk", "r")) == NULL)
{
    .
    .
}
```

Here, junk is a file name, while the string "r" means that the file is to be opened read-only. The string "w" could be used to truncate or create the file for writing. If successful, fopen will initialize a FILE structure and return its address via stream. The stream pointer can then be passed to other routines in the library. It is important to realize that somewhere within the body of fopen, a call to our old friend open is made. As a corollary, somewhere within a FILE structure, there is a file descriptor which ties that structure to the file. The essential point is that Standard I/O routines are written around the system call primitives. The main function of the library is to provide a more programmer-friendly interface and automatic buffering.

Once the file has been opened, many Standard I/O routines are available to access it. One such is getc, which reads a single character; another is putc, which writes a single character. They are used along the following lines:

Usage

```
#include <stdio.h>

int getc(FILE *istream);          /* read a character from istream */

int putc(int c, FILE *ostream);   /* place a character onto ostream */
```

Both routines can be placed into a loop to copy one file to another as follows:

```
int c;
FILE *istream, *ostream;

/* open istream for reading and ostream for writing */
.
.
.
while( ( c = getc(istream)) != EOF)
    putc(c, ostream);
```

EOF is defined in <stdio.h> and is returned by getc when it reaches end of file. The actual value of EOF is −1, which is why the return from getc is defined as an int.

At first sight, getc and putc look worrying because they process single characters, and, as we have seen, this is extremely inefficient for system calls.

Standard I/O avoids this inefficiency by an elegant buffering mechanism, which works along the following lines: the first call to `getc` results in BUFSIZ characters being read from the file via the system call `read` (as we saw in Section 2.1.6, BUFSIZ is a constant defined in <stdio.h>). The data is kept in a buffer set up by the library (but still in the user's address space). Only the first character will be returned via `getc`. All the other internal workings are kept well away from the calling program. Successive calls to `getc` return characters in order from the buffer. When BUFSIZ characters have been passed to the program via `getc`, and another `getc` call is made, the next buffer-full is read in from the file. A similar, outward mechanism is provided for `putc`.

This technique is very useful since it absolves the programmer from worrying about efficiency. However, it also means that data is only written out in large chunks, and files will lag behind programs somewhat (special arrangements are made for terminals). It is very unwise therefore to mix Standard I/O routines and system calls like `read`, `write` and `lseek` for the same file. Unless you know exactly what you are doing, chaos could result. On the other hand, it is perfectly all right to mix system calls and Standard I/O routines for separate files.

Besides the buffering mechanism, Standard I/O provides formatting and conversion utilities; for example, `printf` offers output formatting as in:

```
printf("An integer %d\n", ival);
```

This should be familiar to most readers of this book. (`printf`, by the way, implicitly writes to standard output.)

Writing error messages with `fprintf`

`printf` can be used for displaying diagnostic messages. Unfortunately, it writes to standard output, not standard error. However, we can now use `fprintf`, a generalization of `printf`, to do this. The following program fragment shows how:

```
#include <stdio.h>        /* for stderr definition */
   .
   .
fprintf(stderr, "error number %d\n", errno);
```

The only difference between this use of `fprintf` and a call to `printf` is the `stderr` parameter. This is a pointer to a standard FILE structure which is automatically associated with standard error.

The following routine extends the use of `fprintf` to a more general purpose error routine:

```
/* notfound -- print file error then exit */

#include <stdio.h>
#include <stdlib.h>
```

```
int notfound(const char *progname, const char *filename)
{
 fprintf(stderr, "%s: file %s not found\n", progname,
                                           filename);
 exit(1);
}
```

In later examples we will use `fprintf` for error messages, rather than `printf`. This ensures consistency with most commands and programs, which use standard error for diagnostics.

2.4 The `errno` variable and system calls

As we have seen, all the file access system calls so far described can fail in some way. This is universally indicated by a return value of -1. To help the program gain more information when such an exception occurs, UNIX provides a globally accessible integer variable which contains an error code number. The error code number is related to an error message such as 'no permission' or 'invalid argument'. A complete list of error codes and their meanings is specified in Appendix A. The error number stores the last type of error that occurred during a system call.

The name of the error variable is `errno`. A programmer can use `errno` within a C program by including the header file `<errno.h>`. Many older programs insist that the integer `errno` is declared with external linkage; the *XSI* now makes this declaration obsolete.

The following program calls `open` and if this fails, the program will use `fprintf` to display the value of `errno`:

```
/* err1.c -- open a file with error handling */

#include <stdio.h>
#include <fcntl.h>
#include <errno.h>

main()
{
    int fd;

    if( (fd = open("nonesuch", O_RDONLY)) == -1)
      fprintf(stderr, "error %d\n", errno);
}
```

If, for example, the file `nonesuch` does not exist, the error code displayed on a standard UNIX implementation will be 2. Like all of the possible values of `errno`, this code is also given a symbolic name; in this case ENOENT which simply means 'no such file or directory'. You can make direct use of these symbolic names as they are defined using the pre-processor directive `#define` in the system header file `<errno.h>`.

Care should be exercised when using `errno` since it is not reset when a new system call is made. It is therefore safest to use `errno` immediately after a system call has been made and has failed.

2.4.1 The `perror` subroutine

As well as `errno`, UNIX provides a library routine (not a system call) called `perror`. For most traditional UNIX commands, this is the standard way of reporting errors. It takes a single string argument. When called it will produce a message on standard error consisting of the string argument passed to the routine, a colon and then an additional message associated with the current value of the `errno` variable. Usefully, the error message is printed on standard error, not standard output.

In the example above, the line containing the `printf` call could be replaced with:

```
perror("error opening nonesuch");
```

If `nonesuch` is non-existent then `perror` would display the message:

```
error opening nonesuch: No such file or directory
```

Exercise 2.17 Write routines that mimic the file access primitives described in this chapter, but call `perror` when an exception or error occurs.

CHAPTER 3

The file in context

Files are not completely specified simply by the data they contain. Each UNIX file also possesses a number of additional primitive properties necessary for the administration of what is a complex, multi-user system. It is these additional properties, and the system calls that manipulate them, that we will study in this chapter.

3.1 Files in a multi-user environment

3.1.1 Users and ownerships

Every file on a UNIX system is *owned* by one of the system's users, who is normally the user who created the file. The owner's actual identity is represented by a non-negative integer called the **user-id** (often abbreviated to **uid**) which is associated with the file when it is created.

In a typical UNIX system, the uid associated with a particular username can be found in the third field of the user's entry in the password file; that is, the line in the file `/etc/passwd` that identifies a user to the system. The typical entry:

```
keith:x:35:10::/usr/keith:/bin/ksh
```

indicates that user `keith` has a uid of 35.

The fields in a password file entry are separated by colons. The first gives the username. The second, represented here by x, is a place marker for the user's password. Unlike earlier versions of UNIX, the actual encrypted password is now typically held in a different file, the implementation of which is system dependent. As we have seen, the third field contains the uid. Field four contains the user's default **group-id** (abbreviated to **gid**), explained in more detail in a moment. Field five is an optional comment field. Field six gives the user's home directory. The last field is the pathname of the program started after the user has logged in. For example, /bin/ksh is one of the standard UNIX shells.

In fact, as far as UNIX is concerned, it is the user-id that is really important in identifying a user. Each UNIX process is normally associated with the uid of the user who started that process. (Remember, a process is simply an execution of a program.) The actual username is really just a mnemonic convenience for human beings. When a file is created, the system establishes ownership by referring to the uid of the creating process.

The ownership of a file can be changed later, but only by either the system's privileged superuser or the file's owner. It is worth noting that the superuser has the username **root** and always has a uid of 0.

As well as individual users, files are also associated with **groups**, a group simply being an arbitrary collection of users which offers a straightforward method of controlling projects involving several people. Each user belongs to at least one group, possibly more.

Groups are defined in the file /etc/group. Each group is identified by a **gid**, which like the uid is a non-negative integer. A user's default group is indicated by the fourth field of his or her password file entry.

As with uids, the gid of a user is inherited by the processes that the user initiates. So, when a file is created, the gid associated with the creating process is stored along with the uid.

Effective user- and group-ids

To be a little more precise, we should actually describe file creation in relation to the **effective user-id** (often abbreviated to **euid**) associated with a process. This is because although a process may be started by one user (keith, say), it can under certain very specific circumstances acquire the file system privileges of another user (dina, say). Just how this is done we shall see very shortly. The uid of the user who actually initiated a process is described as the **real user-id** (again often abbreviated to **ruid**) of that process. In most cases, of course, the *effective* and *real* user-ids coincide.

For similar reasons, it is the **effective group-id** (abbreviated to **egid**) of a process that establishes the group associated with the file.

3.1.2 Permissions and file modes

Like any kind of ownership, file ownership gives certain privileges to the owner. In particular, the owner can choose the **permissions** associated with a file.

Permissions determine how different users can access a file. Three types of user are affected:

1. The file's owner.

2. Anyone who belongs to the same group as the one associated with the file. Note that, as far as the file's owner is concerned, the permissions for category 1 override the permissions for the file's group.

3. Anyone who is not covered by categories 1 or 2.

For each category of user, there are three basic types of file permission. These specify whether a user of a particular category can:

1. Read the file.

2. Write to the file.

3. Execute the file. (In this case the file will normally contain a program or a list of shell commands.)

The superuser, as always, is a special case and is able to manipulate any file regardless of the read, write or execute permissions associated with it.

The system stores the permissions associated with a file as a bit pattern called the **file mode**. Although the header file <sys/stat.h> contains symbolic names for the permission bits most UNIX programmers still prefer to use the octal constants shown in Table 3.1 – the symbolic names being a fairly recent and clumsy innovation. Remember that in C octal constants are always indicated by a preceding 0, otherwise the compiler will assume you are speaking decimal.

From the table, it is easy to see that we can make a file readable by all types of user by adding 0400 (read permission for the owner), 040 (read permission for members of the file's group) and 04 (read permission for all other users). This gives

Table 3.1 *Octal values for constructing file permissions*

Octal value	Symbolic mode	Meaning
0400	S_IRUSR	Read allowed by owner
0200	S_IWUSR	Write allowed by owner
0100	S_IXUSR	Owner can execute file
0040	S_IRGRP	Read allowed by group
0020	S_IWGRP	Write allowed by group
0010	S_IXGRP	Group member can execute file
0004	S_IROTH	Other types of user can read file
0002	S_IWOTH	Other types of user can write file
0001	S_IXOTH	Other types of user can execute file

a final file mode of 0444. The mode can also be specified by performing a bitwise OR (|) on the symbolic representations, for example 0444 is equivalent to:

```
S_IRUSR | S_IRGRP | S_IROTH
```

Since none of the other values from the table are involved, this particular mode of 0444 also means that no user is able to write or execute the file, including the owner.

To circumvent this, it is possible to use more than one of the octal values relating to one category of user. For example, adding together 0400, 0200 and 0100 to give the value 0700 means that the file's owner is allowed to read, write or execute the file.

Therefore the more likely mode value:

```
0700 + 050 + 05 = 0755
```

means the owner can read, write or execute the file, while members of the group associated with the file and any other type of user are restricted to just reading or executing the file.

It is quite understandable why UNIX programmers prefer to use the octal constants rather than the names from <sys/stat.h> when the simple value 0755 is represented by:

```
S_IRUSR | S_IWUSR | S_IXUSR | S_IRGRP | S_IXGRP | S_IROTH | S_IXOTH
```

This is not the whole permission story. In the next subsection we will see how three other types of permission affect files containing executable programs. Perhaps more important as far as file access goes, each UNIX directory also has a set of access permissions much like a regular file; this affects the accessibility of files within the directory. We will discuss this issue in detail in Chapter 4.

Exercise 3.1 What do the following permission values mean: 0761, 0777, 0555, 0007 and 0707?

Exercise 3.2 Translate the octal values in Exercise 3.1 into their symbolic equivalents.

Exercise 3.3 Write a routine lsoct which translates a set of permissions, as specified by ls (e.g. rwxr-xr-x) into its octal equivalent. Then write its inverse octls.

3.1.3 Extra permissions for executable files

There are three other types of file permission, which specify special attributes and are usually only relevant when a file contains an executable program. The appropriate octal values and symbolic names, which again correspond to specific bits within the file mode, and their meanings are:

```
04000 S_ISUID    Set user-id on execution
02000 S_ISGID    Set group-id on execution
01000 S_ISVTX    Save-text-image (sticky bit)
```

If the S_ISUID permission is set, then when the program contained in the file is started, the system gives the resulting process an **effective user-id** taken from the *file owner* rather than that of the user who started the process (the latter case being the normal state of affairs). The process then assumes the file system privileges of the file owner, not the user who started the process.

This mechanism can be used to control access to sensitive data; the delicate information can be protected from public gaze or manipulation by use of the standard read-write-execute permissions. The owner of the file can then create a program that accesses the file in a specific, tightly defined manner. When the program is complete, its S_ISUID permission can be set, allowing other users access to the file through that program only. Of course, the program must be carefully written to avoid any temporary privilege being abused.

The classic example of this technique is the passwd program. A system manager is asking for trouble if any user can write to the password file at whim. However, all users must write to this file sometimes in order to change their password. The passwd program circumvents this problem because it is owned by superuser and has the S_ISUID bit set.

Perhaps rather less usefully, the S_ISGID permission does the same thing for the file's group-id. If it is set then, when the file is started, the resulting process acquires the gid of the file's owner, not the user who started up the program.

Historically, the S_ISVTX bit used to be able to be set on executable files and was known as the **save-text-image** permission, or more usually known by its nickname, the **sticky bit**. In earlier systems if the save-text-image bit was set on a file, then, when it was executed, its program-text part would remain in the system's swap area until the system was halted. So, when the program was next invoked the system would not hunt for it through the system's directory structure but instead simply (and quickly) swap it into memory. On modern day UNIX systems this bit is now redundant. The *XSI* only defines the S_ISVTX bit for directories. This use of the S_ISVTX bit will be explained further in Chapter 4.

Exercise 3.4 The following examples show how ls displays the set-user-id and set-group-id permissions, respectively:

```
r-sr-xr-x
r-xr-sr-x
```

Using the command ls -l, examine the contents of /bin, /etc and /usr/bin for files with unusual permissions of this type. The more experienced readers should be able to speed things up by using the grep program. If you do find any files with strange permissions, explain why.

3.1.4 The file creation mask and the `umask` system call

As we very briefly saw in Chapter 2, the initial permissions of a file are set when the file is created via a call to either `creat` or `open` in its extended form. For example:

```
filedes = open("datafile", O_CREAT, 0644);
```

Associated with each process is a value called the **file creation mask**. This is used to turn off permission bits automatically whenever a file is created, whatever the mode given with the appropriate `creat` or `open` call. It is useful in safeguarding all files created during the existence of a process because it prevents the specified permissions from being accidentally turned on.

The basic idea is straightforward: if a permission bit is set in the file creation mask, then it is always turned off when a file is created. The bits in the mask can be set using the same octal constants as described previously for file modes, although only the basic read, write and execute permissions can be used. The more exotic permissions such as `S_ISUID` have no significance in a file creation mask.

In programming terms, the statement:

```
filedes = open(pathname, O_CREAT, mode);
```

is therefore actually equivalent to:

```
filedes = open(pathname, O_CREAT, (~mask)&mode);
```

where `mask` holds the current value of the file creation mask, `~` is the C bitwise negation operator and `&` the bitwise AND operator.

For example, if the value of the mask is $04+02+01=07$ then the permissions normally indicated by these values are turned off whenever a file is created. So, with this value in effect, the file created with the statement:

```
fd = open("/tmp/newfile", O_CREAT, 0644);
```

will actually be given a mode of 0640. This means that the file owner and members of the group associated with the file will be able to use the file, but other types of user will be denied any access at all.

A process' file creation mask can be changed with the `umask` system call.

Usage
``#include <sys/types.h>
#include <sys/stat.h>

mode_t umask(mode_t newmask);``` |

For example:

```
mode_t oldmask;
 .
 .
 .
oldmask = umask(022);
```

The value 022 blocks write permission being given to anyone other than the file owner. The mode_t type is designed specially to hold file modes, that is permission, information. It is defined in the header file <sys/types.h>, which in turn is included in <sys/stat.h>. After the call, oldmask will hold the mask's previous value.

As a corollary to this, if you want to make absolutely sure that files are created with the mode exactly as given in an open or creat call, then you should first call umask with an argument of zero. Since all permission bits in the file creation mask will now be zero, none of the bits in a file mode, passed to open or creat, will be masked. The following example uses this idea to create a file with a guaranteed mode, then restores the old file creation mask. It returns the file descriptor from open.

```
#include <fcntl.h>
#include <sys/stat.h>

int specialcreat(const char *pathname, mode_t mode)
{
 mode_t oldu;
 int filedes;

 /* set file creation mask to zero */
 if( (oldu = umask(0)) == -1)
 {
       perror("saving old mask");
       return (-1);
 }

 /* create the file */
 if((filedes = open(pathname, O_WRONLY|O_CREAT|O_EXCL, mode)) == -1)
       perror("opening file");

 /* restore the old file mode, even if open failed */
 if(umask(oldu) == -1)
       perror("restoring old mask");

 /* return file descriptor */
 return filedes;
}
```

3.1.5 open and file permissions

If open is used to open an existing file for reading or writing, then the system checks whether the mode of access requested by the process (read only, write only or read–write) is allowed by checking the file's permissions. If it is not, open will return −1 indicating failure and `errno` will contain the error code `EACCES`, meaning 'permission denied'.

When `open` is used in its extended mode to create a file, the specification of `O_CREAT`, `O_TRUNC` and `O_EXCL` flags means that the treatment of existing files is very flexible. Example uses of `open` with file permissions are:

```
filedes = open(pathname, O_WRONLY | O_CREAT | O_TRUNC, 0600);
```

and:

```
filedes = open(pathname, O_WRONLY | O_CREAT | O_EXCL, 0600);
```

In the first example, the file in question will be truncated if it exists, providing the file permissions allow the calling process write access. In the second, the call to `open` will fail if the file exists, whatever its permissions, and `errno` will hold `EEXIST`.

Exercise 3.5

(a) Suppose a process has an euid of 100 and an egid of 200. File `testfile` is owned by user 101 and has a gid of 200. For each possible mode of access (read only, write only and read–write) state whether a call to `open` would succeed when `testfile` has the following permissions:

```
rwxr-xrwx      r-xrwxr-x      rwx--x---      rwsrw-r--
--s--s--x      ---rwx---      ---r-x--x
```

(b) What would happen if the process also had *real* user-id 101 and *real* group-id 201?

3.1.6 Determining file accessibility with `access`

`access` is a useful system call that determines whether or not a process can access a file, according to the *real* user-id of the process, rather than the current *effective* user-id. It provides another level of security in a process which has gained powers via the `S_ISUID` bit.

Usage
`#include <unistd.h>`
`int access(const char *pathname, int amode);`

As we have seen, there are several ways of accessing a file, so to give more information to the system the parameter `amode` contains a value indicating the required method of access. The parameter `amode` can take the following values, which are defined in `<unistd.h>`:

R_OK   Has calling process read access?

W_OK   Has calling process write access?

X_OK   Can calling process execute the file?

There is just one set of values for `amode` because we are concerned with only the ability of one user, identified by the ruid of the calling process, to access the file. `amode` can also take the value `F_OK`. This causes access to check for the file's existence only.

The other parameter `pathname` gives, rather unsurprisingly, the name of the file.

The return value from `access` is either 0 (indicating that the user identified by the process' ruid can access the file in the manner indicated by amode) or −1 (indicating that the process cannot). In the latter case, `errno` will contain a value indicating the reason why. A value of `EACCES`, for example, means the file's permissions do not allow the required access, while `ENOENT` means that the file simply does not exist.

The following skeleton program uses `access` to check if its user can read a file, whatever the `S_ISUID` bit setting:

```
/* example use of access */

#include <stdio.h>
#include <stdlib.h>
#include <unistd.h>

main()
{
  char *filename = "afile";

  if(access(filename, R_OK) == -1)
  {
      fprintf(stderr, "User cannot read file %s\n", filename);
      exit(1);
  }

  printf("%s readable, proceeding\n", filename);

  /* rest of program ... */
}
```

Exercise 3.6 Write a program `whatable` which tells you whether you can read, write or execute a file. When a type of access is not available, then `whatable` should say why (use `perror`).

3.1.7 Changing the file permissions with chmod

Usage
| ```
#include <sys/types.h>
#include <sys/stat.h>

int chmod(const char *pathname, mode_t newmode);
``` |

The chmod system call is used to alter the permissions of an existing file. It can be used on a file only by the file's owner or superuser.

The pathname parameter points to the filename. The newmode parameter contains the new file mode, constructed in the way described in the first part of this chapter.

An example use of chmod is:

```
if(chmod(pathname, 0644) == -1)
  perror("call to chmod failed");
```

Exercise 3.7 Write a program setperm that takes two command line arguments. The first is a filename, the second the octal or ls style specification for a set of permissions. If the file exists, then setperm should attempt to reset the file's permissions to the value given. Use the routine lsoct you developed in Exercise 3.3.

3.1.8 Changing ownership with chown

chown is used to alter both the owner and group of a file.

Usage
| ```
#include <sys/types.h>
#include <unistd.h>

int chown(const char *pathname, uid_t owner_id, gid_t group_id);
``` |

For example:

```
int retval;
.
.
.
retval = chown("/usr/dina", 56, 3);
```

As you can see, it has three arguments: `pathname`, which points to the file's pathname, the `owner_id`, which indicates the new owner, and the `group_id`, which gives the new group. The return value in `retval` is either 0 on success or −1 on error. Both `uid_t` and `gid_t` are types defined in the header file `<sys/types.h>`.

On an *XSI* compliant system the calling process must either be the superuser process or it must own the file, and the effective user-id of the calling process must therefore match that of the file owner. The error `EPERM` is always returned on any illegal attempt to change the ownership of a file.

As `chown` can only be used by either the current file owner or superuser it is therefore possible for an ordinary user to give a file of theirs away. However, once done this cannot be undone by the user making the call, since the user's id and the new uid of the file will no longer match! Note also, that to prevent the unscrupulous using `chown` to steal file system privileges, the set-user-id and set-group-id permissions are turned off for a file when the ownership of that file is altered. (What could happen if this was not the case?)

3.2 Files with multiple names

Any UNIX file can be identified by more than one name. In other words, the same *physical* collection of data can be associated with several UNIX pathnames without the need for the file to be duplicated. This may seem strange at first, but it can be very useful in terms of saving disk space or ensuring a number of people all make use of the same file.

Each such name is referred to as a **hard link**. The number of links associated with a file is called the **link count** of that file.

A new hard link is created with the `link` system call, and an existing hard link can be removed with the `unlink` system call.

3.2.1 The `link` system call

Usage

`#include <unistd.h>`
 	
`int link(const char *orginal_path, const char *new_path);`

The first parameter `original_path` is a character pointer that points to a UNIX pathname. It must identify an existing link to a file; that is, an existing name for the file. The second parameter, `new_path` points to the new name or link for the file. Note that `new_path` must not already exist as a file.

The `link` system call will return 0 if the call is successful or −1 if an error occurs. In the latter case no new link will be created.

For example, the statement:

```
link("/usr/keith/chap.2", "/usr/ben/2.chap");
```

will create a new link called /usr/ben/2.chap to the existing file /usr/keith/chap.2. The file can now be referred to using either name. As you can see, links do not have to be in the same directory.

3.2.2 The unlink system call revisited

In Section 2.1.13 we introduced the unlink system call as a simple way of removing a file from the system. For example:

```
unlink("/tmp/scratch");
```

will remove /tmp/scratch.

In fact, the unlink system call removes just the link named, and reduces the file's *link count* by one. Only if the link count is reduced to zero, and no program currently has the file open, will the data in the file be irredeemably lost from the system. In this case, the disk blocks previously allocated to the file are added to a list of free blocks maintained by the system. Although the data may for a time remain in physical existence, it is not recoverable. Since most files have only one link, this is the usual result of a call to unlink. Conversely, if the link count is not reduced to zero, the file data is left untouched and can be accessed through the file's other links.

The following short program renames a file by first linking it to the new desired pathname and if this is successful, unlinking the old pathname. It is a simplified version of the standard UNIX mv command.

```
/* move -- move a file from one pathname to another */

#include <stdlib.h>
#include <stdio.h>
#include <unistd.h>

char *usage = "usage: move file1 file2\n";

/* main uses args passed from command line in
 * standard manner
 */

main(int argc, char **argv)
{
 if(argc != 3)
 {
      fprintf(stderr, usage);
      exit(1);
 }
```

```
if( link(argv[1], argv[2]) == -1)
{
     perror("link failed");
     exit(1);
}

if(unlink(argv[1]) == -1)
{
     perror("unlink failed");
     unlink(argv[2]);
     exit(1);
}

printf("Succeeded\n");
exit(0);
}
```

Before proceeding, one final point. So far we have not mentioned the interaction of unlink and the permissions associated with its filename argument. This is because unlink is simply not affected by these permissions. The success or failure of a call to unlink is instead determined by the permissions of the *directory* containing the file. Again, this is a topic we will explore in Chapter 4.

3.2.3 The rename system call

In fact, the previous example can more easily be achieved by using the rename system call, which is a fairly recent addition to UNIX. The rename system call can also be used to rename directories as well as regular files.

Usage

```
#include <stdio.h>

int rename(const char *oldpathname, const char *newpathname);
```

The argument oldpathname is renamed to the name pointed to by the second argument newpathname. If newpathname already exists then it is removed before oldpathname is renamed.

Exercise 3.8 Using unlink write your own version of the rm command. Your program should check that the user has write permission on the file with access. If not, it should ask for confirmation before attempting to unlink the file. (Why?) Be careful while testing it!

3.2.4 Symbolic links

There are two important limitations in the use of the link call. It is not possible for a normal user to create a link to a directory and no user can create a link to a file across different **file systems**. File systems are the fundamental components of the overall UNIX file structure and will be explored in more detail in Chapter 4.

To overcome these limitations the *XSI* supports the concept of **symbolic links**. A symbolic link is actually a file in its own right, but instead of containing normal file data it contains the path of the file to which it is linked. It could be said that a symbolic link is a pointer to another file.

To create a symbolic link the symlink system call is used.

Usage

```
#include <unistd.h>

int symlink(const char *realname, const char *symname);
```

On completion of symlink the file symname is created and points to the file realname. If there is an error, for example symname is the name of an existing file, then symlink returns −1. Otherwise it returns 0 on success.

If a symbolic link file is ever opened with open then the open system call correctly follows the path to realname. If a programmer wishes to see the data held in symname itself then the system call readlink must be used.

Usage

```
#include <unistd.h>

int readlink(const char *sympath, char *buffer, size_t bufsize);
```

The readlink system call firstly opens sympath, then reads the contents of the file into buffer, and finally closes sympath. Unfortunately the *XSI* does not guarantee that the contents of buffer will be null terminated. The return value from readlink is the number of characters in the buffer, or −1 on error.

A word of caution when using and pursuing symbolic links. If the original file, pointed to by a symbolically linked file, is ever removed, then a somewhat misleading error will be reported if you try to access the file through the symbolic link. A program will still be able to 'see' the symbolic link but unfortunately an open call will not be able to follow the path contained within it and will return with errno set to EEXIST.

3.3 **Obtaining file information:** stat **and** fstat

So far we have only seen how to set or change the basic properties associated with files. The two system calls stat and fstat enable a process to discover the values of these properties for an existing file.

Usage

```#include <sys/types.h>```
```#include <sys/stat.h>```
 	
```int stat(const char *pathname, struct stat *buf);```
 	
```int fstat(int filedes, struct stat *buf);```

The stat system call is given two arguments; pathname as usual points to the pathname that identifies the file. The second buf is a pointer to a stat structure. This structure will hold the information associated with the file after a successful invocation.

The fstat system call is more or less identical in function to the stat system call. The only difference is that, instead of a pathname, fstat expects a file descriptor. fstat can therefore only be used with an open file.

```
        .
        .
        .
struct stat s;
int filedes, retval;

filedes = open("/tmp/dina", O_RDWR);

/* s can now be filled using either ... */
retval = stat("/tmp/dina", &s);

/* ... or */
retval = fstat(filedes, &s);
```

The definition of the structure stat is found in the system header file <sys/stat.h> and includes the following members:

```
dev_t       st_dev;
ino_t       st_ino;
mode_t      st_mode;
nlink_t     st_nlink;
uid_t       st_uid;
gid_t       st_gid;
dev_t       st_rdev;
off_t       st_size;
time_t      st_atime;
time_t      st_mtime;
time_t      st_ctime;
long        st_blksize;
long        st_blocks;
```

The types used by the stat structure are defined in the system header file <sys/types.h>.

The members of the stat structure itself have the following meanings:

1.   st_dev, st_ino   The first of these structure members describes the logical device on which the file resides and the second gives the *inode number* of the file. This, in conjunction with st_dev, identifies a file uniquely. In fact, both st_dev and st_ino are concerned with the underlying management of the UNIX file structure. We will explain these ideas in the next chapter. For the moment, you can safely ignore both these members.

2.   st_mode   This gives the file mode and enables a programmer to calculate the permissions associated with the file. A word of caution is due here. The value contained in st_mode also gives information on the type of file, and only the lowest 12 bits are concerned with permissions. This will become clear in Chapter 4.

3.   st_nlink   The number of non-symbolic links (in other words, the number of different pathnames) associated with the file. This value will be updated with each call of the link and unlink system calls.

4.   st_uid, st_gid   The uid and gid of the file. Initially set by creat or open and altered by the chown system call.

5.   st_rdev   This is meaningful only when the file entry is used to describe a device. Again you can safely ignore this member for the time being.

6.   st_size   The current *logical* size of the file in bytes. You should be aware that when a file is stored on disk it will be placed on the physical boundaries of the disk and therefore the actual physical size of a file may be greater than its logical size. st_size is changed after each write to the end of the file.

7.   st_atime   This records the last time the data in the file was read (although the initial creat or open will also set this value).

8.   st_mtime   This records the time the data in the file was in any way modified and is reset with each write to the file.

9.   st_ctime   This records the time since any of the information returned in the stat structure itself was altered. System calls which change this include link (because of st_nlink), chmod (because of st_mode) and write (because of st_mtime and possibly st_size).

10.   st_blksize   This records the file system specific I/O block size for this file. In some file systems this may vary from file to file.

11.   st_blocks   This records the number of physical file system blocks allocated to this particular file.

The following example subroutine filedata displays details associated with a file identified by pathname. The information printed out consists of the file size, the user and group ids of the file, and the file's read–write–execute permissions.

To help translate the file permissions into a readable form like that produced by ls, we have used an array of short integers octarray, which contains the values for the basic permissions, and a character array perms, which holds the character equivalent.

```c
/* filedata -- display information about a file */

#include <stdio.h>
#include <sys/stat.h>

/*
 * use octarray for determining
 * if permission bits set
 */
static short octarray[9] = { 0400,0200,0100,
                             0040,0020,0010,
                             0004,0002,0001};

/* mnemonic codes for file permissions,
 * 10 chars long because of the terminating null
 */
static char perms[10] = "rwxrwxrwx";

int filedata(const char *pathname)
{
 struct stat statbuf;
 char descrip[10];
 int j;

 if(stat(pathname, &statbuf) == -1)
 {
       fprintf(stderr, "Couldn't stat %s\n", pathname);
       return (-1);
 }

 /* put permissions into readable form */

 for(j=0; j<9; j++)
 {
       /*
        * test whether permission set
        * using bitwise AND
        */
       if(statbuf.st_mode & octarray[j])
             descrip[j] = perms[j];
       else
             descrip[j] = '-';
 }
 descrip[9] = '\0'; /* make sure we've a string */
```

```
/* display file information */

printf("\nFile %s :\n", pathname);
printf("Size %ld bytes\n", statbuf.st_size);
printf("User-id %d, Group-id %d\n\n", statbuf.st_uid,
        statbuf.st_gid);
printf("Permissions: %s\n", descrip);
return (0);
}
```

The following program `lookout` is a more useful tool. Given a list of filenames, it checks once a minute to see if any file in the list has changed. It does this by monitoring the modification time of each file (`st_mtime`). It is a utility intended to be run as a background process.

```
/* lookout -- print message when file changes */

#include <stdlib.h>
#include <stdio.h>
#include <sys/stat.h>

#define MFILE      10

void cmp(const char *, time_t);
struct stat sb;

main(int argc, char **argv)
{
 int j;
 time_t last_time[MFILE+1];

 if(argc < 2)
 {
      fprintf(stderr, "usage: lookout filename ...\n");
      exit(1);
 }

 if(--argc > MFILE)
 {
      fprintf(stderr, "lookout: too many filenames\n");
      exit(1);
 }

 /* initialization */

 for(j=1; j<=argc; j++)
 {
      if(stat(argv[j], &sb) == -1)
      {
           fprintf(stderr, "lookout: couldn't stat %s\n",
                            argv[j]);
           exit(1);
      }
      last_time[j] = sb.st_mtime;
 }
```

```
/* loop until file changes */
for(;;)
{
        for(j=1; j<=argc; j++)
                cmp(argv[j], last_time[j]);

        /*
         * rest for 60 seconds
         * "sleep" is a standard
         * UNIX library routine
         */
        sleep(60);
}
}


void cmp(const char *name, time_t last)
{
/* as long as statistics about the file can be read
 * check the modification time */
if(stat(name, &sb) == -1 || sb.st_mtime != last)
{
        fprintf(stderr, "lookout: %s changed\n", name);
        exit(0);
}
}
```

Exercise 3.9 Write a program which monitors, and records, the alterations in the size of a file over one hour. At the end, it should produce a simple histogram showing any variation over time.

Exercise 3.10 Write a program `slowwatch` which periodically monitors the modification time of a named file (it should not fail if the file does not initially exist). When the file changes, `slowwatch` should copy it to its standard output. How can you ensure (or guess) that the file is fully updated before it is copied?

3.3.1 `chmod` **revisited**

`stat` and `fstat` enhance the use of `chmod` because, since the mode of a file can now be obtained, a program can modify file permissions instead of merely resetting them unconditionally.

The following program `addx` demonstrates this. It first calls `stat` to obtain the current file mode of a file named in the program's argument list. If successful, it then modifies the existing permissions so that the file is executable by its owner. This might be useful if the file contained a 'shell script'.

```
/* addx -- add execute permission to file */

#include <stdlib.h>
#include <stdio.h>
#include <sys/stat.h>

#define XPERM      0100  /* Execute permission for owner */

main(int argc, char **argv)
{
 int k;
 struct stat statbuf;

 /* loop for all files in arg list */
 for(k=1; k<argc; k++)
 {
      /* get current file mode */
      if(stat(argv[k], &statbuf) == -1)
      {
          fprintf(stderr, "addx: couldn't stat %s\n", argv[k]);
          continue;
      }

      /* attempt to add execute permissions
         by using bitwise OR operator */

      statbuf.st_mode |= XPERM;
      if(chmod(argv[k], statbuf.st_mode) == -1)
         fprintf(stderr, "addx: couldn't change mode for %s\n",
                              argv[k]);

 } /* end of loop */

 exit(0);
}
```

The most interesting point here is the way the file mode is modified by using the bitwise OR operator. This ensures that the bit described by XPERM is set. In fact we could have lengthened this statement to:

```
statbuf.st_mode = (statbuf.st_mode) | XPERM;
```

We used the shorter form for clarity. We could also have used the system-defined name S_IXUSR instead of XPERM.

Exercise 3.11   This example is, for the task it performs, over-complex. If you know how, write an equivalent using the shell.

Exercise 3.12   Using your UNIX manual as a specification, write your own version of the chmod command.

CHAPTER 4

Directories, file systems and special files

4.1 Introduction

In the previous two chapters we concentrated on the basic component of the UNIX file structure – the regular file. This chapter will examine the other components of the file structure, namely:

- *Directories* Directories act as repositories for filenames and, consequently, allow users to group together arbitrary collections of files. The notion of directories will be familiar to most users of UNIX and many refugees from other operating systems. As we shall see, UNIX directories can be nested and this gives the file structure a hierarchical, tree-like form.

- *File systems* File systems are collections of directories and files. They represent complete subsections of the hierarchical tree of directories and files that makes up a UNIX file structure. Typically, file systems correspond to physical sections ('partitions') of a disk or an entire disk. They are, for most purposes, invisible to the user.

- *Special files*   UNIX extends the file concept to cover the peripheral devices connected to a system. These peripheral devices, such as printers, disk units and even main memory, are represented by filenames in the file structure. A file which represents a device in this way is called a **special file**. They can be accessed via the file access system calls discussed in Chapters 2 and 3 (for example, open, read and write). Each such call activates the device driver code within the kernel responsible for controlling the particular device. However, the program need not know anything about this; the system ensures that special files can be treated almost identically to regular files.

4.2 Directories: the user view

Even a casual user of UNIX will have some notion of how its directory structure appears at command level. However, for completeness we will briefly review the way the user views the layout of files and directories.

In essence, directories are just collections of filenames, which provide a means of dividing files into logically related groups. For example, each user is usually provided with his or her own **home directory**, where they are 'placed' at login, and where they are allowed to create and manipulate files. This makes obvious sense, since it keeps the files owned by different users separate. Public programs, such as cat or ls, are similarly kept together in just a handful of directories which have names such as /bin and /usr/bin. To use a common metaphor, directories can be compared to the drawers within filing cabinets that are used to group paper files.

However, directories do have some advantages over filing cabinets. As well as containing files, they can also contain other directories, called **subdirectories**, and so allow further levels of grouping. Subdirectories may in turn contain their own subdirectories, and this nesting can continue to any depth.

In fact, the UNIX file structure can be represented as an inverted, hierarchical, tree-like structure. A simplified directory tree is shown in Figure 4.1 (in fact, it is the same example as in Chapter 1). Any real-life system would, of course, have a more complex layout.

At the top of our example tree, and indeed any UNIX directory tree, there is a single directory called the root directory. This is given the rather terse name '/'. The non-terminal nodes within the tree, such as keith or ben, are always directories. The terminal nodes, such as file1 or file2, are either regular files, special files, or empty directories. Most UNIX systems now allow the names of directories to be up to 255 characters, but like the names of files, you should keep them to 14 characters or less for portability.

In our example, keith and ben are subdirectories of their parent directory called usr. In the directory called keith are three entries: two regular files called file1 and file2, and a subdirectory called book. From the viewpoint of book, it is

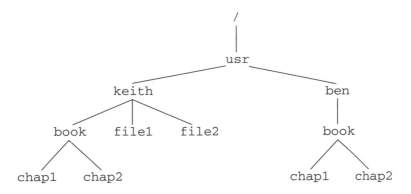

Figure 4.1 *Example directory tree.*

keith that is the parent directory. book in its turn contains two files, chap1 and
chap2. As Chapter 1 showed, the location of a file within the hierarchy can be
specified using a pathname. For example, the full pathname of the chap2 file
contained within keith is /usr/keith/book/chap2. Similarly, directories themselves can also be identified by pathnames. The pathname for the ben directory is
/usr/ben.

Notice that the directory /usr/ben/book also contains two files called
chap1 and chap2. These bear no necessary relation to their namesakes in the
/usr/keith/book directory, since it is only the full pathname that uniquely identifies
a file. The fact that files in different directories can have the same name means it is
unnecessary for users to continually invent weird, wonderful and unique filenames.

The current working directory

A logged-on user will find him or herself working at a particular place in the file
structure called the current working directory or sometimes just the current
directory. This is, for example, the directory from where the ls command will list
files, when run without arguments. The initial setting for a user's current working
directory is that user's home directory, as identified in the system password file. It
can be changed using the cd command. For example:

$ *cd /usr/keith*

changes the current working directory to /usr/keith. When you need to know, the
pwd command (the name pwd stands for 'print working directory') will print out the
name of the current working directory:

$ *pwd*
/usr/keith

As far as the system is concerned, the defining characteristic of the current
working directory is that it is the directory from where the system starts relative

pathname searches; that is, searches involving pathnames that do not begin with a '/'. For example, if the current working directory is /usr/keith, the command:

$ *cat book/chap1*

is equivalent to:

$ *cat /usr/keith/book/chap1*

and the command:

$ *cat file1*

is equivalent to:

$ *cat /usr/keith/file1*

4.3 The implementation of a directory

UNIX directories are, in fact, nothing more than files. In many respects they are treated by the system in the same way as regular files. They have an owner, group, a size and associated access permissions. Many of the system calls used for file manipulation that we covered in previous chapters could be used to manipulate directories, although this is not recommended. For example, directories may be opened for reading using the open system call and the returned file descriptor may be used in subsequent calls to read, lseek, fstat and close.

There are some important differences, however, between directories and regular files that are imposed by the system. Directories may not be created using the creat or open system calls. Nor will open work on a directory when either of the O_WRONLY or O_RDWR flags is set. It will instead fail and set errno to EISDIR. These limitations make it impossible to update a directory using write. In fact because of the special nature of directories it is much better to use a dedicated family of system calls, which we shall explore shortly.

Structurally, directories consist of a series of directory entries, one for each file or subdirectory contained within them. Each directory entry consists of at least a positive number called the file's **inode number**, and a character field which contains the file's name. In the good old days, when filenames were guaranteed to be no more than 14 characters in length, directory entries were set to a fixed length and the majority of UNIX systems used the same method of implementation (Berkeley UNIX was a notable exception). However, when longer filenames were introduced, each directory file entry became variable in length, and this meant that the implementation of a directory became file system dependent. Your programs should therefore never make assumptions about the actual format of a directory and to be truly portable should use the *XSI* directory manipulation system calls.

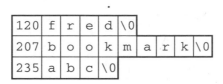

Figure 4.2 *Partial slice of a directory.*

A partial logical slice of a directory containing three files might look something like Figure 4.2. (We have excluded any information required to manage the free space within a directory file.) This directory contains the names of three files (which could be subdirectories) called `fred`, `bookmark` and `abc`. These have inode numbers of 120, 207 and 235, respectively. Figure 4.2 represents the logical structure of a directory; in reality the directory is a continuous stream of bytes.

The inode number uniquely identifies a file (actually, inode numbers are really only unique within a file system, but more of that later). The inode number is used by the operating system to locate a disk-based data structure, called the inode structure, which contains all the administrative information for the file: size, owner's user-id, group-id, permissions, date last accessed, last modified date and the disk addresses of the blocks on disk that hold the file data. Most of the information supplied by the `stat` and `fstat` calls described in the previous chapter is, in fact, obtained directly from the inode structure. We will explain inode structures in more detail in Section 4.5.

It is important to realize that our representation of a directory is only a logical picture. Printing the contents of a directory using the `cat` command can result in garbage being output on the terminal screen. A better way to examine a directory is to use the octal dump command `od` with the `-c` option. For example, to view the contents of the current working directory, try:

```
$ od -c .
```

The '.' in this command is the standard way of referring to the current working directory.

4.3.1 `link` and `unlink` revisited

In the previous chapter we saw how the `link` system call was used to create different names that referred to the same physical file. It should now be clear how this actually works. Each link simply results in a new directory slot with the same inode number as the original, and with a new name.

In the directory in Figure 4.2, if we created a link to the file `abc` called `xyz` with the following call:

```
link("abc", "xyz");
```

.
.

120	f	r	e	d	\0			
207	b	o	o	k	m	a	r	k	\0
235	a	b	c	\0
235	x	y	z	\0

Figure 4.3 *Example directory with new file.*

our partial directory slice might look like Figure 4.3. When a link is removed using the `unlink` system call, the appropriate bytes which held the filename are freed for reuse. If this filename represented the last link to the file, the entire inode structure is cleared. The associated disk blocks, which contained the actual file data, are added to a free list maintained by the system and become available for reuse. In most UNIX systems files cannot be 'undeleted'.

4.3.2 Dot and double-dot

Two strange filenames are always present in every directory. These are '.' and '..' (that is, dot and double-dot). The single dot is the standard UNIX method of referring to the current working directory as in:

   $ *cat ./fred*

which will type the file `fred` from the current directory, or:

   $ *ls .*

which will list the files in the current directory. The double-dot is the standard method of referring to the parent directory of the current working directory; that is, the directory that contains the current directory. So the command:

   $ *cd ..*

moves the user one level up the directory tree.

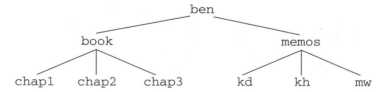

Figure 4.4 *Example section of directory tree.*

Directory ben

123	.	\0			
247	.	.	\0		
260	b	o	o	k	\0
401	m	e	m	o	s	\0

Directory book

260	.	\0			
123	.	.	\0		
566	c	h	a	p	1	\0
567	c	h	a	p	2	\0
590	c	h	a	p	3	\0

Directory memos

401	.	\0		
123	.	.	\0	
800	k	h	\0	
810	k	d	\0	
077	m	w	\0	

Figure 4.5 *Directories* ben, book *and* memos.

In fact, '.' and '..' are simply links to the current working directory and parent directory, respectively, and every UNIX directory contains these two names in its first two slots. To put it another way, every directory, when created, automatically contains these two names.

We can make things clearer by looking at the example section of the directory tree shown in Figure 4.4.

If we were to examine each of the directories ben, book and memos we would see something like Figure 4.5. Notice how in the directory book, '.' has an inode number of 260 and '..' has an inode number of 123 which correspond to the entries book and '.' in the parent directory, ben. Similarly '.' and '..' in memos (401 and 123) correspond to memos and '.' in ben.

4.3.3 Directory permissions

Like regular files, directories have permissions associated with them controlling the way different users can access them.

Directory permissions are organized in exactly the same way as regular file permissions with the three groups of 'rwx' bits specifying the privileges of the directory owner, users in the owner's group and all other system users. However, even though the permissions are represented in exactly the same way, they are interpreted rather differently.

- Read permission on a directory means that the appropriate class of users is able to list the names of files and subdirectories contained within the directory. This does not mean that the users are able to read the information contained in the files themselves – permission for that is controlled by the access permissions of the individual files.

- Write permission on a directory enables a user to create new files and remove existing files in that directory. Again, it does not permit a user to modify the contents of existing files unless the individual file permissions say so. It would, however, be possible to remove an existing file and create a new one with the same name, which really amounts to the same thing.

- Execute permission (also called **search permission**) on a directory allows a user to 'move into' the directory using the cd command, or the chdir system call within a program (we discuss the latter below). In addition, to open a file, or execute a program, a user must have execute permission on all directories leading to the file as specified in the file's absolute pathname.

At shell command level, the permissions associated with directories can be examined using the -l option to the ls command. Subdirectories will be identified by a letter 'd' in the first character position of the listing. For example:

```
$ ls -l
total 168
-rw-r-----   1   ben   other   39846   Oct 12   21:21   dir_t
drwxr-x---   2   ben   other      32   Oct 12   22:02   expenses
-rw-r-----   1   ben   other   46245   Sep 13   10:34   new
-rw-r-----   1   ben   other    3789   Sep  2   18:40   pwd_text
-rw-r-----   1   ben   other    1310   Sep 13   10:38   test.c
```

Here the line describing subdirectory expenses is tagged with a leading letter 'd'. It shows that the directory has access permissions of read, write and execute (search) for its owner (user ben), read and execute permissions for users in the file's group (called other), and no access permissions at all for other users.

If you want to obtain listing information about the current working directory you can give the -d option to ls as well as the -l option. For example:

```
$ ls -ld
drwxr-x---   3   ben   other     128   Oct 12   22:02   .
```

Remember that the name '.' at the end of the listing is used to refer to the current working directory.

4.4 Programming with directories

As mentioned earlier, there is a special family of calls to do with directories. These generally centre around the structure of type dirent, which is defined in the header file <dirent.h> and includes the following members:

```
ino_t       d_ino;      /* inode number */
char        d_name[];   /* filename, null terminated */
```

The data type ino_t is defined in the header file <sys/types.h>, which itself is included in the <dirent.h> header file. The *XSI* does not specify the size of d_name but it does guarantee that the number of bytes preceding the terminating null will be less than the number held in the variable _PC_NAME_MAX, which is defined in <unistd.h>. Note that a zero value of d_ino denotes an empty slot in the directory.

4.4.1 Creating and removing directories

As previously mentioned, directories cannot be created using the creat or open system calls. A special system call, mkdir, is available for this task.

Usage
| ```
#include <sys/types.h>
#include <sys/stat.h>

int mkdir(const char *pathname, mode_t mode);
``` |

The first parameter pathname points to a character string which contains the pathname of the directory to be created. The second parameter mode is the set of access permissions for the directory. The permissions will be modified by the process' umask value. For example:

```
int retval;
retval = mkdir("/tmp/dir1", 0777);
```

You will not be surprised to learn that a successful call to mkdir will return 0, an unsuccessful call −1. Much more importantly, you should note that mkdir also places the two links '.' and '..' into the newly created directory. If these two did not exist, the entry would be unusable as a directory.

When a directory is no longer needed it can be removed with the rmdir function.

Usage
| ```
#include <unistd.h>

int rmdir(const char *pathname);
``` |

The parameter `pathname` specifies the path of the directory to be removed. This function is only successful if the directory is empty (that is, only contains . (dot) and .. (double-dot)).

4.4.2 Opening and closing directories

To open any UNIX directory the *XSI* defines a specific function called `opendir`.

Usage

```
#include <sys/types.h>
#include <dirent.h>

DIR *opendir(const char *dirname);
```

The parameter passed to `opendir` is the pathname of the directory to be opened. If `dirname` is successfully opened then `opendir` returns a pointer to a `DIR` type. The `<dirent.h>` header file includes a type definition for `DIR` which represents a directory stream. It works in a similar way to the `FILE` type used in the Standard I/O Library, as described in Chapters 2 and 11. The pointer to the directory stream is positioned at the first entry of the directory. If the call to `opendir` fails then the system returns a null pointer. You should always write the appropriate error checking code to test for the null pointer before trying to read from the directory stream.

When the program has finished accessing the directory it should be closed. This can be achieved with the `closedir` function.

Usage

```
#include <dirent.h>

int closedir(DIR *dirptr);
```

The `closedir` function closes the directory stream pointed to by the argument `dirptr`. This will normally be the value returned from the `opendir` call, as the following code fragment demonstrates:

```
#include <stdlib.h>
#include <dirent.h>

main()
{
  DIR *dp;
```

```
if((dp = opendir("/tmp/dir1")) == NULL)
{
        fprintf(stderr, "Error on opening directory /tmp/dir1\n");
        exit(1);
}

/* processing code for the directory */

    .
    .
    .
closedir(dp);
}
```

4.4.3 Reading directories: `readdir` and `rewinddir`

Once the directory has been opened with `opendir`, each directory entry can then be read into a `dirent` structure.

Usage

`#include <sys/types.h>`
`#include <dirent.h>`
 	
`struct dirent *readdir(DIR *dirptr);`

The `readdir` function should be passed a valid directory stream pointer, normally the one returned from the call to `opendir`. On the first call of `readdir` the first directory entry will be read into the `struct dirent`. On completion the directory pointer will be moved onto the next entry in the directory.

If after successive calls to `readdir` the end of the directory is reached then the null pointer will be returned. If at any stage the program wishes to start rereading from the beginning of the directory the `rewinddir` call can be made, which is defined as follows:

Usage

`#include <sys/types.h>`
`#include <dirent.h>`
 	
`void rewinddir(DIR *dirptr);`

Following the `rewinddir` call the next `readdir` will return the first entry of the directory pointed to by `dirptr`.

In the following example, the function `my_double_ls` will list the names of all the files in a given directory, twice. It accepts a directory name as a parameter, and returns −1 on error.

```
#include <dirent.h>

int my_double_ls(const char *name)
{
 struct dirent *d;
 DIR *dp;

 /* open the directory and check for failure */
 if((dp=opendir(name)) == NULL)
      return (-1);

 /* continue looping through the directory,
  * printing out the directory entry name as long
  * as the inode number is valid
  */
 while(d = readdir(dp))
 {
     if(d->d_ino != 0)
          printf("%s\n", d->d_name);
 }

 /* now go back to the beginning of the directory ... */
 rewinddir(dp);

 /* ... and print out the directory again */
 while(d = readdir(dp))
 {
     if(d->d_ino != 0)
          printf("%s\n", d->d_name);
 }

 closedir(dp);
 return (0);
}
```

The order of the filenames printed by the my_double_ls function will reflect the order in which the files were placed in the directory. If my_double_ls is executed in a directory containing the three files abc, bookmark and fred the output might appear as follows:

```
.
..
fred
bookmark
abc
.
..
fred
bookmark
abc
```

A second example: `find_entry`

The next example routine `find_entry` will search through a directory looking for the next occurrence of a file (or subdirectory) ending with a specified suffix. The function takes three parameters: a directory name to be searched, the suffix string and a flag indicating whether the search should continue from the last slot found. If a suitable name is found, a pointer to the name is returned, otherwise the null pointer is returned.

    `find_entry` uses a string-matching routine called `match` to check whether a particular filename ends with the desired suffix. `match` in turn calls two standard routines from the C library found in all UNIX systems: `strlen`, which returns the length of a string in characters, and `strcmp`, which compares two strings, returning zero if they match exactly.

```
#include <stdio.h>  /* for NULL */
#include <dirent.h>
#include <string.h> /* for string functions */

int match(const char *, const char *);

char *find_entry(char *dirname, char *suffix, int cont)
{
 static DIR *dp=NULL;
 struct dirent *d;

 if(dp == NULL || cont == 0){
     if(dp != NULL}
         closedir(dp)
     if((dp = opendir(dirname)) -- NULL)
         return (NULL);
 }

 while(d = readdir(dp))
 {
     if(d->d_ino == 0)
         continue;
     if(match(d->d_name, suffix))
         return (d->d_name);
 }
 closedir(dp);
 dp = NULL
 return(NULL);
}

int match(const char *s1, const char *s2)
{
 int diff = strlen(s1) - strlen(s2);

 if(strlen(s1) > strlen(s2))
     return(strcmp(&s1[diff], s2) == 0);
 else
     return (0);
}
```

Exercise 4.1 Modify the `my_double_ls` function in the earlier example to accept a second parameter – an integer called `skip`. When `skip` is set to 0, `my_double_ls` should perform as before. When skip is set to 1, `my_double_ls` should skip any files with names that begin with a dot '.'.

Exercise 4.2 In the previous chapter, we introduced the `stat` and `fstat` system calls as a means of obtaining file information. The `stat` structure returned by `stat` and `fstat` contains a field called `st_mode`, which contains the file mode. This is made up of the file permissions bitwise ORed with a constant that determines whether the data structure represents a regular file, a directory, a special file or an inter-process communication mechanism such as a named pipe. The best way to test whether a file is a directory is to use the macro `S_ISDIR` as follows:

```
/* buf comes from a call to stat */
if(S_ISDIR(buf.st_mode))
    printf("It's a directory\n");
else
    printf("It's not\n");
```

Modify the `my_double_ls` routine so that it calls `stat` for every file found, and prints an asterisk after every filename that refers to a directory.

4.4.4 The current working directory

As we saw in Section 4.2, each logged-in user works within a current working directory. In fact each UNIX process, that is, each program execution, has its own current working directory. This is used as the starting point for all relative pathname searches in `open` calls and the like. The current directory apparently associated with a user is actually the current working directory associated with the shell process that interprets his or her commands.

Initially, the current working directory of a process is set to the current working directory of the process from which it was started, usually the shell. However, it is possible for a process to change its current working directory via the system call `chdir`.

4.4.5 Changing directories with `chdir`

Usage
`#include <unistd.h>`
`int chdir(const char *path);`

The chdir system call causes path to become the new current working directory of the calling process. It is important to note that this change applies only to the process that makes the chdir call. In particular, a program that changes directory will not disturb the shell that started the program. So, when a program exits, the user will find the shell in the place where it started, regardless of the wanderings of the program.

chdir will fail, and consequently return a value of −1, if path does not define a valid directory or if execute permission does not exist at every component directory along the path for the calling process.

chdir can be usefully invoked when a program needs to access a number of files in a given directory. Changing directory and using filenames relative to this new directory will be more efficient than using absolute filenames. This is because the system has to scan each directory in a pathname in turn until the final filename is located, so reducing the number of components in a pathname saves time. For example, instead of using the following program fragment:

```
fd1 = open("/usr/ben/abc", O_RDONLY);
fd2 = open("/usr/ben/xyz", O_RDWR);
```

a programmer could use:

```
chdir("/usr/ben");
fd1 = open("abc", O_RDONLY);
fd2 = open("xyz", O_RDWR);
```

4.4.6 Finding the name of the current working directory

The *XSI* defines a function (not a system call) called getcwd which returns the name of the current working directory.

Usage

```#include <unistd.h>```
 	
```char *getcwd(char *name, size_t size);```

The getcwd function returns a pointer to the current directory pathname. You should remember that the size argument should be at least one greater than the length of the pathname to be returned. On success the current directory name is copied into the array pointed to by name. The call will fail if size is 0 and will return the null pointer. On some implementations if name is the null pointer, getcwd will allocate size bytes of dynamic memory; however, because the implementation is system dependent, invoking getcwd with a null pointer is not recommended.

An example: my_pwd

This short program imitates the pwd command:

```
/* my_pwd -- print working directory */

#include <stdio.h>
#include <unistd.h>
#define VERYBIG 200

void my_pwd(void);

main()
{
 my_pwd();
}

void my_pwd(void)
{
 char dirname[VERYBIG];

 if( getcwd(dirname, VERYBIG) == NULL)
      perror("getcwd error");
 else
      printf("%s\n", dirname);
}
```

4.4.7 Walking a directory tree

Sometimes it is necessary to perform an operation on a directory hierarchy beginning at some starting directory, and working down through all files and subdirectories. To this end, UNIX provides a routine called ftw which performs a directory tree walk starting at any directory and calls a user-defined routine for each directory entry found.

Usage

```
#include <ftw.h>

int ftw(const char *path, int(*func)(), int depth);
```

The first parameter path defines the directory pathname at which the recursive tree walk should begin. The depth parameter is a rather strange beast that controls the number of different file descriptors used by ftw. The larger the value of depth, the fewer directories have to be reopened, therefore increasing the speed of the call. Although only one file descriptor will be used at each level in the tree you must ensure that the value of depth is not greater than the number of file descriptors available. The system call, getrlimit, discussed in Chapter 12, can be used to determine the maximum number of file descriptors a process may allocate.

The second parameter, `func` is a user-defined function that will be called for every file or directory found in the hierarchy that starts at `path`. As can be seen in the usage description, `func` is passed to the `ftw` routine as a function pointer. It needs, therefore, to be declared prior to the call to `ftw`. At each call, `func` will be called with three arguments: a null-terminated string holding the object name, a pointer to a `stat` structure containing data about the object, and an integer code. `func` should therefore be constructed as follows:

```
int func(const char *name, const struct stat *sptr, int type)
{
 /* body of function */
}
```

The integer argument (`type` above) contains one of several possible values (all defined in the header file `<ftw.h>`), which describe the object encountered. These values are:

FTW_F   The object is a file.

FTW_D   The object is a directory.

FTW_DNR   The object is a directory that could not be read.

FTW_SL   The object is a symbolic link.

FTW_NS   The object is not a symbolic link and is one for which `stat` could not be executed successfully.

If the object was a directory that could not be read (FTW_DNR), then descendants of that directory will not be processed. If the `stat` function could not be executed successfully (FTW_NS), then the `stat` structure passed to the user-defined structure will contain undefined values.

The tree walk continues until the bottom of the tree is reached or an error is encountered in `ftw`. The walk can also be terminated if the user-defined function returns a non-zero value. At this point, `ftw` halts execution and returns the value returned to it by the user function. Errors within `ftw` cause a value of −1 to be returned and the error type is set in `errno`.

The next example uses `ftw` to descend a directory hierarchy, printing out the name of the files it encounters on the way, along with their access permissions, and indicating which files are directories (or symbolic links) by appending an asterisk to their name.

First, let us look at the function `list` that will be passed as an argument to `ftw`.

```
#include <sys/stat.h>
#include <ftw.h>

int list(const char *name, const struct stat *status,
         int type)
{
 /* if the stat call failed, just return */
 if(type == FTW_NS)
       return 0;
```

```
/*
 * otherwise print object name,
 * permissions and "*" postfix
 * if object is a directory or symbolic link
 */
if(type == FTW_F)
        printf("%-30s\t0%3o\n", name, status->st_mode&0777);
else
        printf("%-30s*\t0%3o\n", name, status->st_mode&0777);

return 0;
}
```

The next task is to write a main program that accepts a pathname as an argument and uses it as the starting point for the tree walk. If no argument is supplied, the walk will begin at the current working directory.

```
main(int argc, char **argv)
{
 int list(const char *, const struct stat *, int);

 if(argc == 1)
        ftw(".", list, 1);
 else
        ftw(argv[1], list, 1);
 exit(0);
}
```

The output from our list program might look something like:

```
$ list
.                              *    0755
./list                         *    0755
./file1                             0644
./subdir                       *    0777
./subdir/another                    0644
./subdir/subdir2               *    0755
./subdir/yetanother                 0644
```

for a simple directory hierarchy. Notice the order in which directories are processed.

4.5 UNIX file systems

We have seen that files may be organized into different directories and that directories form part of an overall hierarchical tree structure. Directories can themselves be grouped together into a **file system**. File systems are generally only of concern to the UNIX System Administrator. They allow the directory structure to be accommodated across several distinct, physical disks or disk partitions, while retaining the uniform user view of the structure.

Each file system starts at a directory node within the hierarchy tree. This facility allows system administrators to divide up a UNIX file hierarchy and allocate parts of it to specific areas of a disk or indeed to split a complete file structure across several physical disk devices. The physical division of file systems is, for the most part, invisible to users.

File systems are also called **demountable volumes** because it is possible to dynamically introduce complete subsections of the hierarchy anywhere into the tree structure. More to the point, it is also possible to dynamically disconnect, or unmount, a complete file system from the hierarchy and, therefore, make it temporarily inaccessible to users. At any given moment in time several file systems may be online, but not all of them will necessarily be visible as part of the tree-structured hierarchy.

The information contained in a file system resides on a disk partition that is identified by an entity called a UNIX **device file** (also called a **special file**), the idea of which is discussed in detail below. For the time being, just note that file systems are in some way uniquely identified by UNIX filenames.

The actual low-level layout of the data held in a file system is completely different from the high-level hierarchical view of directories presented to the user. In addition, this layout is not part of the *XSI* and a variety of different forms exist. The kernel can concurrently support file systems with different layouts. For discussion purposes we will describe the traditional layout.

The traditional file system is divided into a number of logical blocks. Every such file system contains four distinct sections: a **bootstrap** area, a file system **super block**, a number of blocks reserved for file system inode structures and the area reserved for the data blocks that make up the files on that particular file system. Pictorially, this layout is as shown in Figure 4.6. The first of these blocks (logical

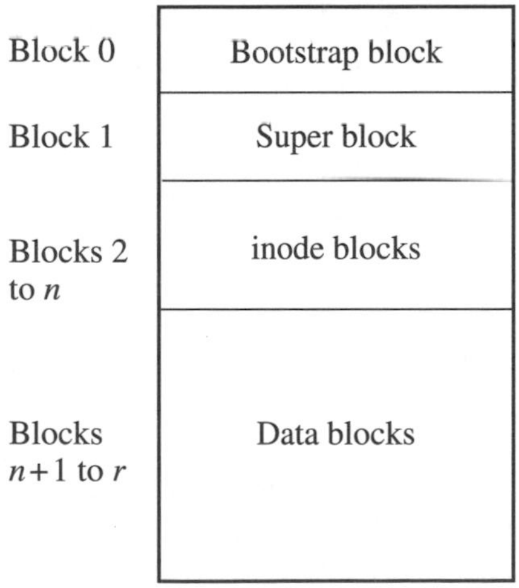

Figure 4.6 *Traditional file system layout.*

block 0 in the file system but physically wherever the disk partition begins) is reserved for use as the bootstrap block. That is, it may contain a hardware-specific boot program that is used to load UNIX at system startup time.

Logical block 1 on the file system is called the file system super block. It contains all the vital information about the file system, for example the total file system size (r blocks in the diagram), the number of blocks reserved for inodes ($n - 2$), and the date and time that the file system was last updated. The super block also contains two lists. The first holds part of a chain of free data block numbers, and the second part of a chain of free inode numbers for fast access when allocating new disk blocks for data or creating a new directory slot. The super block for a mounted file system is kept in memory to give fast access into the free block and free inode lists. The in-memory lists are replenished from disk when they become exhausted.

The size of an inode structure is file system dependent; for example, in some systems they are 64 bytes in size and on others they can be 128 bytes. Inodes are numbered sequentially from 1 onwards, and so a simple algorithm is used to determine the location of an inode structure given the inode number that is extracted from a directory slot.

File systems are created using the `mkfs` program and it is when this program is executed that the sizes of the inode areas and data areas for the file system must be specified. In traditional file systems these sizes could not be changed dynamically and it was possible to run out of space on a file system in two ways. First, all the data blocks may have been used up (even though there may have still been available inode numbers). Second, it was possible to use up all the inode numbers (by creating lots of small files) and consequently not be able to create any new files on the file system but still have data blocks free. Today, however, more modern file systems can be resized and inodes are often allocated dynamically.

You should be able to see from this discussion that inode numbers are only unique within a file system and that it is therefore impossible to link files across file systems unless symbolic links are used.

4.5.1 Caching: `sync` and `fsync`

For efficiency reasons, with the traditional file system structure copies of the super blocks of mounted file systems are kept in a UNIX machine's main memory. Updates to these super blocks can then occur quickly without the need to access the disk directly. Similarly, all transfers from memory to disk, that is, writes, are typically cached in the operating system's data space instead of being written out to disk immediately. Reads as well are buffered within the cache. At any given moment, therefore, the actual data on disk may be out of date with respect to the cache stored in main memory. UNIX provides two functions to allow a process to ensure that things are set up to date. `sync` is used to flush, to disk, all the main memory buffers containing information about file systems and `fsync` is called to flush out all data and attributes associated with a particular file.

Usage

`#include <unistd.h>`
 	
`void sync(void);`
 	
`int fsync(int filedes);`

The important difference between these two calls is that `fsync` will not return until all the file data has been written to disk whereas the `sync` call may return when the writing of the data has been scheduled, but not necessarily completed (and in some specific implementations, `sync` may be unnecessary, and have no effect).

As can be seen the `sync` function returns no value. However, the `fsync` call will return 0 if successful and −1 on error. `fsync` may fail for example if `fildes` is not a valid file descriptor.

In order to ensure that file systems are not out of date for too long, the UNIX system continually runs a piece of code that repeatedly calls `sync`, pausing for a specified period of time between each call. Typically, this period is 30 seconds, although the time interval is a configurable parameter under the control of the system administrator.

4.6 UNIX device files

The peripheral devices attached to UNIX systems (disks, terminals, printers, tape units and so on) are accessed through filenames in the file system. These files are called device files. The disk partitions corresponding to file systems are among the objects represented by these special files.

Unlike ordinary disk files, reads and writes to these device files cause data to be transferred directly between the system and the appropriate peripheral device.

Typically, these special files are stored in a directory called /dev. So, for example:

```
/dev/tty00
/dev/console
/dev/pts/as        (a pseudo-terminal, for network access)
```

could be the names given to three of a system's terminal ports, and:

```
/dev/lp
/dev/rmt0
/dev/rmt/0cbn
```

could refer to a line printer and two magnetic tape drives.

Names for disk partitions are much more variable. Possibilities include:

```
/dev/dsk/c0b0t0d0s3
/dev/dsk/hd0d
```

Device files may be used at command level or within programs just like regular files. For example:

```
$ cat fred > /dev/lp
$ cat fred > /dev/rmt0
```

would cause the file `fred` to be written to a line printer and magnetic tape unit, respectively (access permissions permitting). It is obviously madness to try to manipulate disk partitions containing file systems directly in this way. Much valuable information could be accidentally destroyed with a careless command. In addition, if the permissions on such a device file are too permissive, then it is possible for sophisticated users to bypass the permissions of files held on the file system. System administrators should set the appropriate access permissions on disk partition device files to ensure that this is impossible.

From within a program, `open`, `close`, `read` and `write` can all be used on device files. For example:

```
#include <fcntl.h>

main()
{
 int i, fd;

 fd = open("/dev/tty00", O_WRONLY);

 for(i=0; i<100; i++)
      write(fd, "x", 1);

 close(fd);
}
```

would cause 100 xs to be written to terminal port `tty00`. Terminal handling is obviously an important topic and we will go into this in much greater detail in Chapter 9.

4.6.1 Block and character device files

UNIX device files are divided into two categories: **block devices** and **character devices**.

1. *Block device files* include devices such as disk or magnetic tape units. The transfer of data between these devices and the kernel occurs in standard-sized

blocks. All block devices will support random access. Inside the kernel, access to these devices is controlled by a highly structured set of kernel data structures and routines. This common interface to block devices means that, typically, block device drivers are very similar, varying only in their low-level control over the device in question.

2. *Character device files* include devices such as terminal lines, modem lines and printer devices that do not share this structured transfer mechanism. Random access may, or may not, be supported. Data transfer is not performed in fixed size blocks, but in terms of byte streams of arbitrary length.

It is important to note that file systems can only exist on block devices and therefore these block devices have associated character devices for fast access often known as the **raw** device. Utilities such as mkfs and fsck use the raw interface.

UNIX uses two operating system configuration tables called the **block device switch** and **character device switch** tables to associate a peripheral device with the device-specific code to drive the particular peripheral. These tables and the device-specific code are held within the kernel itself. Both tables are indexed using a value called the **major device number**, which is stored in the device file's inode. The sequence for transmitting data to or from a peripheral device is as follows:

1. read or write system calls access the device file's inode in the normal way.

2. The system checks a flag within the inode structure to see whether the device is a block or a character device. The major number is also extracted.

3. The major number is used to index into the appropriate device configuration table and the device-specific driver routine is called to perform the data transfer.

In this way accesses to peripheral devices can be entirely consistent with accesses to normal disk files.

As well as the major device number, a second value called the **minor device number** is also stored in the inode and is passed to the device driver routines in order to identify exactly which port is being accessed on those devices which support more than one peripheral port. For example, on an 8-line terminal board each terminal line would share the same major number (and consequently the same set of device driver routines), but would each have its own unique minor number in the range 0 to 7 to identify the particular line being accessed.

4.6.2 The stat structure revisited

The stat structure, which we first discussed in Chapter 3, has a provision for storing device file information in two fields:

st_mode   In the case of a device file, this contains the file's permissions added to a value of octal 060000 for block devices or 020000 for character devices. There are symbolic constants defined in <stat.h> which can be used instead of these actual numbers, namely: S_IFBLK and S_IFCHR.

st_rdev   This contains the major and minor device numbers.

This information can be displayed by using the ls command with the -l option. For example:

```
$ ls -l /dev/tty3
    crw--w--w-   1   ben   other   8,3   Sep 13 10:19   /dev/tty3
```

Notice the letter 'c' in the first column of the output, which specifies that /dev/tty3 is a character device file. The integer values 8 and 3 represent the major and minor device numbers, respectively.

Within a program, st_mode can be tested using the technique introduced in Exercise 4.2:

```
if(S_ISCHR(buf.st_mode))
 printf("It's a character device\n");
else
 printf("It's not\n");
```

Remember that S_ISCHR is a macro defined in <stat.h>.

4.6.3 File system information

For devices that hold file systems, two functions, statvfs and fstatvfs, can be called to obtain basic file system information such as the total number of free disk blocks and the number of free inodes.

Usage

#include <sys/statvfs.h>
 	
int statvfs(const char *path, struct statvfs *buf);
 	
int fstatvfs(int fd, struct statvfs *buf);

Both functions return information about the file system which holds the file referenced by the path parameter for statvfs or for the open file referenced by fd for fstatvfs. The buf parameter is an occurrence of the statvfs structure type which is defined in the <sys/statvfs.h> header file. The statvfs structure includes at least the following members:

`unsigned long f_bsize`	the file system block size used by the system to get better performance. For example, `f_frsize` may be set to 1K, but `f_bsize` may be set to 8K in order that the system may perform more efficient I/O.
`unsigned long f_frsize`	the fundamental file system block size (as specified when the file system was created)
`unsigned long f_blocks`	total number of blocks on the file system in units of `f_frsize`
`unsigned long f_bfree`	total number of free blocks
`unsigned long f_bavail`	number of free blocks available to non-privileged processes
`unsigned long f_files`	total number of inode numbers
`unsigned long f_ffree`	total number of free inode numbers
`unsigned long f_favail`	number of inode numbers available to non-privileged processes
`unsigned long f_fsid`	file system id
`unsigned long f_flag`	bit mask of flag values
`unsigned long f_namemax`	maximum file length

The following example in this chapter parallels the standard df command. It uses statvfs to print the number of free blocks and free inodes on a file system.

```
/* fsys -- print file system information. */
/* the file system name is passed in as an argument */

#include <sys/statvfs.h>
#include <stdlib.h>
#include <stdio.h>

main(int argc, char **argv)
{
 struct statvfs buf;

 if(argc != 2)
 {
      fprintf(stderr, "usage: fsys filename\n");
      exit(1);
 }
```

```
if(statvfs(argv[1], &buf) != 0)
{
      fprintf(stderr, "statvfs error\n");
      exit(2);
}
printf("%s:\tfree blocks %d\tfree inodes %d\n",
                 argv[1], buf.f_bfree, buf.f_ffree);
exit(0);
}
```

4.6.4 File and directory limits: `pathconf` and `fpathconf`

POSIX and other standards activity have introduced more formality over certain system limits. Since a system can support multiple file system types, certain limits can vary across files and directories. Two routines, `pathconf` and `fpathconf` can be used to interrogate these limits for your particular system on a file or directory basis.

Usage

`#include <unistd.h>`
 	
`long int pathconf(const char *pathname, int name);`
 	
`long int fpathconf(int filedes, int name);`

The two routines work in the same way and return the value for a requested limit or variable. The difference between the two is in the first parameter: for `pathconf` a valid pathname of a file or directory should be given, and for `fpathconf` the file descriptor of an open file should be given. The second parameter is the symbolic name of the variable to be interrogated for that particular file or directory, taken from `<unistd.h>`.

The following routine, `lookup`, can be used on a file to print out system limits for that particular file. In this example `lookup` displays the more interesting of those values for the standard directory `/tmp`:

```
/* lookup -- displays the settings of file limits */

#include <unistd.h>
#include <stdio.h>

typedef struct{
 int val;
 char *name;
} Table;
```

```
main()
{
 Table *tb;
 static Table options[] = {
        { _PC_LINK_MAX, "Maximum number of links"},
        { _PC_NAME_MAX, "Maximum length of a filename"},
        { _PC_PATH_MAX, "Maximum length of pathname"},
        {-1, NULL}
 };

 for(tb=options; tb->name != NULL; tb++)
        printf("%-28.28s\t%ld\n", tb->name,
                                   pathconf("/tmp", tb->val));
}
```

When this program was run on one system it produced the following output:

```
Maximum number of links      32767
Maximum length of a filename 256
Maximum length of a pathname 1024
```

/tmp is a directory. The maximum number of links refers to the directory itself. The maximum filename length, however, refers to files in the directory. In general, *system-wide* limits are documented in <limits.h> and values can be found dynamically using a similar routine called sysconf.

CHAPTER 5

The process

5.1 Review of the notion of a process

As we saw in Chapter 1, a process, in UNIX terms, is simply an instance of an executing program, corresponding to the notion of a task in other environments. Each process incorporates program code, the data values within program variables, and more exotic items such as the values held in hardware registers, the program stack and so on.[†]

[†] This is not to be confused with the notion of a thread, where several copies of code only execute on a single set of data. Threads are now commonly available in some UNIX implementations, and are covered in recent extensions to *POSIX* and latest updates to the *XSI*. However, we will not describe the complexities of the thread-based model further. For more information, try your local manual.

The shell creates a new process each time it starts up a program in response to a command. For example, the command line:

$ *cat file1 file2*

results in the shell creating a process especially to run the cat command. The slightly more complex command line:

$ *ls | wc -l*

results in two processes being created to run the commands ls and wc concurrently. (In addition, the output of the directory listing program ls is **piped** into the word count program wc.)

Because a process corresponds to an execution of a program, processes should not be confused with the programs they run; indeed, several processes can concurrently run the same program. For example, several users may be running the same editor program simultaneously, each invocation of the one program counting as a separate process.

Any UNIX process may in turn start other processes. This gives the UNIX process environment a hierarchical structure paralleling the directory tree of the file system. At the top of the process tree is a single controlling process, an execution of an extremely important program called init, which is ultimately the ancestor of all system and user processes.

For the programmer, UNIX provides a handful of system calls for process creation and manipulation. Excluding the various facilities for inter-process communication, the most important of these are:

fork Used to create a new process by duplicating the calling process. fork is the basic process creation primitive.

exec A family of library routines and one system call, each of which performs the same underlying function: the transformation of a process by overlaying its memory space with a new program. The differences between exec calls lie mainly in the way their argument lists are constructed.

wait This call provides rudimentary process synchronization. It allows one process to wait until another related process finishes.

exit Used to terminate a process.

In the rest of this chapter we will discuss the UNIX process in general and these four important calls in particular.

5.2 Creating processes

5.2.1 The `fork` system call

The fundamental process creation primitive is the `fork` system call. It is the mechanism which transforms UNIX into a multitasking system.

Usage

`#include <sys/types.h>`
`#include <unistd.h>`
 	
`pid_t fork(void);`

A successful call to `fork` causes the kernel to create a new process which is a (more or less) exact duplicate of the calling process. In other words the new process runs a copy of the same program as its creator, the variables within this having the same values as those within the calling process, with a single important exception, which we shall discuss shortly.

The newly created process is described as the **child process**, the one that called `fork` in the first place is called, not unnaturally, its **parent**.

After the call the parent process and its newly created offspring execute concurrently, both processes resuming execution at the statement immediately after the call to `fork`.

For those used to a purely sequential programming environment, the idea of `fork` can be a little difficult at first. Figure 5.1 demonstrates the notion more clearly. The figure centres around three lines of code, consisting of a call to `printf`, followed by a call to `fork` and then another call to `printf`.

There are two sections to the figure, *Before* and *After*. The *Before* section shows things prior to the invocation of `fork`. There is a single process labelled *A* (we are using the label *A* purely for convenience; it means nothing to the system). The arrow labelled *PC* (for program counter) shows the statement currently being executed. Since it points to the first `printf`, the rather trivial message One is displayed on standard output.

The *After* section shows the situation immediately following the call to `fork`. There are now two processes *A* and *B* running together. Process *A* is the same as in the *Before* part of the figure. *B* is the new process spawned by the call to `fork`. With one major exception, the value of `pid`, it is a copy of *A* and is executing the same program as *A*, hence the duplication of the three lines of source code in the figure. Using the terminology we introduced above, *A* is the parent process while *B* is its child.

The two *PC* arrows in this part of the figure show that the next statement executed by both parent and child after the `fork` invocation is a call to `printf`. In other words, both *A* and *B* pick up at the same point in the program code, even though *B* is new to the system. The message Two is therefore displayed twice.

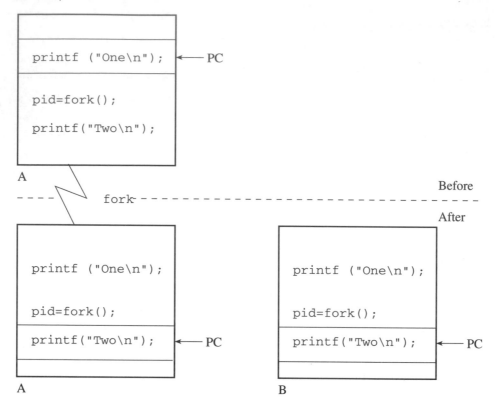

Figure 5.1 *The* fork *call.*

Process-ids

As you can see from the usage description at the beginning of this section, fork is called without arguments and returns a pid_t. The special pid_t type is defined in <sys/types.h> and is typically integer. An example call would be:

```
#include <unistd.h>      /* includes pid_t definition */

pid_t pid;
.
.
.
pid = fork();
```

It is the value of pid that distinguishes child and parent. In the parent, pid is set to a non-zero, positive number. In the child it is set to zero. Because the return value in parent and child differ, the programmer is able to specify different actions for the two processes.

The number returned to the parent in pid is called the **process-id** of the child process. It is this number that identifies the new process to the system, rather like a user-id identifies a user. Since all processes are born through a call to fork, every

UNIX process has its own process-id, which at any one time is unique to that process. A process-id can therefore best be thought of as the identifying signature of its process.

The following short program demonstrates the action of fork, and the use of the process-id, perhaps a little more clearly:

```
/* spawn -- demonstrates fork */
#include <unistd.h>

main()
{
 pid_t pid;    /* hold process-id in parent */

 printf("Just one process so far\n");
 printf("Calling fork...\n");

 pid = fork();  /* create new process */

 if(pid == 0)
      printf("I'm the child\n");
 else if(pid > 0)
      printf("I'm the parent, child has pid %d\n", pid);
 else
      printf("Fork returned error code, no child\n");
}
```

There are three branches to the if statement after the fork. The first specifies the child process, corresponding to a zero value for the variable pid. The second gives the action for the parent process, corresponding to a positive value for pid. The third branch deals, implicitly, with a negative value (in fact −1) for pid, which can arise when fork has failed to create a child. This can indicate that the calling process has tried to breach one of two limits; the first is a system-wide limit on the number of processes; the second restricts the number of processes an individual user may run simultaneously. In both circumstances, the error variable errno contains the error code EAGAIN. Also notice that, since the two processes generated by the example program will run concurrently and without synchronization, there is no guarantee that the output from parent and child will not become confusingly intermingled.

Before we move on, it is worth discussing why fork is a useful call, since it may seem a little pointless in isolation. The essential point is that fork becomes valuable when combined with other UNIX facilities. For example, it is possible to have a child and parent process perform different but related tasks, cooperating by using one of the UNIX inter-process communication mechanisms such as signals or pipes (described in later chapters). Another facility often used in combination with fork is the exec system call, which we shall discuss in the next section, and which enables other programs to be executed.

Exercise 5.1 A program can call fork several times. Similarly, each child process can use fork to spawn children of its own. To prove this, write a program which creates two subprocesses. Each of these should then create one subprocess of its own. After each `fork`, each parent process should use `printf` to display the process-ids of its offspring.

5.3 **Running new programs with** exec

5.3.1 The exec **family**

If `fork` was the only process creation primitive available to the programmer, UNIX would be a little boring since only copies of the same program could be created. Thankfully, a member of the `exec` family can be used to initiate the execution of a new program. Figure 5.2 shows the family tree for the `exec` calls. The main difference between them is the way parameters can be passed. As you can see from the figure, all of these functions eventually make a call to `execve` – the real system call.

The following usage description shows most of the members of the family. (We will return to `execle` and `execve` shortly.)

Usage

```
#include <unistd.h>

/* The execl family of calls must be given the arguments as
   a NULL terminated list */

/* execl must be given a valid pathname for the executable */
int execl(const char *path,
          const char *arg0, ..., const char *argn,
          (char *)0);

/* execlp only needs the filename of the executable */
int execlp(const char *file,
           const char *arg0, ..., const char *argn,
           (char *)0);

/* The execv family of calls must be given an array of arguments */

/* execv must be given a valid pathname for the executable */
int execv(const char *path, char *const argv[]);

/* execvp only needs the filename of the executable */
int execvp(const char *file, char *const argv[]);
```

All varieties of `exec` perform the same function: they transform the calling process by loading a new program into its memory space. If the `exec` is successful the calling program is completely overlaid by the new program, which is then

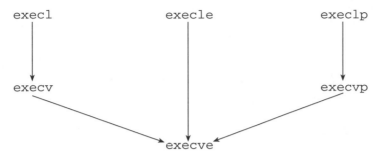

Figure 5.2 *The* exec *family tree.*

started from its beginning. The result can be regarded as a new process, but one that retains the same process-id as the calling process.

It is important to stress that exec does not create a new subprocess to run concurrently with the calling process. Instead the old program is obliterated by the new. So, unlike fork there is no return from a successful call to exec.

To simplify matters, we spotlight just one of the exec calls, namely execl.

All parameters for execl are character pointers. The first, path in the usage description, gives the name of the file containing the program to be executed; with execl this must be a valid pathname, absolute or relative. The file itself must also contain a true program or a shell script with execute permission. (The system tells whether a file contains a program by looking at its first two bytes or so. If these contain a special value, called a **magic number**, then the system treats the file as a program.) The second parameter arg0 is, by convention, the name of the program or command stripped of any preceding pathname element. This and the remaining variable number of arguments (arg1 to argn) are available to the invoked program, corresponding to command line arguments within the shell. Indeed, the shell itself invokes commands by using one of the exec calls in conjunction with fork. Because the argument list is of arbitrary length, it must be terminated by a null pointer to mark the end of the list.

As always a short example is worth a thousand words, and the following program uses execl to run the directory listing program ls:

```
/* runls -- use "execl" to run ls */

#include <unistd.h>

main()
{
 printf("executing ls\n");

 execl("/bin/ls", "ls", "-l", (char *)0);

 /* If execl returns, the call has failed, so ... */
 perror("execl failed to run ls");
 exit(1);
}
```

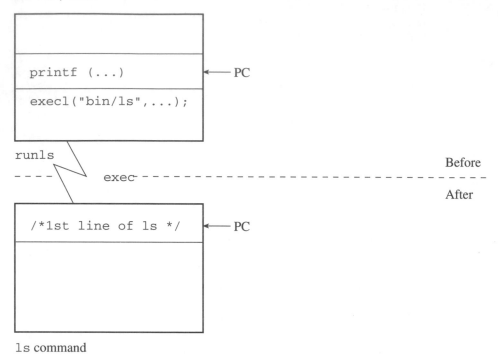

Figure 5.3 *The* exec *call.*

The action of this example program is shown in Figure 5.3. The *Before* section shows the process immediately before the call to execl. The *After* section shows the transformed process, after the call to execl, which now runs the ls program. The program counter *PC* points at the first line of ls, indicating that execl causes the new program to start from its beginning.

Notice that in the example, the call to execl is followed by an unconditional call to the library routine perror. This reflects the way a successful call to execl (and for that matter all its relations) obliterates the calling program. If the calling program does survive and execl returns, then an error must have occurred. As a corollary to this, when execl and its relatives do return, they will always return −1.

The execv, execlp *and* execvp *calls*

The other forms of exec give the programmer flexibility in the construction of parameter lists. execv takes just two arguments: the first (path in the usage description above) is a string containing the pathname of the program to be executed. The second (argv) is an array of strings, declared as:

```
char * const argv[];
```

The first member of this array points, again purely by convention, to the name of the program to be executed (excluding any pathname prefix). The remaining members point to any additional arguments for the program. Since this list is of indeterminate length, it must always be terminated by a null pointer.

The next example uses execv to run the same ls command as the previous example:

```
/* runls2 -- uses execv to run ls */

#include <unistd.h>

main()
{
 char * const av[]={"ls","-l",(char *)0};

 execv("/bin/ls", av);

 /* again - getting this far implies error */
 perror("execv failed");
 exit(1);
}
```

execlp and execvp are almost identical to execl and execv. The main difference is that the first argument for both execlp and execvp is a simple filename, not a pathname. The path prefix for this filename is found by a search of the directories denoted by the shell environment variable PATH. PATH of course can be simply set at shell level with a sequence of commands such as:

$ *PATH* = */bin:/usr/bin:/usr/keith/mybin*
$ *export PATH*

This means that both the shell and execvp will search for commands first in /bin, then /usr/bin and finally /usr/keith/mybin.

Exercise 5.2 In what circumstances would you use execv instead of execl?

Exercise 5.3 Assume that execvp and execlp do not exist. Write subroutine equivalents using execl and execv. The parameters for these routines should consist of a list of directories and a set of command line arguments.

5.3.2 Accessing arguments passed with exec

Any program can gain access to the arguments in the exec call that invoked it through parameters passed to the main function of the program. These parameters can be used by defining the program's main function as follows:

```
main(int argc, char **argv)
{
 /* body of program */
}
```

This should look familiar to many of you, since the same technique is used for accessing arguments from the command line that started a program, another indication that the shell itself uses exec to start processes. (We have, not unreasonably, assumed a knowledge of command line parameters in a few of the preceding examples and exercises. This section should therefore clarify things for those who had any problems with these.)

In the main function declaration above, argc is an integer count of the number of arguments. argv points to the array of arguments themselves. So, if a program is executed through a call to execvp as follows:

```
char * const argin[] = {"command","with","arguments",(char *)0};

execvp("prog", argin);
```

then within prog we would find the following conditions holding true:

```
argc == 3

argv[0] == "command"

argv[1] == "with"

argv[2] == "arguments"

argv[3] == (char *)0
```

As a simple demonstration of this technique, consider the next program, which prints its arguments, excluding its first, on standard output:

```
/* myecho -- echo command line arguments */

main(int argc, char **argv)
{
 while(--argc > 0)
      printf("%s ", *++argv);

 printf("\n");
}
```

If this program is invoked with the following program fragment:

```
char * const argin[]={"myecho", "hello", "world", (char *)0};

execvp(argin[0], argin);
```

then `argc` in `myecho` would be set to 3, and the following output would result:

```
hello world
```

which is the same result as would be obtained by the shell command:

$ *myecho hello world*

Exercise 5.4 Write `waitcmd`, a program which, when a file changes, executes an arbitrary command. It should pick up both the name of the file to watch and the command to execute from its command line arguments. The calls `stat` and `fstat` can be used to monitor the file. The program should not unnecessarily waste system resources; therefore use the standard `sleep` subroutine (introduced in Exercise 2.16) to make `waitcmd` pause for a decent interval after it has examined the file. How should it cope if the file does not exist initially?

5.4 **Using** exec **and** fork **together**

`fork` and `exec` combined offer the programmer a powerful tool. By forking, then using `exec` within the newly created child, a program can run another program within a subprocess and without obliterating itself. The following example shows how. In it we also introduce a simple error routine called `fatal` and, rather prematurely, the system call `wait`. This system call makes a process wait for its child to finish what it is doing – a common experience of any parent. It is discussed in detail later.

```c
/* runls3 -- run ls in a subprocess */

#include <unistd.h>

main()
{
 pid_t pid;

 switch(pid = fork()){
 case -1:
        fatal("fork failed");
        break;
 case 0:
        /* child calls exec */
        execl("/bin/ls", "ls", "-l", (char *)0);
        fatal("exec failed");
        break;
```

```
default:
      /* parent uses wait to suspend execution
       * until child finishes
       */
      wait((int *)0);
      printf("ls completed\n");
      exit(0);
   }
}
```

`fatal` simply uses `perror` to display a message, then exits. (The `break` following the call to `fatal` insures the code against any future changes to the subroutine.) `fatal` is implemented as follows:

```
int fatal(char *s)
{
 perror(s);
 exit(1);
}
```

Again, we will use a diagram for clarity in explaining the program's action, in this case Figure 5.4. This is divided into three parts: *Before* `fork`, *After* `fork` and *After* `exec`.

In the initial state, *Before* `fork`, there is a single process *A* and the program counter *PC* points at the `fork` statement, indicating that this is the next statement due to be executed.

After the `fork` call, there are two processes *A* and *B*. *A*, the parent process, is executing the `wait` system call. This will cause the execution of *A* to be suspended until *B* terminates. Meanwhile, *B* is using `execl` to load the `ls` command.

What happens next is shown in the *After* `exec` part of Figure 5.4. Process *B* has been transformed and now executes the `ls` program. The program counter for *B* has been set to the first statement of `ls`. Because *A* is waiting for *B* to terminate, its *PC* arrow has not changed position.

You should now be able to see the outline of some of the mechanisms employed by the shell. For example, when a command is executed, in the normal fashion, the shell uses `fork`, `exec` and `wait` as above. When a command is placed in the background the call to `wait` is omitted until later and both shell and command processes run concurrently.

The `docommand` *example*

UNIX provides a library routine called `system` which allows a shell command to be executed from within a program. Using `fork` and `exec` we will implement a rudimentary version of this called `docommand`. We will invoke a standard shell (identified by the pathname `/bin/sh`) as an intermediary, rather than attempt to run the command directly. This allows `docommand` to take advantage of the features offered by the shell such as filename expansion. The `-c` argument used in the

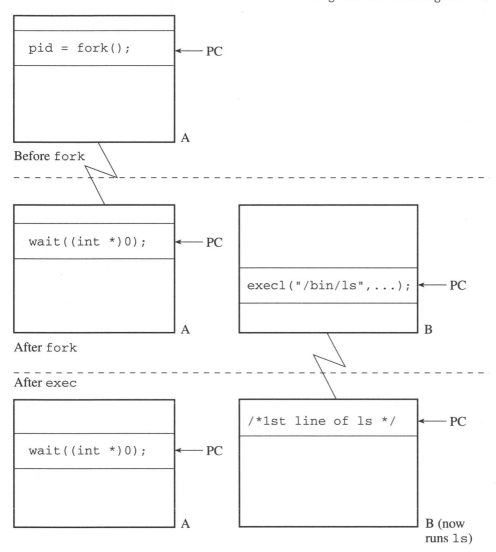

Figure 5.4 *The* fork *and* exec *calls combined.*

invocation of the shell tells it to take commands from the next string argument, rather than standard input.

```
/* docommand -- run shell command, first version */

#include <unistd.h>

int docommand(char *command)
{
  pid_t pid;
```

```
if ((pid = fork()) < 0 )
      return (-1);

if (pid == 0) /* child */
{
      execl("/bin/sh", "sh", "-c", command, (char *)0);
      perror("execl");
      exit(1);
}

/* code for parent */
/* wait until child exits */
      wait((int *)0);
      return(0);
}
```

This, it must be said, is only a first approximation to the proper library routine system. For example, if the end user of the program hit the interrupt key while the shell command was running, then both the command and the calling program would be stopped. There are ways to circumvent this, but we will delay discussing these until the next chapter.

5.5 Inherited data and file descriptors

5.5.1 fork, files and data

A child process created with fork is an almost perfect copy of its parent. In particular all variables within the child will retain the values they held in the parent (the one exception is the return value from fork itself). Since the data available to the child is a *copy* of that available to the parent, and occupies a different absolute place in memory, it is important to realize that subsequent changes in one process will not affect the variables in the other.

Similarly, all the files open in the parent are also open in the child; the child maintaining its own copy of the file descriptors associated with each file. However, files kept open across a call to fork remain intimately connected in child and parent. This is because the read–write pointer for each file is shared between the child and the parent. This is possible because the read–write pointer is maintained by the system; it is not embedded explicitly within the process itself. Consequently, when a child process moves forward in a file, the parent process will also find itself at the new position. The following short program demonstrates this. In it we use the routine fatal introduced earlier in this chapter, and a new routine called printpos. In addition, we are assuming the existence of a file called data which is at least 20 characters in length.

```
/* proc_file -- shows how files are handled across forks */
/* assume "data" is at least 20 chars long */
```

```
#include <unistd.h>
#include <fcntl.h>

main()
{
 int fd;
 pid_t pid;                      /* process-id */
 char buf[10];                   /* buffer to hold file data */

 if(( fd = open("data", O_RDONLY)) == -1)
      fatal("open failed");

 read(fd, buf, 10);             /* advance file pointer */

 printpos("Before fork",  fd);

 /* now create two processes */
 switch(pid = fork()){
 case -1:                       /* error */
      fatal("fork failed");
      break;
 case 0:                        /* child */
      printpos("Child before read", fd);
      read(fd, buf, 10);
      printpos("Child after read", fd);
      break;
 default:                       /* parent */
      wait((int *)0);
      printpos("Parent after wait", fd);
 }
}
```

printpos simply displays the current position within a file together with a short message. It can be implemented as follows:

```
/* print position in file */
int printpos(const char *string, int filedes)
{
 off_t pos;

 if(( pos = lseek(filedes, 0, SEEK_CUR)) == -1)
      fatal("lseek failed");
 printf("%s:%ld\n", string, pos);
}
```

When we ran this example we obtained the following results, fairly conclusive proof that the read−write pointer is shared by both processes:

```
Before fork:10
Child before read:10
Child after read:20
Parent after wait:20
```

Exercise 5.5   Write a program that demonstrates that program variables in a parent and child process have the same initial values but are independent of each other.

Exercise 5.6   Discover what happens within a parent process when a child closes a file descriptor inherited across a fork. In other words, does the file remain open in the parent, or is it closed there?

5.5.2 `exec` and open files

Open file descriptors are also normally passed across calls to `exec`. That is, files open in the original program are kept open when an entirely new program is started through `exec`. The read–write pointers for such files are unchanged by the `exec` call. (It obviously makes no sense to talk about the values of variables being preserved across an `exec` call, since the original and newly loaded programs will in general be entirely different.)

However, the all-purpose, all-weather routine `fcntl` can be used to set the **close-on-exec** flag associated with a file. If this is on (the default is off), then the file is closed when any member of the `exec` family is invoked. The following code fragment shows how the close-on-exec flag is enabled:

```
#include <fcntl.h>

    .
    .
    .

int fd;

fd = open("file", O_RDONLY);

    .
    .
    .

/* set close-on-exec flag on */
fcntl(fd, F_SETFD, 1);
```

The close-on-exec flag can be turned off with:

```
fcntl(fd, F_SETFD, 0);
```

Its value can be obtained as follows:

```
res = fcntl(fd, F_GETFD, 0);
```

The integer `res` will be 1 if the close-on-exec flag is on for the file descriptor `fd`, 0 otherwise.

5.6 Terminating processes with the `exit` system call

Usage
`#include <stdlib.h>`
`void exit(int status);`

The `exit` system call is an old friend, but we can now place it into its proper context. It is used to terminate a process, although a process will also stop when it runs out of program by reaching the end of the `main` function, or when `main` executes a `return` statement.

The single, integer argument to `exit` is called the process' **exit status**, the low-order eight bits of which are available to the parent process, providing it has executed a `wait` system call (more details of this in the next section). The value returned through `exit` in this way is normally used to indicate the success or failure of the task performed by the process. By convention a process returns zero on normal termination, some non-zero value if something has gone wrong.

As well as stopping the calling process, `exit` has a number of other consequences: most importantly, all open file descriptors are closed. If the parent process has executed a `wait` call, as in the last example, it will be restarted. `exit` will also call any programmer-defined exit handling routines and perform what are generally described as clean-up actions. These can, for example, be concerned with buffering in the Standard I/O Library. A programmer can also set at least 32 exit handling routines with the `atexit` function.

Usage
`#include <stdlib.h>`
`int atexit(void (*func)(void));`

The `atexit` routine registers the function pointed to by `func`, to be called with no parameters. Each of the exit handling functions recorded by `atexit` will be called on exit in the reverse order to which they were set.

For completeness, we should also mention the system call `_exit`, which is distinguished from `exit` by the leading underscore in its name. This is used in exactly the same way as `exit`. However, it circumvents the clean-up actions we described earlier. The `_exit` call should be avoided by most programmers.

Exercise 5.7 The exit status of a program can be obtained by using the '$?' variable within the shell, for example:

```
$ ls nonesuch
  nonesuch: No such file or directory
$ echo $?
  2
```

Write a program called fake which uses the integer value of its first argument as its exit status. Using the method outlined above, try out fake using a variety of arguments, including negative and large values. Is fake a useful program?

5.7 Synchronizing processes

5.7.1 The wait system call

Usage

```#include <sys/types.h>```
 ```#include <sys/wait.h>```
 	
 ```pid_t wait(int *status);```

As we have already seen briefly, wait temporarily suspends the execution of a process while a child process is running. Once the child has finished, the waiting parent is restarted. If more than one child is running then wait returns as soon as any one of the parent's offspring exits.

wait is often called by a parent process just after a call to fork. For example:

```
   .
   .
   .
int status;
pid_t cpid;

cpid = fork(); /*create new process */

if(cpid == 0){

 /* child */
 /* do something .... */

}else{

 /* parent, so wait for child */
 cpid = wait(&status);
 printf("The child %d is dead\n",cpid);

}
   .
   .
   .
```

This combination of fork and wait is most useful when the child process is intended to run a completely different program by calling exec.

The return value from wait is normally the process-id of the exiting child. If wait returns (pid_t)-1, it can mean that no child exists and in this case errno will contain the error code ECHILD. Being able to tell if any child has terminated individually means that the parent process can sit in a loop waiting for each of its offspring. When the parent realizes that all the children have terminated, it can continue.

wait takes one argument, status, a pointer to an integer. If the pointer is NULL then the argument is simply ignored. If, however, wait is passed a valid pointer, status will contain useful status information when wait returns. Normally this information will be the exit-status of the child passed through exit.

The following program status demonstrates how wait is used in these circumstances:

```
/* status -- how to get hold of a child's exit status */

#include <sys/wait.h>
#include <unistd.h>
#include <stdlib.h>

main()
{
 pid_t pid;
 int status, exit_status;

 if((pid = fork())< 0)
      fatal("fork failed");

 if(pid == 0)              /* child */
 {
      /* now call the library routine sleep
       * to suspend execution for 4 seconds
       */
      sleep(4);
      exit(5);             /* exit with non-zero value */
 }

 /* getting this far means this is the parent */
 /* so wait for child */

 if((pid = wait(&status)) == -1)
 {
      perror("wait failed");
      exit(2);
 }

 /* test to see how the child died */
 if(WIFEXITED(status))
```

```
{
        exit_status = WEXITSTATUS(status);
        printf("Exit status from %d was %d\n",pid, exit_status);
}

exit(0);
}
```

The value returned to the parent via `exit` is stored in the high-order eight bits of the integer `status`. For these to be meaningful the low-order eight bits must be zero. The macro `WIFEXITED` (defined in `<sys/wait.h>`) tests to see if this is in fact the case. The macro `WEXITSTATUS` returns the value stored in the high-order bits of `status`. If `WIFEXITED` returns 0 then it means that the child was stopped in its tracks by another process, using a communication method called a **signal**. Signals will be discussed in Chapter 6.

Exercise 5.8 Adapt the `docommand` routine so that it returns the `exit` status of the command it executes. What should happen if the `wait` call involved returns −1?

5.7.2 Waiting for a particular child: `waitpid`

The `wait` system call allows a parent to wait for any child. However, if the parent wants to be more particular it can use the `waitpid` system call to wait for a specific child process.

Usage

`#include <sys/types.h>`
`#include <sys/wait.h>`
 	
`pid_t waitpid(pid_t pid, int *status, int options);`

The first argument, `pid` specifies the process-id of the child process that the parent wishes to wait for. If this is set to −1 and the `options` argument is set to 0 then `waitpid` behaves exactly the same as `wait`, since −1 denotes an interest in any child process. If `pid` is greater than 0 then the parent will wait for the child with a process-id of `pid`. The second argument, `status`, will hold the status of the child when `waitpid` returns.

The final argument, `options`, can take a variety of values defined in `<sys/wait.h>`. The most useful of these options is `WNOHANG`. This allows `waitpid` to sit in a loop monitoring a situation but not blocking if the child process is still running. If `WNOHANG` is set then `waitpid` will return 0 if the child has not yet terminated.

The functionality of `waitpid` with the `WNOHANG` option can be demonstrated by rewriting the previous example. This time the parent process checks to see if the child has finished. If not, it outputs a message to say that it is still waiting, it then sleeps for a second and again calls `waitpid` to see if the child has completed. Notice that the child process gets its process-id by calling `getpid`. We will explain this in Section 5.10.1.

```
/* status2 --
 * how to obtain a child's exit status using waitpid */

#include <sys/wait.h>
#include <unistd.h>
#include <stdlib.h>

main()
{
 pid_t pid;
 int status, exit_status;

 if((pid = fork())< 0)
       fatal("fork failed");

 if(pid == 0)              /* child */
 {
       /* now call the library routine sleep
        * to suspend execution for 4 seconds
        */
       printf("Child %d sleeping...\n",getpid());
       sleep(4);
       exit(5);           /* exit with non-zero value */
 }

 /* getting this far means this is the parent */
 /* so see if the child has exited if not sleep for */
 /* one second and recheck */

 while(waitpid(pid, &status, WNOHANG) == 0)
 {
       printf("Still waiting...\n");
       sleep(1);
 }

 /* test to see how the child died */
 if(WIFEXITED(status))
 {
       exit_status = WEXITSTATUS(status);
       printf("Exit status from %d was %d\n",pid, exit_status);
 }

 exit(0);
}
```

Running this program produced the following output:

```
Still waiting...
Child 12857 sleeping...
Still waiting...
Still waiting...
Still waiting...
Exit status from 12857 was 5
```

5.8 Zombies and premature exits

So far, we have assumed that exit and wait are used in an orderly fashion, where each subprocess is waited for. However, there are two other situations worth discussing:

1.   A child exits when its parent is not currently executing wait.

2.   A parent exits while one or more children are still running.

In case 1, the exiting process is placed into a kind of limbo and becomes a **zombie**. A zombie process is one that occupies a slot in a table maintained in the kernel for process control, but uses no other kernel resources. It will be finally put to rest if its parent claims the child by executing wait. The parent will then be able to read the exit status and the slot will become available for reuse. In case 2, the parent is allowed to exit normally. The children (including zombies) of the parent process are adopted by the init process (process-id = 1).

5.9 smallsh: a command processor

In this section we will construct a simple command processor called smallsh. This example has two advantages. The first is that it develops the concepts we have introduced in this chapter. The second is that it demonstrates that there is really nothing special about standard UNIX commands and utilities. In particular it shows that the shell is just an ordinary program that happens to be invoked when you login.

The demands that we shall make of smallsh are straightforward. The program should assemble commands and execute them, either in the background or foreground. It should also be able to deal with lines consisting of several commands, separated by semicolons. Other facilities, such as filename expansion or I/O redirection, could be added later.

The basic logic is clear:

```
while(EOF not typed)
{
  get command line from user
  assemble command args and execute
  wait for child
}
```

We shall give the *get command line* function the name userin, which should print a prompt, then wait for a line of input from the keyboard. Any input it does receive it should place into a program buffer. We have implemented userin as follows:

```
/* include file for example */
#include "smallsh.h"

/* program buffers and work pointers */
static char inpbuf[MAXBUF], tokbuf[2*MAXBUF],
      *ptr = inpbuf, *tok = tokbuf;

/* print prompt and read a line */
int userin(char *p)
{
 int c, count;

 /* initialization for later routines */
 ptr = inpbuf;
 tok = tokbuf;

 /* display prompt */
 printf("%s", p);

 count = 0;

 while(1)
 {
      if((c = getchar()) == EOF)
            return(EOF);

      if(count < MAXBUF)
            inpbuf[count++] = c;

      if( c == '\n' && count < MAXBUF)
      {
            inpbuf[count] = '\0';
            return count;
      }

      /* if line too long restart */
      if(c == '\n')
      {
            printf("smallsh: input line too long\n");
            count = 0;
            printf("%s ",p);
      }
 }
}
```

Some of the initialization detail you can ignore for now. The essential point is that userin first prints a prompt (which is passed as a parameter), then reads a character at a time from the user, returning when it encounters a newline or end of file (the latter case denoted by the symbol EOF).

The Standard I/O Library routine we have used is getchar. It reads a single character from the program's standard input, which normally corresponds to the keyboard. userin places each new character (where possible) into the character array inpbuf. When it completes, userin returns either a count of the number of characters read or EOF to signify end of file. Note that newlines are added to inpbuf and not discarded.

The include file smallsh.h referenced within userin contains definitions for some useful constants (such as MAXBUF). Its actual contents are:

```
/* smallsh.h -- defs for smallsh command processor */

#include <unistd.h>
#include <stdio.h>
#include <sys/wait.h>

#define EOL        1      /* end of line */
#define ARG        2      /* normal arguments */
#define AMPERSAND  3
#define SEMICOLON  4

#define MAXARG     512    /* max. no. command args */
#define MAXBUF     512    /* max. length input line */

#define FOREGROUND 0
#define BACKGROUND 1
```

The other constants not referenced within userin we will meet in later routines.

smallsh.h also includes the standard header file <stdio.h>. This gives us the definition of getchar and the constant EOF.

The next routine we shall look at is gettok. This extracts individual **tokens** from a command line constructed by userin. (A token is a lexical unit such as a command name or argument.) gettok is invoked as follows:

```
toktype = gettok(&tptr);
```

toktype is an integer which will contain a value denoting the type of the token. The range of possible values is taken from smallsh.h and includes EOL (for end of line), SEMICOLON, etc. tptr is a character pointer which will point to the actual token itself after the call to gettok. Because gettok will allocate its own storage for the token string we must pass the address of tptr rather than its value.

The source code for gettok follows. Note that since it references the character pointers tok and ptr, it must be included in the same source file as userin. (You should now also be able to see the reason for the initialization of tok and ptr at the beginning of userin.)

```
/* get token, place into tokbuf */
int gettok(char **outptr)
{
 int type;

 /* set the outptr string to tok */
 *outptr = tok;
```

```
/* strip white space from the buffer containing the tokens */
while( *ptr == ' ' || *ptr == '\t')
        ptr++;

/* set the token pointer to the first token in the buffer */
*tok++ = *ptr;

/* set the type variable depending
 * on the token in the buffer */
switch(*ptr++){
case '\n':
            type = EOL;
            break;
case '&':
            type = AMPERSAND;
            break;
case ';':
            type = SEMICOLON;
            break;
default:
            type = ARG;
            /* keep reading valid ordinary characters */
            while(inarg(*ptr))
                  *tok++ = *ptr++;
}

*tok++ = '\0';
return type;
}
```

inarg is used for determining whether a character can be part of an 'ordinary' argument. For the present, we need just check whether the character is special to smallsh or not:

```
static char special [] = {' ', '\t', '&', ';', '\n', '\0'};

int inarg(char c)
{
 char *wrk;

 for(wrk = special; *wrk; wrk++)
 {
      if(c == *wrk)
            return (0);
 }

 return (1);
}
```

We are now ready to introduce the function that does the real work. procline will parse a command line using gettok, constructing an argument list in the process. When it encounters a newline or semicolon it invokes a routine called runcommand to execute the command. It assumes that an input line has already been read with userin.

```
#include "smallsh.h"

int procline(void)          /* process input line */
{
 char *arg[MAXARG + 1];     /* pointer array for runcommand */
 int toktype;               /* type of token in command */
 int narg;                  /* number of arguments so far */
 int type;                  /* FOREGROUND or BACKGROUND */

 narg=0;

 for(;;)                    /* loop forever */
 {
      /* take action according to token type */
      switch(toktype = gettok(&arg[narg])){
      case ARG:   if(narg < MAXARG)
                      narg++;
                  break;
      case EOL:
      case SEMICOLON:
      case AMPERSAND:
                  if ( toktype == AMPERSAND)
                      type = BACKGROUND;
                  else
                      type = FOREGROUND;

                  if(narg != 0)
                  {
                      arg[narg] = NULL;
                      runcommand(arg, type);
                  }

                  if(toktype == EOL)
                      return;

                  narg = 0;
                  break;
      }
 }
}
```

The next stage is to specify the runcommand routine, which actually starts any command processes. runcommand is essentially an adaptation of the routine docommand we met earlier. It has an extra integer parameter called where. If where is set to the value BACKGROUND as defined in smallsh.h, then the waitpid call is omitted and runcommand simply prints the process-id and returns.

```
#include "smallsh.h"

/* execute a command with optional wait */
int runcommand(char **cline, int where)
```

```
{
 pid_t pid;
 int status;

 switch(pid = fork()){
 case -1:
        perror("smallsh");
        return (-1);
 case 0:
        execvp(*cline, cline);
        perror(*cline);
        exit(1);
 }

 /* code for parent */
 /* if background process print pid and exit */
 if(where == BACKGROUND)
 {
        printf("[Process id %d]\n", pid);
        return (0);
 }

 /* wait until process pid exits */
 if(waitpid(pid, &status, 0) == -1)
        return (-1);
 else
        return (status);
 }
```

Notice that the simple wait call of docommand has been replaced with a call to waitpid. This ensures that runcommand exits only when the child it last started terminates and avoids problems with background commands that terminate in the interim. (If this seems unclear, remember that wait returns the process-id of the first child process to exit, not the last to be started.)

runcommand also makes use of the execvp system call. This ensures that the program identified by a command is hunted for along the string of directories in the current PATH, although, unlike a real shell, smallsh does not have any means of manipulating PATH.

The last step is to write the main function which ties everything together. This is a trivial exercise:

```
/* smallsh -- simple command processor */

#include "smallsh.h"

char *prompt = "Command> ";     /* prompt */

main()
{
 while(userin(prompt) != EOF)
        procline();
}
```

This routine completes the first version of smallsh. Again, it must be stressed that it is only a skeleton of any finished solution. As with docommand, the behaviour of smallsh is less than ideal when the user types the current interrupt character, since this causes smallsh to terminate. We will see how to make smallsh more robust in the next chapter.

Exercise 5.9   Add to smallsh a mechanism for escaping special characters such as ampersand and semicolon so that they can be included within program arguments. Also make it correctly interpret comments, as indicated by a leading hash (#) character. What should happen to the prompt when a newline is escaped?

Exercise 5.10   The fcntl routine can be used to duplicate an open file descriptor. In this context, it is called as follows:

```
newfdes = fcntl(filedes, F_DUPFD, reqvalue);
```

filedes is the original file descriptor for the open file. The constant F_DUPFD is taken from the system include file <fcntl.h>. reqvalue should be a small integer. After a successful call newfdes will contain a file descriptor which refers to the same file as filedes and has the same numeric value as reqvalue (assuming reqvalue is not already a file descriptor). The following program fragment shows how to reassign standard input; that is, file descriptor 0.

```
fd1 = open("somefile", O_RDONLY);
close(0);
fd2 = fcntl(fd1, F_DUPFD, 0);
```

After this call the value of fd2 will be 0.

Using this call in conjunction with the open and close system calls, adapt smallsh so that it supports redirection of standard input and standard output using the same notation as the conventional UNIX shell. Remember that standard input and output correspond to file descriptors 0 and 1, respectively.

Note that this method of duplicating file descriptors can also be achieved by the dup2 system call. (A close relative dup is also available.)

5.10 Process attributes

Each UNIX process is associated with a number of attributes which help the system control the running and scheduling of processes, maintain the security of the file system and so on. One attribute we have already met is the process-id, a number which uniquely identifies a process. Other attributes range from the environment, which is a collection of strings maintained outside the data areas defined by the programmer, to the effective user-id which determines the file system privileges of the process. In the rest of this chapter we will look at the more important process attributes.

5.10.1 The process-id

As we saw at the beginning of this chapter, the system gives each process a non-negative number called a process-id. At any one time a process-id is unique although it will eventually be reused when the process has terminated. The system reserves some process-ids for special processes. Process 0 (although named the scheduler) is actually the swapper process. Process 1 is the initialization process which is actually an execution of the program /etc/init. Process 1 is, directly or indirectly, the ancestor of every other process on a UNIX system.

A program can obtain its own process-id by using the following system call:

```
pid = getpid();
```

Similarly, the getppid call returns the process-id of the calling process' parent:

```
ppid = getppid();
```

The following example routine gentemp uses getpid to generate a unique, temporary filename. This name has the form:

```
/tmp/tmp<pid>.<no>
```

The suffix number is incremented on each call to gentemp. The routine also calls access to check if the file already exists:

```
#include <string.h>
#include <unistd.h>

static int num = 0;

static char namebuf[20];
static char prefix[] = "/tmp/tmp";

char *gentemp(void)
{
 int length;
 pid_t pid;

 pid = getpid();    /* get process-id */

 /* standard string-handling routines */
 strcpy(namebuf, prefix);
 length = strlen(namebuf);

 /* add pid to filename */
 itoa(pid, &namebuf[length]);

 strcat(namebuf, ".");
 length = strlen(namebuf);
```

```
do{
      /* add suffix number */
      itoa(num++, &namebuf[length]);
} while (access(namebuf, F_OK) != -1);

return (namebuf);
}
```

The routine `itoa` simply converts an integer into its string equivalent:

```
/* itoa -- convert int to string */

int itoa(int i, char *string)
{
 int power, j;

 j = i;

 for(power = 1; j >= 10; j /= 10)
      power *= 10;

 for( ; power > 0; power /= 10)
 {
      *string++ = '0' + i/power;
      i %= power;
 }

 *string = '\0';
}
```

Notice the way we convert a digit into its character equivalent with the first statement inside the second `for` loop. You should also note that the routine `sprintf` could do much of the above work more easily. See Chapter 11 for a description of `sprintf`.

Exercise 5.11 Adapt `gentemp` so that it takes a prefix for the temporary filename as an argument.

5.10.2 Process groups and process group-ids

UNIX allows processes to be usefully placed into groups. For example, when processes are connected by pipes from the command line, they are typically placed into a process group. Figure 5.5 shows such a typical process group set up by a shell command line.

Process groups are useful when you want to handle a set of processes as a whole using an inter-process communication mechanism called signals, which we

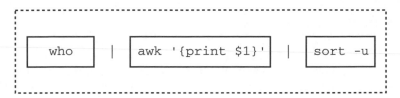

Figure 5.5 *A process group.*

explore in Chapter 6. A signal is normally 'sent' to a single process, usually resulting in process termination, but they can easily be sent to an entire group.

Each **process group** is denoted by a **process group-id** of type `pid_t`. If a process has the same process-id as the process group-id then it is deemed the leader of the process group (and some special actions are taken when it exits). Initially a process inherits its process group-id across a `fork` or `exec`.

A process can obtain its current process group-id with the `getpgrp` system call:

Usage
| ```
#include <sys/types.h>
#include <unistd.h>

pid_t getpgrp(void);
``` |

5.10.3 Changing process group

In a UNIX shell which supports job control, a process may wish to place itself in a new process group. Job control allows a shell to start multiple process groups (jobs) and to control which of the process groups should run in the foreground and therefore have access to the terminal, and which should run in the background. Job control is orchestrated through the use of signals.

A process can join or create a new process group by invoking the `setpgid` system call:

Usage
| ```
#include <sys/types.h>
#include <unistd.h>

int setpgid(pid_t pid, pid_t pgid);
``` |

The `setpgid` call sets the process group-id of the process with an id of `pid` to `pgid`. If the `pid` is set to 0 the process-id of the *calling* process is used. If `pid` and `pgid` are the same then the process will become the process group leader. −1 is returned on error. If `pgid` is zero, the process-id indicated by `pid` is used as the process group-id.

5.10.4 Sessions and session-ids

Each process group in turn belongs to a session. A session is really about a process's connection to a **controlling terminal**. When users log on, the processes and process groups they explicitly or implicitly create will belong to a session linked to their current terminal. A session is typically a collection of a single foreground process group using the terminal and one or more background process groups. A session is identified by a **session-id** of type `pid_t`.

A process can obtain its current session-id with a call to `getsid` as follows:

Usage
| ```
#include <sys/types.h>
#include <unistd.h>

pid_t getsid(pid_t pid);
``` |

If `getsid` is passed a value of 0 then it returns the session-id of the calling process otherwise the session-id of the process identified by `pid` is returned.

The idea of a session is useful with background or **daemon** processes. A daemon process is simply a process which does not have a controlling terminal. An example is `cron`, which executes commands at specified times and dates. A daemon can set itself to be in a session *without a controlling terminal* by calling the `setsid` system call, and moving itself into a new session.

Usage
| ```
#include <sys/types.h>
#include <unistd.h>

pid_t setsid(void);
``` |

If the calling process is not a process group leader then a new process group and session will be created and the process-id of the calling process will become the session-id. It will also have no controlling terminal. The daemon process will now be in a strange state in that it will be the only process in the process group contained in the new session, and its `pid` will also be the process group-id and the session-id.

The `setsid` function will fail if the calling process is already a process group leader returning `(pid_t)-1`.

5.10.5 The environment

The **environment** of a process is simply a collection of null-terminated strings, represented within a program as a null-terminated array of character pointers. By convention, each environment string has the form:

name = something

A programmer can make direct use of the environment of a process by adding an extra parameter envp to the parameter list of the main function within a program. The following program fragment shows the type of envp:

```
main(int argc, char **argv, char **envp)
{
 /* do something */
}
```

As a trivial example, the next program simply prints out its environment and exits:

```
/* showmyenv.c -- show environment */

main(int argc, char **argv, char **envp)
{
 while(*envp)
       printf("%s\n",*envp++);
}
```

Running this program on one machine produced the following results:

```
CDPATH=:..:/
HOME=/usr/keith
LOGNAME=keith
MORE=-h -s
PATH=/bin:/etc:/usr/bin:/usr/cbin:/uor/lbin
SHELL=/bin/ksh
TERM=vt100
TZ=GMT0BST
```

This layout may well look familiar to you. It is the environment of the shell process that invoked the showmyenv program and includes important variables used by the shell such as HOME and PATH.

What this example shows is that the default environment of a process is the same as the process that created it through a call to exec or fork. Since the environment is passed on in this way, it allows information to be recorded semi-permanently which would otherwise have to be respecified for each new process. The TERM environment variable, which stores the current terminal type, is a good example of how useful this can be.

To actually specify a new environment for the process you must use one of two new members of the exec family: execle and execve. These are called as follows:

```
execle(path, arg0, arg1, ..argn, (char *)0, envp);
```

and:

```
execve(path, argv, envp);
```

These duplicate, respectively, the actions of the system calls `execv` and `execl`. The one difference is the addition of the `envp` parameter, which is a null-terminated array of character pointers that specifies the environment for the new program. The next example uses `execle` to pass a new environment to the `showmyenv` program:

```
/* setmyenv.c -- set environment for program */

main()
{
 char *argv[2], *envp[3];

 argv[0] = "showmyenv";
 argv[1] = (char *)0;

 envp[0] = "foo=bar";
 envp[1] = "bar=foo";
 envp[2] = (char *)0;

 execve("./showmyenv", argv, envp);

 perror("execve failed");
}
```

Although it is acceptable to use the parameters passed to the `main` function, the preferred way a process can gain access to its environment is through the global variable:

```
extern char **environ;
```

A standard library function `getenv` can be used to scan `environ` for the name of an environment variable in the form `name = string`.

Usage

```
#include <stdlib.h>

char *getenv(const char *name);
```

Here the argument to `getenv` is the name of the variable you wish to find. If the search is successful, `getenv` returns a pointer to the value part of the string, otherwise it returns the `NULL` pointer. The following code shows an example of its use:

```
/* find the value of the PATH environment variable */

#include <stdlib.h>
```

```
main()
{
  printf("PATH=%s\n", getenv("PATH"));
}
```

A companion routine putenv is also provided to change or extend the environment. It is called along the following lines:

```
putenv("NEWVARIABLE = value");
```

putenv returns zero if it was successful. It alters the environment pointed to by environ. It does not alter the envp pointer in the current main function.

5.10.6 The current working directory

As we saw in Chapter 4, each process is associated with a current working directory. The initial setting for the current working directory is inherited across the fork or exec that started the process. To put it another way, a process is initially placed in the same directory as its parent.

The fact that the current working directory is a per-process attribute is important. If a child process changes position by calling chdir (defined in Chapter 4), the current working directory in the parent process is unchanged. For this reason the standard cd command is actually a 'built-in' command within the shell itself and docs not correspond to a program.

5.10.7 The current root directory

Each process is also associated with a root directory used in absolute pathname searches. As with the current working directory, the root directory of a process is initially determined by that of its parent. UNIX provides a system call for changing a process' idea of where the start of the file system hierarchy is. This system call is chroot.

Usage

`#include <unistd.h>`
 	
 `int chroot(const char *path);`

path points to a pathname naming a directory. If chroot succeeds, path will become the starting point for those file searches that begin with a '/' (for the calling process only, the system as a whole is not affected). chroot returns −1 and the root directory remains unchanged if the call fails. The calling process must have the appropriate privileges to change the root directory.

Exercise 5.12   Add the `cd` command to the `smallsh` command processor.

Exercise 5.13   Write your own version of the `getenv` function.

5.10.8 User- and group-ids

Each process is associated with a real user-id and a real group-id. These are always the user and current group-ids of the user who invoked the process.

The effective user- and group-ids are used to determine whether a process can access a file. More often than not, these are the same as the real user- and group-ids. However, a process, or one of its ancestors, can have its set-user-id or set-group-id permission bit set. For example, if the program file's set-user-id bit is set, then when the program is invoked through a call to `exec`, the effective user-id of the process becomes that of the file owner, not that of the user who started the process.

There are several system calls available for obtaining the user- and group-ids associated with a process. The following program fragment demonstrates these:

```
#include <unistd.h>

main()
{
 uid_t uid, euid;
 gid_t gid, egid;

 /* get real user-id */
 uid = getuid();

 /* get effective user-id */
 euid = geteuid();

 /* get real group-id */
 gid = getgid();

 /* get effective group-id */
 egid = getegid();
}
```

Two calls are also available for setting the effective user- and group-ids of a process:

```
#include <unistd.h>

uid_t newuid;
gid_t newgid;
 .
 .
 .
/* set effective user-id */
status = setuid(newuid);
```

```
/* set effective group-id */
status = setgid(newgid);
```

A process invoked by a non-privileged user (that is, anybody who is not superuser) can only reset its effective user- and group-ids back to their real counterparts. Superuser as usual is allowed free rein. The return value from both routines is 0 on successful completion, −1 otherwise.

Exercise 5.13 Write a routine that obtains the real user- and group-ids of the calling process, then writes the ASCII equivalents of these onto the end of a log file.

5.10.9 File size limits: ulimit

There is a per-process limit on the size of a file that can be created with the write system call. This limit also covers the situation where a pre-existing file, shorter than the limit, is extended.

The file size limit can be manipulated with the ulimit system call.

Usage

`#include <ulimit.h>`
 	
`long ulimit(int cmd, [long newlimit]);`

To obtain the current file size limit, a programmer can call ulimit with the parameter cmd set to UL_GETFSIZE. The value returned is in units of 512-byte blocks.

To change the file size limit, a programmer should set cmd to UL_SETFSIZE and place the new file size limit, again in 512-byte blocks, into newlimit. For example:

```
if(ulimit(UL_SETFSIZE, newlimit) < 0)
 perror("ulimit failed");
```

Only superuser can actually increase a file size limit in this way. Processes that have the effective user-ids of other users are, however, allowed to decrease their limit.

5.10.10 Process priorities: nice

The system decides the proportion of cpu time a particular process is allocated partly on the basis of an integer **nice** value. Nice values range from 0 to a system-dependent maximum. The higher the number, the lower the process' priority.

Socially aware processes can lower their priority, and thus allocate more resources to other processes, by using the `nice` system call. This takes one argument, a positive increment to be added to the current nice value; for example:

```
nice(5);
```

Superuser (and only superuser) processes can increase their priority by using a negative value as the `nice` call parameter. `nice` is a useful call if all you want to do is calculate π to a hundred million places and not impact the system's responsiveness to other users. `nice` is an old call. Recent optional real-time extensions in *POSIX* give far more fine grain control. However, this is a specialist topic which we will not consider further.

CHAPTER 6

Signals and signal processing

6.1 Introduction

It is often desirable to construct software systems that consist of several cooperating processes rather than just a single, monolithic program. There are many possible reasons for this: a single program might, for example, be too large for the machine it is running on, either in terms of physical memory or available address space; part of the required functionality may already reside in an existing program; the problem might be best solved with a server process that cooperates with an arbitrary number of client processes, you might want to utilize multiple processes, and so on.

Luckily, UNIX is rich in inter-process communication mechanisms. In this and the following chapter, we will discuss three of the most widely used of these facilities: **signals**, **pipes** and **FIFOs**. Together with the more complex facilities we highlight in Chapters 8 and 10, they offer a wide choice for the software developer who wants to build multi-process systems.

We shall start, in this chapter, by looking at signals.

Suppose you are running a UNIX command that seems likely to take a long time:

```
$ cc verybigprog.c
```

Then you realize that something is wrong, and the command will eventually fail. To save time, you can stop the command by hitting the current **interrupt** key, which is often *Del* or *Ctrl-C*. The command will be terminated, and you will be returned to the shell prompt.

What actually happens is this: the part of the kernel responsible for keyboard input sees the interrupt character. The kernel then sends a signal called SIGINT to all processes that recognize the terminal as their control terminal. This includes the invocation of cc. When cc receives the signal, it performs the default action associated with SIGINT and terminates. It is interesting to note that the shell process associated with the terminal is also sent SIGINT. However, because it has to stay around to interpret later commands it sensibly ignores the signal. As we shall see, programs can also elect to 'catch' SIGINT, which means they perform a special interrupt routine whenever the user presses interrupt.

Signals are also used by the kernel to deal with certain kinds of severe error. For example, suppose a program file has become corrupted in some way and contains illegal machine instructions. When a process executes the program, the kernel will detect the attempt to execute illegal instructions and send the process the signal SIGILL (the ILL here stands for 'illegal') to terminate it. The resulting dialogue could look like:

```
$ badprog
Illegal instruction - core dumped
```

We will explain the phrase 'core dumped' in due course.

As well as being sent from the kernel to a process, signals can be sent from process to process. This is easiest to show with the kill command. For example, suppose a programmer starts off a long-running command in the background:

```
$ cc verybigprog.c &
[1] 1098
```

and then decides to terminate it. The command kill can then be used to send the signal SIGTERM to the process. Like SIGINT, SIGTERM will terminate a process unless it has made explicit arrangements otherwise. The process-id must be given to the kill command as an argument:

```
$ kill 1098
Terminated
```

Signals provide a simple method for transmitting software interrupts to UNIX processes. If you need a metaphor, think of a signal as a kind of software tap on the shoulder, which interrupts a process whatever it may be doing. Because of their nature, signals tend to be used for handling abnormal conditions rather than the straightforward transmission of data between processes.

In short a process can do three things with signals, it can:

1.   Choose the way it responds when it receives a particular signal (signal handling).

2.   Block out signals (that is, leave them to later) for a specified piece of critical code.

3.   Send a signal to another process.

The remainder of this chapter looks at each of these in more detail.

6.1.1 Signal names

Signals cannot carry information directly, which limits their usefulness as a general inter-process communication mechanism. However, each type of signal is given a mnemonic name − SIGINT is an example − which indicates the purpose for which the signal is normally used. Signal names are defined in the standard header file <signal.h> with the pre-processor directive #define. As you might expect, these names just stand for small, positive integers. For example, SIGINT is usually defined as:

```
#define    SIGINT    2    /* interrupt (rubout) */
```

Most of the signal types provided by UNIX are intended for use by the kernel, although a few are provided to be sent from process to process. The complete list of standard signals, as described in the *XSI*, and their meanings follows. The list of signals has been put in alphabetical order for ease of reference. On first reading you can safely skip this list.

● SIGABRT *Process abort signal*. This is sent by a call to the abort function by the current process. SIGABRT will result in what the *XSI* describes as **abnormal termination**. The actual effect on UNIX implementations is a **core dump**, indicated by the message Quit - core dumped, where the process image is dumped into a disk file for debugging purposes. More of this later.

● SIGALRM *Alarm clock*. This is sent by the kernel to a process after a timer has expired. All processes can set at least three interval timers. The first of these can be set to measure real elapsed time. The timer is actually set by the process itself using the alarm system call (or setting the first parameter to the more exotic setitimer system call to ITIMER_REAL). We will describe alarm in Section 6.4.2. See your local manual if you want to know more about setitimer.

● SIGBUS *Bus error*. This error is sent if a hardware fault is detected. A bus error is implementation defined and, like SIGABRT, causes an abnormal termination.

- SIGCHLD *Child process terminated or stopped.* Whenever a child process terminates or stops, the kernel will inform its parent by sending it SIGCHLD, the death of child signal. By default the parent will ignore the signal, and therefore a parent must explicitly catch the SIGCHLD signal if it wishes to know about any child processes which have completed.

- SIGCONT *Continue executing if stopped.* This is a job control signal which will continue the process if it is stopped; otherwise the process will ignore the signal. It is the inverse of SIGSTOP.

- SIGFPE *Floating-point exception.* This is sent by the kernel when a floating-point error occurs (such as overflow or underflow). It causes abnormal termination.

- SIGHUP The *hangup* signal. This is sent by the kernel to all processes attached to a **control terminal** when that terminal is disconnected. (Normally, a process group's control terminal will be the user's own terminal, although this is not always the case. The concept is further explored in Chapter 9.) It is also sent to all members of a session when the session leader, normally a shell process, exits, providing the session is associated with a control terminal. This ensures background processes are terminated when a user logs out, unless explicit arrangements have been made otherwise (see Section 5.10 for more details).

- SIGILL *Illegal instruction.* This is sent by the operating system when a process attempts to execute an illegal instruction. It is possible that the program has corrupted its own code, but this is unlikely. Other causes, such as an attempt to execute floating-point instructions without the right hardware support, are more probable. SIGILL results in abnormal termination.

- SIGINT *Interrupt.* This is sent by the kernel to all processes associated with a terminal session when a user hits the interrupt key. It is the conventional way of halting a running program.

- SIGKILL *Kill.* This is a rather special signal that is sent from one process to another to terminate the receiver. It is also occasionally sent by the system (that is, during system shutdown). SIGKILL is one of only two signals that cannot be ignored or 'caught' (that is, handled via a user-defined interrupt routine).

- SIGPIPE *Write on a pipe or socket when recipient has terminated.* A pipe and a socket are other inter-process communication mechanisms, which we will discuss in later chapters. SIGPIPE will be properly examined then.

- SIGPOLL *Pollable event.* This signal is generated by the kernel when an open file descriptor is ready for input or output. However, an easier way to implement polling is to use the select system call, which we describe in detail in Chapter 7.

- SIGPROF *Profiling time expired.* As mentioned above for SIGALRM, all processes can set at least three interval timers. The second of these timers can be set to measure the time the process is executing in user and system mode. A SIGPROF signal is generated when this timer expires and can therefore be used by interpreters to profile the execution of a program. (The timer is set by setting the first parameter of the function setitimer to ITIMER_PROF.)

- SIGQUIT *Quit.* Very similar to SIGINT, this is sent by the kernel when the user hits the quit key associated with his or her terminal. The default value for the quit key is ASCII FS or *Ctrl-*. Unlike SIGINT, this signal will cause an abnormal termination and therefore a core dump.

- SIGSEGV *Invalid memory reference.* SEGV stands for segmentation violation and is generated when a process tries to access an invalid memory address. SIGSEGV results in abnormal termination.

- SIGSTOP *Stop executing.* This is a job control signal which will stop the process. It is similar to SIGKILL in that it cannot be caught or ignored.

- SIGSYS *Invalid system call.* This is sent by the kernel if a process attempts to execute a machine instruction which is not a system call. This is another signal that results in abnormal termination.

- SIGTERM *Software termination signal.* By convention, it is used to terminate a process (as you might guess from its name!). The programmer can use this signal to allow a process some tidying up time before sending SIGKILL.

- SIGTRAP *Trace trap.* This is a special signal used by debuggers such as sdb and adb, in conjunction with the ptrace system call. Because of its specialized nature, we will not discuss it further. By default, SIGTRAP results in abnormal termination.

- SIGTSTP *Terminal stop signal.* This signal is generated by the user typing the suspend key (normally *Ctrl-Z*). SIGTSTP is similar to SIGSTOP; however, it can be caught and ignored.

- SIGTTIN *Background process attempting read.* Whenever a process is executing in the background and attempts to read from its controlling terminal the SIGTTIN signal will be sent. The default action is to stop the process.

- SIGTTOU *Background process attempting write.* This is similar to SIGTTIN except that this signal will be generated when the background process attempts to write to the controlling terminal. Again, the default action is to stop the process.

- SIGURG *High bandwidth data is available at a socket.* This signal tells a process that urgent or out of band data has been received on a network connection.

- SIGUSR1 and SIGUSR2 Like SIGTERM, these are never sent by the kernel and may be used for whatever purpose a user wishes.

- SIGVTALRM *Virtual timer expired.* As mentioned for SIGALRM and SIGPROF, all processes have at least three interval timers. The last of these timers can be set to measure the time the process is executing in user mode. (The timer is set by setting the first parameter of the function setitimer to ITIMER_VIRTUAL.)

- SIGXCPU *CPU time limit exceeded.* This signal is generated if a process exceeds its maximum CPU time limit. The default action is an abnormal termination.

- SIGXFSZ *File size limit exceeded.* This signal is generated if a process exceeds its maximum file size limit. The default action is an abnormal termination.

There are a number of other signals that you may encounter which are implementation dependent and lie outside the territory of *XSI*. Again, most of these are used by the kernel to indicate error conditions, for example: SIGEMT (*emulator trap*) often indicates an implementation-defined hardware fault.

6.1.2 Normal and abnormal termination

For most signals **normal termination** occurs when a signal is received. The effect is roughly the same as if the process had executed an impromptu _exit call. The exit status returned to the parent in this circumstance tells the parent what happened. There are macros defined in <sys/wait.h> which allow the parent to determine the cause of termination and in this particular case the value of the signal which was responsible. The following code extract shows the parent testing for the cause of termination and printing out an appropriate message.

```
#include <sys/wait.h>

  .

  .
if((pid=wait(&status)) == -1)
{
 perror("wait failed");
 exit(1);
}

/* test to see if the child exited normally */
if(WIFEXITED(status))
{
 exit_status = WEXITSTATUS(status);
 printf("Exit status from %d was %d\n", pid, exit_status);
}
```

```
/* test to see if the child received a signal */
if(WIFSIGNALED(status))
{
 sig_no = WTERMSIG(status);
 printf("Signal number %d terminated child %d\n", sig_no, pid);
}

/* test to see if the child has been stopped */
if(WIFSTOPPED(status))
{
 sig_no = WSTOPSIG(status);
 printf("Signal number %d stopped child %d\n", sig_no, pid);
}
```

As we saw above, the signals SIGABRT, SIGBUS, SIGSEGV, SIGQUIT, SIGILL, SIGTRAP, SIGSYS, SIGXCPU, SIGXFSZ and SIGFPE cause an abnormal termination, and the usual effect of this is a core dump. This means that a memory dump of the process is written to a file called core in the process' current working directory ('core', of course, is a rather old-fashioned way of describing main memory). The core file will include, in binary form, the values of all program variables, hardware registers and control information from the kernel at the moment termination occurred. The exit status of a process that abnormally terminates will be the same as it would be for normal termination by a signal, except that the seventh low-order bit is set. Most UNIX systems now define a macro WCOREDUMP, which will return true or false depending on whether the appropriate bit is set in the status variable. Beware, however, that WCOREDUMP is not defined by the *XSI*. If the macro is available the previous example could be expanded as follows:

```
/* test to see if the child received a signal */
if(WIFSIGNALED(status))
{
 sig_no = WTERMSIG(status);
 printf("Signal number %d terminated child %d\n", sig_no, pid);
 if(WCOREDUMP(status))
       printf("...core dump created\n");
}
```

The format of a core file is known to the UNIX debuggers and these programs can be used to examine the state of a process at the point it core dumped. This can be extremely useful since debuggers will allow you to pinpoint the spot where the problem occurred.

It is also worth mentioning the abort routine, called straightforwardly:

```
abort();
```

abort will send the SIGABRT signal to the calling process, causing abnormal termination; that is, a core dump. abort is useful as a debugging aid since it allows a process to record its current state when something goes wrong. It also illustrates the fact that a process can send a signal to itself.

6.2 Signal handling

On the receipt of a signal, a process has three choices to the way in which it will act:

1. Take the default action. The default action is normally to terminate the process. However, for SIGUSR1 and SIGUSR2 it is to ignore the signal. For SIGSTOP it is stop the process (that is, suspend).

2. Ignore the signal altogether and carry on processing. In larger programs, unexpected signals can cause problems. It makes no sense, for example, to allow a program to be halted by a careless press of an interrupt key during an important database update.

3. Take a specified user-defined action. Whenever a program exits, whatever the cause, a programmer might want to perform clean-up operations such as removing work files.

In older versions of UNIX, signal handling was relatively straightforward. However, the mechanisms were not that reliable and the newer routines we will explore are tighter but more complex. Before we set to our first examples, some explanations are needed. We will start with **signal sets**.

6.2.1 Signal sets

Signal sets are one of the main parameters passed to system calls that deal with signals. They simply specify a list of signals you want to do something with.

Signal sets are defined using the type sigset_t, which is itself defined in the header file <signal.h>. This is guaranteed to be large enough to hold a representation for all of the system's defined signals. You now have a number of choices in the way in which you wish to indicate an interest in particular signals. You can either start with a full set of signals and then delete the ones you do not want, or you can start with an empty set of signals and turn on the ones that you do want. The initialization steps are done with the routines sigemptyset and sigfillset. The relevant signal sets can then be manipulated with sigaddset and sigdelset, which add and remove signals respectively.

Usage

```
#include <signal.h>

/* initialize */
int sigemptyset(sigset_t *set);
int sigfillset(sigset_t *set);

/* manipulate */
int sigaddset(sigset_t *set, int signo);
int sigdelset(sigset_t *set, int signo);
```

sigemptyset and sigfillset take one parameter, a pointer to a variable of type sigset_t. The call sigemptyset initializes the set so that all signals are excluded. Conversely, sigfillset initializes the parameter pointed to by set so that all signals are included. Applications should call sigemptyset or sigfillset at least once for any variable of type sigset_t.

sigaddset and sigdelset take a pointer to an initiated signal set and a signal number to be added or deleted as appropriate. The second parameter signo can be the signal's symbolic constant name, such as SIGINT, or, less portably, the actual signal number.

In the following example we create two signal sets, the first one starts empty and then the SIGINT and SIGQUIT signals are added to the set. In the second, the set starts full and the signal SIGCHLD is deleted from the set.

```
#include <signal.h>

sigset_t mask1, mask2;
.
.
.

/* create empty set */
sigemptyset(&mask1);

/* add signal */
sigaddset(&mask1, SIGINT);
sigaddset(&mask1, SIGQUIT);

/* create full set */
sigfillset(&mask2);

/* remove signal */
sigdelset(&mask2, SIGCHLD);
.
.
.
```

6.2.2 Setting the signal action: sigaction

Once you have defined a signal set, you can choose a particular method of handling a signal using sigaction.

Usage
``#include <signal.h>

int sigaction(int signo, const struct sigaction *act,
                         struct sigaction *oact);``` |

As we shall see in a moment, the sigaction structure contains a signal set. The first parameter signo identifies an individual signal for which we want to specify an action. To have any effect, sigaction must be called before a signal of type signo is received. signo can be set to any of the signal names defined previously, with the exceptions of SIGSTOP and SIGKILL, which are provided exclusively to stop (that is, suspend) or terminate a process, respectively, and cannot be handled in any other way.

The second parameter, act, gives the actions you want to set for signo. If you need to know, the third parameter oact will simply be filled out with the current settings. Either one can be set to NULL. Let us investigate the sigaction structure. This is defined in <signal.h> as:

```
struct sigaction{
  void (*sa_handler)(int); /* the action to be taken */
  sigset_t sa_mask;        /* additional signals to be blocked
                              during the handling of the signal */
  int    sa_flags;         /* flags which affect the behaviour of
                              the signal */
  void (*sa_sigaction)(int, siginfo_t *, void *);
                           /* pointer to signal handler */
};
```

This looks very complex, but let us decompose it step by step. The first field sa_handler identifies the action to be taken on receipt of the signal signo. It can take three values:

1. SIG_DFL A special symbolic name which restores the system's default action (normally termination of the process).

2. SIG_IGN Another symbolic name, which simply means 'ignore this signal'. In future, the process will do just that. This cannot be used for SIGSTOP and SIGKILL.

3. The address of a function which takes an integer argument. As long as it is declared before sigaction is called, sa_handler can be simply set to the name of a function. The compiler will assume you mean the function's address. The function will be executed when a signal of type signo is received, and the value of signo itself will then be passed to the function. Control will be passed to the function as soon as the process receives the signal, whatever part of the program it is executing. When the function returns, control will be passed back to the point at which the process was interrupted. This mechanism will become clearer in our next example.

The second field, sa_mask, demonstrates our first practical use of a signal set. The signals specified in sa_mask will be blocked during the time spent in the function specified by sa_handler. This does not mean they are ignored. It means they are put on hold until the handling function finishes. When the process enters the function the caught signal will also be added to the current signal mask. This turns signals into a more (but not completely) reliable communication mechanism.

The sa_flags field can be used to modify the behaviour of signo – the originally specified signal. For example a signal's action can be reset to SIG_DFL on return from the handler, by setting sa_flags to SA_RESETHAND. If sa_flags is set to SA_SIGINFO, extra information will be passed to the signal handler. In this case sa_handler is redundant and the final field sa_sigaction is used. The siginfo_t structure passed to this handler contains additional information about the signal; for example, its number, the sending process-id and the real user-id of the sending process. For a truly portable program the *XSI* specifies that your process should use either sa_handler or sa_sigaction, but never both.

This is all heavy going, so let us now consider some examples. It really is much simpler than it seems.

Example 1: catching SIGINT

This example shows how a signal can be caught, and also sheds more light on the underlying signal mechanism. It centres around the program sigex, which simply associates a function called catchint with SIGINT, then executes a series of sleep and printf statements. Notice how we define the sigaction structure act as static. This forces initialization of the structure – and sa_flags in particular – to zero.

```
/* sigex -- shows how sigaction works */

#include <signal.h>

main()
{
 static struct sigaction act;

 /* declare catchint, later to be used as the handler */
 void catchint(int);

 /* set up the action to be taken on receipt of SIGINT */
 act.sa_handler = catchint;

 /* create a full mask */
 sigfillset(&(act.sa_mask));

 /* before sigaction call, SIGINT will
  * terminate process (default action)
  */

 sigaction(SIGINT, &act, NULL);

 /* on receipt of SIGINT control will be passed
  * to catchint
  */

 printf("sleep call #1\n");
 sleep(1);
 printf("sleep call #2\n");
 sleep(1);
```

```
printf("sleep call #3\n");
sleep(1);
printf("sleep call #4\n");
sleep(1);

printf("Exiting \n");
exit(0);
}

/* trivial function to handle SIGINT */
void catchint(int signo)
{
printf("\nCATCHINT: signo=%d\n", signo);

printf("CATCHINT: returning\n\n");
}
```

If left alone sigex produces the following output:

```
$ sigex
sleep call #1
sleep call #2
sleep call #3
sleep call #4
Exiting
```

The user can, however, interrupt the progress of sigex by typing the interrupt key. If typed before sigex has had a chance to execute sigaction, the process will simply terminate. If typed after the sigaction call, control will be passed to the function catchint, as follows:

```
$ sigex
sleep call #1
 < interrupt >                    (user presses interrupt key)

CATCHINT: signo = 2
CATCHINT: returning

sleep call #2
sleep call #3
sleep call #4
Exiting
```

Notice how control is passed from the main body of the program to catchint. When catchint has finished, control is passed back to the point at which the program was interrupted. sigex could equally easily be interrupted at a different place:

```
$ sigex
sleep call #1
sleep call #2
 <interrupt>                    (user presses interrupt key)

CATCHINT: signo=2
CATCHINT: returning

sleep call #3
sleep call #4
Exiting
```

Example 2: *ignoring* `SIGINT`

Suppose we want a process to ignore the interrupt signal `SIGINT`. All we need do is replace the following line in the program:

```
act.sa_handler = catchint;
```

with:

```
act.sa_handler = SIG_IGN;
```

After this is executed the interrupt key will be ineffective. It can be enabled again with:

```
act.sa_handler = SIG_DFL;
sigaction(SIGINT, &act, NULL);
```

It is perfectly possible to ignore several signals simultaneously. For example,

```
act.sa_handler = SIG_IGN;
sigaction(SIGINT, &act, NULL);
sigaction(SIGQUIT, &act, NULL);
```

deals with both `SIGINT` and `SIGQUIT`. This is useful for programs which do not want to be interrupted from the keyboard.

Certain shells use this technique to ensure that background processes are not stopped when the user presses the interrupt key. This is possible because signals that are ignored by a process are still ignored after an `exec` call. The shell can therefore call `sigaction` to make sure `SIGQUIT` and `SIGINT` are ignored, then `exec` the new program.

Example 3: *restoring a previous action*

As we saw above, `sigaction` can fill out its third parameter `oact`. This allows us to save and restore the previous state of the signal, as the next example shows:

```
#include <signal.h>

static struct sigaction act,oact;

/* save the old action for SIGTERM */
sigaction(SIGTERM, NULL, &oact);

/* set new action for SIGTERM */
act.sa_handler = SIG_IGN;
sigaction(SIGTERM, &act, NULL);

/* do the work here... */

/* now restore the old action */
sigaction(SIGTERM, &oact, NULL);
```

Example 4: a graceful exit

Suppose a program uses a temporary workfile. The following simple routine removes the file:

```
/* exit from program gracefully */
#include <stdio.h>
#include <stdlib.h>

void g_exit(int s)
{
 unlink("tempfile");
 fprintf(stderr, "Interrupted -- exiting\n");
 exit(1);
}
```

This could be associated with a particular signal as follows:

```
extern void g_exit(int);
 .
 .
 .
static struct sigaction act;
act.sa_handler = g_exit;
sigaction(SIGINT, &act, NULL);
```

After this call, control will pass automatically to g_exit when the user presses the interrupt key. The contents of g_exit could be expanded depending on the number of clean-up operations required.

6.2.3 Signals and system calls

In most cases, if a process is sent a signal when it is executing a system call, the signal has no effect until the system call completes. However, a few system calls behave differently, and they can be interrupted by a signal. This is true for a `read`, `write` or `open` on a slow device (such as a terminal, but not a disk file), a `wait`, or a `pause` call (which we will discuss in due course). In all cases, if the process traps the call, the interrupted system call returns −1 and places `EINTR` into `errno`. This sort of situation can be handled with code like:

```
if( write(tfd, buf, size) < 0)
{
 if( errno == EINTR )
 {
        warn("Write interrupted");
        .
        .
        .
 }
}
```

In this case, if the progam wanted to rerun the `write` system call it would have to use a loop and a `continue` statement. However, `sigaction` allows you to automatically restart the system call if it is interrupted in this way. This is achieved by setting the `sa_flags` variable in the `struct sigaction` to `SA_RESTART`. If this flag is set then the system call will restart and `errno` will not be set.

It is important to note that UNIX signals cannot normally be stacked. To put it another way, there can never be more than one signal of each type outstanding at any moment for a given process, although there can be more than one type of signal outstanding. The fact that signals cannot be stacked means that they can never be used as a fully reliable method of inter-process communication, since a process can never be sure that a signal it has sent has not been 'lost'.

Exercise 6.1 Alter `smallsh` from the last chapter so that it handles interrupts more like a real shell. Make sure background processes are not halted by either `SIGINT` or `SIGQUIT`. Some variants of the shell (namely the *C-shell* and the *Korn shell*) handle background processes by placing them into a different process group. What are the advantages and disadvantages of this approach? (In recent POSIX work, the possibility of stackable signals has been introduced – but as an option.)

6.2.4 `sigsetjmp` and `siglongjmp`

Sometimes it makes sense to jump back to a previous position in a program when a signal is received. You might want, for example, to allow a user to go back to a program's main menu when he or she presses the interrupt key. This can be done using two special subroutines called `sigsetjmp` and `siglongjmp`. (Alternatives called `setjmp` and `longjmp` exist, with different signal handling.) `sigsetjmp` 'saves' the current program position and signal mask by saving the stack environment, and `siglongjmp` passes control back to the saved position. In a sense `siglongjmp` is a kind of long-distance, non-local goto. It is important to realize that `siglongjmp` never returns because the stack frames are collapsed back to the point where the position was saved. As we shall see, it is the corresponding `sigsetjmp` that appears to return.

Usage

```
#include <setjmp.h>

/* save location in program */
int sigsetjmp(sigjmp_buf env, int savemask);

/* go back to a saved location */
void siglongjmp(sigjmp_buf env, int val);
```

A program position is saved in an object of type `sigjmp_buf`, which is defined in the standard header file `<setjmp.h>`. In the `sigsetjmp` call if the value of `savemask` is non-zero, in other words TRUE, then `sigsetjmp` will save the current signal mask (that is, the state and actions associated with all signals) as well as the environment so that they may be restored when `siglongjmp` passes control back to this saved position. The return of `sigsetjmp` is significant: if `sigsetjmp` has been called from a `siglongjmp` then it will return a non 0 value, in fact the value of `val` in `siglongjmp`. However, if it is called as the next sequential instruction it will return 0.

The following example shows things more clearly:

```
/* example use of sigsetjmp and siglongjmp */

#include <sys/types.h>
#include <signal.h>
#include <setjmp.h>
#include <stdio.h>

sigjmp_buf position;

main()
{
 static struct sigaction act;
 void goback(void);
 .
 .
 .

 /* save current position */
 if(sigsetjmp(position, 1) == 0)
 {
      act.sa_handler = goback;
      sigaction(SIGINT, &act, NULL);
 }
```

```
domenu();
   .
   .
   .

}

void goback(void)
{
 fprintf(stderr, "\nInterrupted\n");

 /* go back to saved position */
 siglongjmp(position, 1);
}
```

If the user types an interrupt after the `sigaction` call, control is passed first to `goback`. This in turn calls `siglongjmp` and control is passed back to where `sigsetjmp` recorded the program position. So program execution continues as if the corresponding call to `sigsetjmp` had just returned. The return value from `sigsetjmp` is in this case taken from the second `siglongjmp` parameter.

6.3 Signal blocking

If a program is performing a sensitive task, like updating a database, it may well need to be protected from interruption in the crucial stages. Rather than ignore any incoming signals, as we saw above, a process can block the signals, which means that they will not be handled until the process has completed its delicate operations.

The system call which allows a process to block out specific signals is `sigprocmask`, which is defined as follows:

Usage
`#include <signal.h>`
`int sigprocmask(int how, const sigset_t *set, sigset_t *oset);`

The `how` parameter tells `sigprocmask` what specific action to take. For example this could be `SIG_SETMASK`, which means block out the signals in the second parameter `set` from now on. The third parameter is simply filled with the current 'mask' of blocked signals – if you do not want to know this simply set it to `NULL`. To make this clearer, here is an example:

```
sigset_t set1;
   .
   .
```

```
/* completely fill the signal set */
sigfillset(&set1);

/* set the block */
sigprocmask(SIG_SETMASK, &set1, NULL);

/* perform extremely critical code .... */

/* remove the signal block */
sigprocmask(SIG_UNBLOCK, &set1, NULL);
```

Notice the use of SIG_UNBLOCK to remove the signal block. Also note that giving a value of SIG_BLOCK instead of SIG_SETMASK for the first parameter will *add* the signals specified in set to the current signal set.

This more complex example shows all signals being blocked for an extremely critical piece of code, and then just SIGINT and SIGQUIT being blocked for a less critical piece of code.

```
/* signal blocking -- demonstrates the use of sigprocmask */

#include <signal.h>

main()
{
 sigset_t set1, set2;

 /* completely fill the signal set */
 sigfillset(&set1);

 /* create a signal set which
  * does not include SIGINT and SIGQUIT
  */
 sigfillset(&set2);
 sigdelset(&set2, SIGINT);
 sigdelset(&set2, SIGQUIT);

 /* perform non critical code ... */

 /* set the block */
 sigprocmask(SIG_SETMASK, &set1, NULL);

 /* perform extremely critical code .... */

 /* set less of a block */
 sigprocmask(SIG_UNBLOCK, &set2, NULL);

 /* perform less critical code ... */

 /* remove all signal blocks */
 sigprocmask(SIG_UNBLOCK, &set1, NULL);
}
```

Exercise 6.2 Make the g_exit routine introduced in Example 4 in Section 6.2.2 ignore both SIGINT and SIGQUIT for the duration of the function.

6.4 Sending signals

6.4.1 Sending signals to other processes: kill

A process calls sigaction to handle signals sent by other processes. The inverse operation of actually sending a signal is performed by the dramatically named kill system call. kill is used as follows:

Usage

```
#include <sys/types.h>
#include <signal.h>

int kill(pid_t pid, int sig);
```

The first parameter pid determines the process, or processes, to which the signal sig will be sent. Normally pid will be a positive number and in this case it will be taken to be an actual process-id. So the statement:

```
kill(7421, SIGTERM);
```

means *send signal* SIGTERM *to the process with process-id 7421.* Because the process that calls kill needs to know the id of the process it is sending to, kill is most often used between closely related processes, for example parent and child. It is also worth noting that processes can send signals to themselves.

There are some privilege issues here. In order to send a signal to a process, the real or effective user-id of the sending process must match the real or effective user-id of the receiver. Superuser processes, naturally enough, can send signals to any other process. If a non-superuser process does try to send to another process which belongs to a different user, then kill fails, returns −1 and places EPERM into errno. (The other possible values for errno with kill are ESRCH, meaning no such process, or EINVAL if sig is not a valid signal number.)

The pid parameter to kill can take other values which have special meanings:

1. If pid is zero, the signal will be sent to all processes that belong to the same process group as the sender. This includes the sender.

2. If pid is −1, and the effective user-id of the process is not superuser, then the signal is sent to all processes with a real user-id equal to the effective user-id of the sender. Again, this includes the sender.

3. If `pid` is −1, and the effective user-id of the process is superuser, then the signal will be sent to all processes with the exception of some special system processes (this last prohibition actually applies to all attempts to send a signal to a group of processes, but is most important here).

4. Finally, if `pid` is less than zero but not −1, the signal will be sent to all processes with a process group-id equal to the absolute value of `pid`. This includes the sender if appropriate.

An example is called for; synchro will create two processes. Both will write messages alternately to standard output. They synchronize themselves by using kill to send the signal SIGUSR1 to each other.

```
/* synchro -- example for kill */

#include <unistd.h>
#include <signal.h>

int ntimes = 0;

main()
{
 pid_t pid, ppid;
 void p_action(int), c_action(int);
 static struct sigaction pact, cact;

 /* set SIGUSR1 action for parent */
 pact.sa_handler = p_action;
 sigaction(SIGUSR1, &pact, NULL);

 switch(pid = fork()){
   case -1:        /* error */
       perror("synchro");
       exit(1);
   case 0:         /* child */

       /* set action for child */
       cact.sa_handler = c_action;
       sigaction(SIGUSR1, &cact, NULL);

       /* get parent process-id */
       ppid = getppid();

       for(;;)
       {
           sleep(1);
           kill(ppid, SIGUSR1);
           pause();
       }
       /* never exits */
```

```
    default:        /* parent */

        for(;;)
        {
            pause();
            sleep(1);
            kill(pid, SIGUSR1);
        }
        /* never exits */
    }
}

void p_action(int sig)
{
 printf("Parent caught signal #%d\n", ++ntimes);
}

void c_action(int sig)
{
 printf("Child caught signal #%d\n", ++ntimes);
}
```

Each process sits in a loop, pausing until it receives a signal from the other. This is done with the system call pause which simply suspends execution until a signal arrives (see Section 6.4.3). Each process then prints a message and takes its turn to send a signal with kill. The child process kicks things off (notice the ordering of statements in each loop). Both processes are terminated when the user hits the interrupt key. An example dialogue might look like:

```
$ synchro
Parent caught signal #1
Child caught signal #1
Parent caught signal #2
Child caught signal #2
< interrupt >                (user hits interrupt key)
$
```

6.4.2 Sending signals to yourself: raise and alarm

The raise function simply sends a signal to the executing process.

Usage
#include <signal.h>
int raise(int sig);

The parameter sig is sent to the calling process and raise returns 0 on success.

alarm is a simple and useful call that sets up a process alarm clock. Signals are used to tell the program that the clock's timer has expired.

Usage

```
#include <unistd.h>

unsigned int alarm(unsigned int secs);
```

Here, secs gives the time in seconds to the alarm. When this interval has expired the process will be sent a SIGALRM signal. So the call:

```
alarm(60);
```

arranges for a SIGALRM signal in 60 seconds. Note that alarm is not like sleep, which suspends process execution; alarm instead returns immediately and the process continues execution in the normal manner, or at least until SIGALRM is received. In fact an active alarm clock will also continue across an exec call. After a fork, however, the alarm clock is turned off in a child process.

An alarm can be turned off by calling alarm with a zero parameter:

```
/* turn alarm clock off */
alarm(0);
```

alarm calls are not stacked: in other words if you call alarm twice, the second call supersedes the first. However, the return value from alarm does give the time remaining for any previous alarm timer, which can be recorded if necessary.

alarm is useful when a programmer needs to place a time limit on some activity. The basic idea is simple: alarm is called, and the process carries on with the task. If the task is completed in good time, the alarm clock is turned off. If it takes too long, the process is interrupted by SIGALRM and takes corrective action.

The following function quickreply uses this approach to force an answer from the user. It takes one argument, a prompt, and returns a pointer to a string containing the input line, or the null pointer if nothing is typed after five retries. Note that each time quickreply reminds the user, it sends *Ctrl-G* to the terminal. This will ring the bell on most terminal hardware or emulators.

quickreply calls a routine gets which comes from the **Standard I/O Library**. gets places the next line from standard input into a char array. It returns either a pointer to the array, or the null pointer on end of file or error. Notice how SIGALRM is caught by the interrupt routine catch. This is important, since the default action associated with SIGALRM is, of course, termination. catch sets a flag called timed_out. quickreply checks this within the body of quickreply to see if it has indeed been timed out.

```c
#include <stdio.h>
#include <signal.h>


#define TIMEOUT     5               /* in seconds */
#define MAXTRIES    5
#define LINESIZE    100
#define CTRL_G      '\007'      /* ASCII bell */
#define TRUE        1
#define FALSE       0


/* used to see if timeout has occurred */
static int timed_out;

/* will hold input line */
static char answer[LINESIZE];


char *quickreply(char *prompt)
{
 void catch(int);
 int ntries;
 static struct sigaction act, oact;

 /* catch SIGALRM + save previous action */
 act.sa_handler = catch;
 sigaction(SIGALRM, &act, &oact);

 for(ntries=0; ntries<MAXTRIES; ntries++)
 {
      timed_out - FALSE,
      printf("\n%s > ", prompt);

      /* set alarm clock */
      alarm(TIMEOUT);

      /* get input line */
      gets(answer);

      /* turn off alarm */
      alarm(0);

      /* if timed_out TRUE, then no reply */
      if(!timed_out)
           break;
 }

 /* restore old action */
 sigaction(SIGALRM, &oact, NULL);

 /* return appropriate value */
 return (ntries == MAXTRIES ? ((char *)0) : answer);
}
```

```
/* executed when SIGALRM received */
void catch(int sig)
{
 /* set timeout flag */
 timed_out = TRUE;

 /* ring bell */
 putchar(CTRL_G);
}
```

6.4.3 The `pause` system call

As a companion to `alarm`, UNIX provides the `pause` system call, which is invoked very simply as follows:

Usage

```
#include <unistd.h>

int pause(void);
```

`pause` suspends the calling process (in such a way that it will not waste CPU time) until any signal, such as `SIGALRM`, is received. If the signal causes normal termination then that is just what will happen. If the signal is ignored by the process, `pause` ignores it too. If the signal is caught, however, then when the appropriate interrupt routine has finished, `pause` returns −1 and places `EINTR` into errno (why?).

The following program `tml` (for 'tell me later') uses both `alarm` and `pause` in order to display a message in a given number of minutes. It is called as follows:

$ *tml # minutes message-text*

For example:

$ *tml 10 time to go home*

The message is preceded with three *Ctrl-G*s or bells for dramatic effect. Note how `tml` forks to create a background process to do the work, allowing the user to continue with other tasks.

```
/* tml -- tell-me-later program */

#include <stdio.h>
#include <stdlib.h>
#include <sys/types.h>
#include <signal.h>
#include <unistd.h>
```

```
#define TRUE        1
#define FALSE       0
#define BELLS       "\007\007\007"     /* ASCII bells */


int alarm_flag = FALSE;


/* routine to handle SIGALRM */
void setflag(int sig)
{
 alarm_flag = TRUE;
}


main(int argc, char **argv)
{
 int nsecs,j;
 pid_t pid;
 static struct sigaction act;

 if( argc<=2 )
 {
      fprintf(stderr, "Usage: tml #minutes message\n");
      exit(1);
 }


 if( (nsecs=atoi(argv[1])*60) <= 0)
 {
      fprintf(stderr, "tml: invalid time\n");
      exit(2);
 }

 /* fork to create background process */
 switch(pid = fork()){
   case -1:            /* error */
      perror("tml");
      exit(1);
   case 0:             /* child */
      break;
   default:            /* parent */
      printf("tml process-id %d\n", pid);
      exit(0);
 }

 /* set action for alarm */
 act.sa_handler = setflag;
 sigaction(SIGALRM, &act, NULL);


 /* turn on alarm clock */
 alarm(nsecs);


 /* pause until signal ... */
 pause();
```

```
/* if signal was SIGALRM, print message */
if(alarm_flag == TRUE)
{
      printf(BELLS);
      for(j = 2; j < argc; j++)
            printf("%s ",argv[j]);
      printf("\n");
}

exit(0);
}
```

From this example you should get an insight into how the `sleep` subroutine works by calling first `alarm`, then `pause`.

Exercise 6.3 Write your own version of `sleep`. Make sure it saves the previous state of the alarm clock and restores it when it exits. (Look at your system's manual for a full specification of `sleep`.)

Exercise 6.4 Rewrite `tml` using your version of `sleep`.

CHAPTER 7

Inter-process communication using pipes

It is inevitable that for two or more processes to cooperate in performing a task, they need to share data. Useful though they are for dealing with unusual events or errors, signals are entirely unsuited for transmitting large amounts of information from one process to another. One possible way of solving this problem is for processes to share files, since there is nothing to prevent several processes from reading or writing the same file simultaneously. However, this can be inefficient and care has to be taken to avoid contention problems.

In order to solve this problem, UNIX provides a construct called the **pipe** (as well as other constructs we shall explore in later chapters). A pipe is typically used as a one-way communications channel which couples one related process to another, and is yet another generalization of the UNIX file concept. As we shall see, a process can send data 'down' the pipe by using the write system call, and another process can receive the data by using read at the other end.

7.1 Pipes

7.1.1 Pipes at command level

Most UNIX users will have come across pipes at command level. For example,

```
$ pr doc | lp
```

causes the shell to start the commands pr and lp simultaneously. The ' | ' symbol in the command line tells the shell to create a pipe to couple the standard output of pr to the standard input of lp. The final result of this command should be a nicely paginated version of the file doc sent to the line printer.

Let us dissect the command further. The pr program on the left-hand side of the pipe symbol does not know that its standard output is being sent to a pipe. It just writes to standard output as normal, making no special arrangements. Similarly, lp on the right-hand side reads from the pipe just as if its standard input is coming from the keyboard or ordinary disk file. The overall effect is logically as if the following sequence had been executed:

```
$ pr doc > tmpfile
$ lp < tmpfile
$ rm tmpfile
```

Flow control along the pipe is handled automatically and invisibly. So if pr produces information too quickly, its execution is suspended. It is restarted when lp catches up and the amount of data in the pipe falls to an acceptable level.

Pipes are one of the strongest and most distinctive features of UNIX, especially at command level. They allow arbitrary sequences of commands to be simply coupled together. UNIX programs can therefore be developed as general tools which read from their standard input, write to their standard output and perform a single, well-defined task. More complex command lines can be built up from these basic building blocks using pipes. For example:

```
$ who | wc -l
```

pipes the output of who into the word count program wc, the -1 option telling wc just to count lines. The number finally output by wc is therefore a count of the number of logged-on users.

7.1.2 Programming with pipes

Within a program a pipe is created using a system call named pipe. If successful, this call returns two file descriptors: one for writing down the pipe, and one for reading from it. pipe is defined as follows:

Usage
#include <unistd.h>   int pipe(int filedes[2]);

filedes is a two-integer array that will hold the file descriptors that will identify the pipe. If the call is successful, filedes[0] will be open for reading from the pipe and filedes[1] will be open for writing down it.

pipe can fail and so return −1. This can happen if the call would cause more file descriptors to be opened than the per-user process limit (in which case errno will contain EMFILE), or if the kernel's open file table would overflow (errno would then contain ENFILE).

Once created, a pipe can be straightforwardly manipulated with read and write. The following example shows this; it creates a pipe, writes three messages down it, then reads them back:

```c
/* first pipe example */
#include <unistd.h>
#include <stdio.h>

/* this figure includes terminating null */
#define MSGSIZE    16

char *msg1 = "hello, world #1";
char *msg2 = "hello, world #2";
char *msg3 = "hello, world #3";

main()
{
 char inbuf[MSGSIZE];
 int p[2], j;

 /* open pipe */
 if(pipe(p) == -1)
 {
      perror("pipe call");
      exit(1);
 }

 /* write down pipe */
 write(p[1], msg1, MSGSIZE);
 write(p[1], msg2, MSGSIZE);
 write(p[1], msg3, MSGSIZE);

 /* read from pipe */
 for(j = 0; j < 3; j++)
 {
      read(p[0], inbuf, MSGSIZE);
      printf("%s\n", inbuf);
 }

 exit(0);
}
```

The output from this program is:

```
hello, world #1
hello, world #2
hello, world #3
```

Process

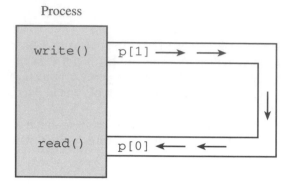

Figure 7.1 *First pipe example.*

Notice the way the messages are read in the order in which they were written. Pipes treat data on a *first-in first-out* or *FIFO* basis. In other words, what you place first into a pipe is what is read first at the other end. This order cannot be altered since lseek will not work on a pipe.

Although we do so in the example, a process does not have to read from a pipe in the same size chunks as the pipe was written. A pipe could, for example, be written in 512-byte blocks and then read a character at a time, just like a regular file. There are advantages in using fixed sized chunks however, as we see in Section 7.2.

The action of the example is shown pictorially in Figure 7.1. This diagram should make it clear that the process is just sending data to itself using the pipe as a kind of loop-back mechanism. This may seem a little pointless, since the process is only talking to itself.

A pipe's true value only becomes apparent when it is used in conjunction with the fork system call, where the fact that file descriptors remain open across a fork can be exploited. The next example shows this. It creates a pipe, and calls fork. The child process then writes a series of messages to its parent.

```
/* second pipe example */
#include <unistd.h>
#include <stdio.h>

#define MSGSIZE    16

char *msg1 = "hello, world #1";
char *msg2 = "hello, world #2";
char *msg3 = "hello, world #3";

main()
{
 char inbuf[MSGSIZE];
 int p[2], j;
 pid_t pid;
```

```
/* open pipe */
if(pipe(p) == -1)
{
      perror("pipe call");
      exit(1);
}


switch(pid = fork()){
case -1:
      perror("fork call");
      exit(2);
case 0:
      /* if child then write down pipe */
      write(p[1], msg1, MSGSIZE);
      write(p[1], msg2, MSGSIZE);
      write(p[1], msg3, MSGSIZE);
      break;
default:
      /* if parent then read from pipe */
      for(j = 0; j < 3; j++)
      {
            read(p[0], inbuf, MSGSIZE);
            printf("%s\n",inbuf);
      }
      wait(NULL);
}

exit(0);
}
```

This example is represented in diagram form in Figure 7.2. It shows how the pipe now connects two processes. As you can see, both parent and child have two open file descriptors, allowing reading and writing on the pipe. So, either process could write down file descriptor p[1] and read from file descriptor p[0]. There is a problem here. Pipes are intended to be used as unidirectional communication

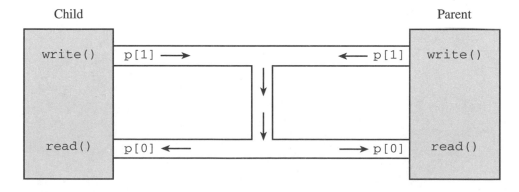

Figure 7.2 *Second pipe example.*

channels. If both processes freely read and write on the pipe at the same time, confusion will result.

To avoid this, it is customary for each process to either just read or just write to or from the pipe and close the file descriptor it does not need. In fact, a program really has to do this to avoid problems when the sending process closes its write end – Section 7.1.4 explains why. The examples shown so far only work because the receiving processes know exactly how much data to expect. The next example shows the finished solution:

```
/* third pipe example */
#include <unistd.h>
#include <stdio.h>

#define MSGSIZE    16

char *msg1 = "hello, world #1";
char *msg2 = "hello, world #2";
char *msg3 = "hello, world #3";

main()
{
 char inbuf[MSGSIZE];
 int p[2], j;
 pid_t pid;

 /* open pipe */
 if(pipe(p) == -1)
 {
       perror("pipe call");
       exit(1);
 }

 switch(pid = fork()){
 case -1:
       perror("fork call");
       exit(2);
 case 0:
       /* if child then closes read file
        * descriptor and writes down the pipe
        */
       close(p[0]);
       write(p[1], msg1, MSGSIZE);
       write(p[1], msg2, MSGSIZE);
       write(p[1], msg3, MSGSIZE);
       break;
 default:
       /* if parent then closes write file
        * descriptor and reads from the pipe
        */
       close(p[1]);
```

```
        for(j = 0; j < 3; j++)
        {
                read(p[0], inbuf, MSGSIZE);
                printf("%s\n",inbuf);
        }
        wait(NULL);
    }

    exit(0);
}
```

The end result is a one-way pathway between parent and child. This simplified situation is shown in Figure 7.3.

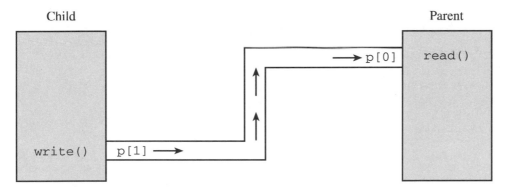

Figure 7.3 *Third pipe example.*

Exercise 7.1 In the last example, a pipe was used to establish a link between a parent and a child process. In fact, a pipe's file descriptors can be passed across several calls to fork. This means that more than one process can read the pipe, and more than one process can write the pipe. To demonstrate this, write a program that creates three processes, two that write down the pipe and one that reads from the pipe. Make the reading process print any messages it receives on its standard output.

Exercise 7.2 To establish two-way communications between processes, two pipes operating in different directions can be created. Devise a possible conversation between two processes and implement it using pipes in this way.

7.1.3 The size of a pipe

So far our examples have transmitted only small amounts of data. In practice, it is important to note that the size of a pipe is finite. In other words, only a certain number of bytes can be in the pipe before a subsequent write will block. The minimum limit is defined by POSIX as 512 bytes. However, in reality most systems make this figure much greater. It is important that you know the maximum size of a pipe when programming as it has implications for both `write` and `read`. If a `write` is made on a pipe and there is enough space, then the data is sent down the pipe and the call returns immediately. If, however, a `write` is made that would overfill the pipe, process execution is normally suspended until room is made by another process reading from the pipe.

As an example, the next program writes down a pipe character by character until the `write` call blocks. It uses `alarm` to prevent the process waiting too long after `write` blocks for a `read` that will never happen. Note the use of `fpathconf` (as described in Section 4.4.8), which is used to determine the maximum number of bytes that can be written to a pipe in one go.

```
/* write down a pipe until we get blocked */

#include <signal.h>
#include <unistd.h>
#include <limits.h>

int count;
void alrm_action(int);

main()
{
 int p[2];
 int pipe_size;
 char c = 'x';
 static struct sigaction act;

 /* set up the signal handler */
 act.sa_handler = alrm_action;
 sigfillset(&(act.sa_mask));

 /* create the pipe */
 if(pipe(p) == -1)
 {
      perror("pipe call");
      exit(1);
 }

 /* determine the size of the pipe */
 pipe_size = fpathconf(p[0], _PC_PIPE_BUF);
 printf("Maximum size of write to pipe: %d bytes\n", pipe_size);

 /* set the signal handler */
 sigaction(SIGALRM, &act, NULL);

 while(1)
 {
      /* set alarm */
      alarm(20);
```

```
                    /* write down pipe */
                    write(p[1], &c, 1);

                    /* reset alarm */
                    alarm(0);

                    if((++count % 1024) == 0)
                            printf("%d characters in pipe\n", count);
    }
}

/* called when SIGALRM received */
void alrm_action(int signo)
{
 printf("write blocked after %d characters\n", count);
 exit(0);
}
```

On many systems, this will produce the following output:

Maximum size of write to pipe: 32768 bytes
1024 characters in pipe
2048 characters in pipe
3072 characters in pipe
4096 characters in pipe
5120 characters in pipe
.

.

.
31744 characters in pipe
32768 characters in pipe
write blocked after 32768 characters

Notice how much bigger the real limit is compared with the POSIX minimum size.

Things get a little more complicated when a process attempts a single write of more data than the pipe can hold even when empty. In this case, the kernel will first write as much as it can into the pipe. It then suspends execution of the process until room becomes available for the rest of the data. This is important; normally a write on a pipe will execute **atomically**, all the data being transferred in a single, uninterrupted kernel operation. If a write of more data than the pipe can hold is made, the write has to be performed in stages. If several concurrent processes were writing the same pipe in this way, data could get confusingly intermingled.

The interaction of read and pipes is simpler. When a read call is made, the system checks whether the pipe is empty. If it is empty, the read will (normally) block until data is written into the pipe by another process. If there is data waiting in the pipe, then the read returns, even if there is less data than the amount requested.

7.1.4 Closing pipes

What happens if the file descriptor that represents one end of a pipe is closed? There are two cases:

1. *Closing the write-only file descriptor* If there are other processes that still have the pipe open for writing, then nothing will happen. However, if there are no more processes capable of writing to the pipe and the pipe is empty, any processes that attempt to read from the pipe will return no data. Processes that were asleep waiting to read from the pipe will be woken up, their `read` calls returning zero. The effect for the reading processes is therefore much like reaching the end of a regular file.

2. *Closing the read-only file descriptor* If there are still processes that have the pipe open for reading, then again nothing will happen. If no other process is reading the pipe, however, all processes waiting to write to the pipe are sent the signal `SIGPIPE` by the kernel. If this signal is not caught, a process will terminate. If it is caught then, after the interrupt routine has completed, `write` will return −1 and `errno` will contain `EPIPE`. Processes that attempt to write to the pipe later will also be sent `SIGPIPE`.

7.1.5 Non-blocking `reads` and `writes`

As we have seen, both `read` and `write` can block when used on a pipe. Sometimes this is not desirable. You may want a program, for example, to execute an error routine, or maybe poll through several pipes until it receives data through one of them. Luckily, there are two simple ways of making sure that a `read` or `write` on a pipe will not hang.

The first method is to use `fstat` on the pipe. The `st_size` field in the returned `stat` structure gives the number of characters currently in the pipe. If only one process is reading the pipe, this is fine. However, if several processes are reading the pipe, another process could read from a pipe in the gap between `fstat` and `read`.

The second method is to use `fcntl` (again). Among its many roles, it allows a process to set the `O_NONBLOCK` flag for a file descriptor. This stops a future `read` or `write` on a pipe from blocking. In this context, `fcntl` can be used as follows:

```
#include <fcntl.h>
.
.
.
if(fcntl(filedes, F_SETFL, O_NONBLOCK) == -1)
 perror("fcntl");
```

If `filedes` was the write-only file descriptor for a pipe, then future calls to `write` would never block if the pipe was full. They would instead return a value of −1 immediately and set `errno` to `EAGAIN`. Similarly, if `filedes` represented the reading end of a pipe, then the process would immediately return a value of −1 if there was no data in the pipe, rather than sleeping. As with the `write` call, `errno` would be set to EAGAIN. (If another flag O_NDELAY is set instead, the behavior of `read` is different. It will return 0 if the pipe is empty. We will not consider this case further.)

The following program demonstrates this variation on the `fcntl` theme. It creates a pipe, sets the O_NONBLOCK flag for the read file descriptor, then forks. The child process sends messages to the parent, which sits in a loop polling the pipe to see if any data has arrived.

```
/* O_NONBLOCK example */

#include <fcntl.h>
#include <errno.h>

#define MSGSIZE 6

int parent(int *);
int child(int *);

char *msg1 = "hello";
char *msg2 = "bye!!";

main()
{
 int pfd[2];

 /* open pipe */
 if(pipe(pfd) == -1)
      fatal("pipe call");

 /* set O_NONBLOCK flag for p[0] */
 if(fcntl(pfd[0], F SETFL, O_NONBLOCK) == -1)
      fatal("fcntl call");

 switch(fork()){
 case -1:                   /* error */
      fatal("fork call");
 case 0:                    /* child */
      child(pfd);
 default:                   /* parent */
      parent(pfd);
 }
}

int parent(int p[2])       /* code for parent */
{
 int nread;
 char buf[MSGSIZE];

 close(p[1]);
```

```
for(;;)
{
     switch(nread = read(p[0], buf, MSGSIZE)){
     case -1:
           /* check to see if nothing is in the pipe */
           if(errno == EAGAIN)
           {
                 printf("(pipe empty)\n");
                 sleep(1);
                 break;
           }
           else
                 fatal("read call");
     case 0:
           /* pipe has been closed */
           printf("End of conversation\n");
           exit(0);
     default:
           printf("MSG=%s\n",buf);
     }
 }
}

int child(int p[2])
{
 int count;

 close(p[0]);

 for(count = 0; count < 3; count++)
 {
     write(p[1], msg1, MSGSIZE);
     sleep(3);
 }

 /* send final message */
 write(p[1], msg2, MSGSIZE);
 exit(0);
}
```

The example makes use of an error routine called `fatal`. We introduced this in the previous chapter. To save you looking back, it is implemented as follows:

```
int fatal(char *s)        /* print error message and die */
{
 perror(s);
 exit(1);
}
```

The output of the example is not entirely predictable since the number of 'pipe empty' messages may vary. On one machine however it produced:

MSG = hello
(pipe empty)
(pipe empty)
(pipe empty)
MSG = hello
(pipe empty)
(pipe empty)
(pipe empty)
MSG = hello
(pipe empty)
(pipe empty)
(pipe empty)
MSG = bye!!
End of conversation

7.1.6 Using `select` to handle multiple pipes

The use of non-blocking reads and writes is fine for simple applications. Another solution suitable for handling multiple pipes simultaneously is to use a system call named `select`.

Imagine the situation where a parent process is acting as a server process and could have an arbitrary number of client (child) processes communicating with it, as shown in Figure 7.4.

Here the server process needs to be able to cope with the situation where there is information pending on more than one pipe. In addition, if there is nothing pending on any of the pipes then it makes sense for the server process to block until there is – without polling. If information arrives on more than one pipe, then the server process needs to know which pipes, so that it can deal with them in the right order.

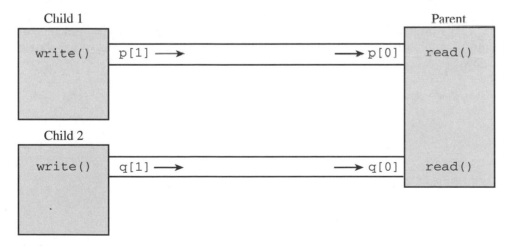

Figure 7.4 *Client/server using pipes.*

The system call which makes this all possible is called `select` (a similar call named `poll` also exists). The `select` system call is not only used for pipes, it can also be used for regular files, terminal devices, FIFOs (discussed in Section 7.2) and sockets (discussed in Chapter 10). The `select` system call works by indicating which of a specified set of file descriptors is ready for reading, or writing, or has an error condition pending. Obviously, we would not want the server process to block forever if none of these conditions was ever true and therefore `select` can also be made to timeout after a specified period.

Usage

```
#include <sys/time.h>

int select(int nfds, fd_set *readfds, fd_set *writefds,
           fd_set *errorfds, struct timeval *timeout);
```

The first parameter `nfds` tells `select` the number of file descriptors which are potentially of interest to the server. For example, if file descriptors 0, 1 and 2 are assigned to `stdin`, `stdout` and `stderr`, respectively, and we have opened two further files which have been allocated file descriptors 3 and 4, then we would need to set `nfds` to 5. As a programmer you can either work this value out for yourself or use the constant FD_SETSIZE defined in `<sys/time.h>`. FD_SETSIZE is defined to be the maximum number of file descriptors usable with `select`.

Parameters 2 through 4 of `select` are pointers to **bit masks**, each bit representing a file descriptor. If a bit is turned on, it denotes interest in the relevant file descriptor. `readfds` asks if there is anything worth reading; `writefds` asks if any of the given file descriptors are ready to accept a write; and `errorfds` asks if an exceptional condition has been raised on any of the given file descriptors, for example, out of band data may have arrived on a network connection. Since bit manipulation is rather ugly and potentially non-portable, an abstract data type `fd_set` is provided, along with macros (or functions depending on the implementation) to manipulate instances of this type. These bit manipulation macros are shown below:

```
#include <sys/time.h>

/* initialize the mask pointed to by fdset */
void FD_ZERO(fd_set *fdset);

/* set the bit, fd, in the mask pointed to by fdset */
void FD_SET(int fd, fd_set *fdset);

/* is the bit, fd, set in the mask pointed to by fdset */
int FD_ISSET(int fd, fd_set *fdset);

/* turn off the bit, fd, in the mask pointed to by fdset */
void FD_CLR(int fd, fd_set *fdset);
```

The following example shows how to express an interest in two open file descriptors:

```c
#include <sys/time.h>
#include <sys/types.h>
#include <fcntl.h>
.
.
.
int fd1, fd2;
fd_set readset;

fd1 = open("file1", O_RDONLY);
fd2 = open("file2", O_RDONLY);

FD_ZERO(&readset);
FD_SET(fd1, &readset);
FD_SET(fd2, &readset);

switch(select(5, &readset, NULL, NULL, NULL))
{
 /* logic */
}
```

The trick to understanding this is to remember that fd1 and fd2 are themselves small integers that represent the first open slots for the file descriptors, and are used as indexes into the bit masks. Notice how the arguments to writefds and errorfds, within select, are set to NULL. This means we are interested only in reading from fd1 and fd2.

The fifth parameter to select, timeout, is a pointer to a struct timeval which has the following structure:

```c
#include <sys/time.h>

struct timeval {
 long tv_sec;            /* seconds */
 long tv_usec;           /* and microseconds */
};
```

If the pointer is null, as in our example, select will block forever or until something of interest turns up. If timeout points at a structure containing 0 seconds, select returns immediately (without blocking). Finally, if the timeout structure contains a non-zero value, select will return after that number of seconds or microseconds specified if there is no file descriptor activity.

The return value of select is −1 on error, 0 upon timeout, or an integer indicating the number of 'interesting' file descriptors. A word of warning, however: when select returns it resets the bit masks pointed to by readfds, writefds or errorfds, as appropriate, by clearing the mask and resetting it with the file descriptors which contain the sought-after information. Therefore, it is essential to keep a copy of your original mask.

Here is a more complex example, based on using three pipes to connect to three child processes. The parent process also keeps an eye on standard input.

```
/* server -- creates three children and then services them */
#include <sys/time.h>
#include <sys/wait.h>

#define MSGSIZE     6

char *msg1 = "hello";
char *msg2 = "bye!!";

void parent(int [][]);
int child(int []);

main()
{
 int pip[3][2];
 int i;

 /* create three communication pipes, and spawn three children */
 for(i = 0; i < 3; i++)
 {
      if(pipe(pip[i]) == -1)
            fatal("pipe call");

      switch(fork()){
      case -1:                    /* error */
            fatal("fork call");
      case 0:                     /* child */
            child(pip[i]);
      }
 }

 parent(pip);

 exit(0);
}

/* parent sits listening on all three pipes */
void parent(int p[3][2])          /* code for parent */
{
 char buf[MSGSIZE], ch;
 fd_set set, master;
 int i;

 /* close all unwanted write file descriptors */
 for(i = 0; i < 3; i++)
      close(p[i][1]);

 /* set the bit masks for the select system call */
 FD_ZERO(&master);
 FD_SET(0, &master);
```

```
    for(i = 0; i < 3; i++)
            FD_SET(p[i][0], &master);


    /* select is called with no timeout,
     * it will block until an event occurs */
    while(set = master, select(p[2][0]+1, &set, NULL, NULL, NULL) > 0)
    {
            /* we mustn't forget information on standard input,
             * i.e. fd=0 */
            if(FD_ISSET(0, &set))
            {
                    printf("From standard input...");
                    read(0, &ch, 1);
                    printf("%c\n", ch);
            }


            for(i = 0; i < 3; i++)
            {
                    if(FD_ISSET(p[i][0], &set))
                    {
                            if(read(p[i][0], buf, MSGSIZE)>0)
                            {
                                    printf("Message from child%d\n", i);
                                    printf("MSG=%s\n",buf);
                            }
                    }
            }


            /* The server will return to the main program if all its
               children have died
            */
            if(waitpid(-1,NULL,WNOHANG) == -1)
                    return;
    }
}


int child(int p[2])
{
 int count;

 close(p[0]);

 for(count = 0; count < 2; count++)
 {
        write(p[1], msg1, MSGSIZE);
        /* pause for a random amount of time */
        sleep(getpid() % 4);
 }

 /* send final message */
 write(p[1], msg2, MSGSIZE);
 exit(0);
}
```

A typical output from running this program would be:

```
Message from child 0
MSG = hello
Message from child 1
MSG = hello
Message from child 2
MSG = hello
```

d	(user hits *d* and then Return)
From standard input d	(d echoed)
From standard input	(Return echoed)

```
Message from child 0
MSG = hello
Message from child 1
MSG = hello
Message from child 2
MSG = hello

Message from child 0
MSG = bye
Message from child 1
MSG = bye
Message from child 2
MSG = bye
```

Notice how in this example the user types the letter d followed by a carriage return, which is detected on standard input in the select call.

7.1.7 Pipes and the `exec` system call

Remember how a pipe can be set up between two programs at shell level:

```
$ ls | wc
```

How is this achieved? The answer has two parts. First, a shell takes advantage of the fact that open file descriptors are kept open (by default) across exec calls. This means that two pipe file descriptors opened prior to a fork/exec combination will still be open when the child process begins execution of the new program. Second, before invoking exec, the shell couples the standard output of ls to the write end of the pipe, and the standard input of wc to the read end. This can be done by using either fcntl or dup2 as shown in Exercise 5.10. Since standard input, standard output and standard error have values 0, 1 and 2, respectively, a programmer could, for example, couple standard output to another file descriptor as follows (assuming standard input is open) using dup2. Note that dup2 closes the file represented by its second parameter before the reassignment.

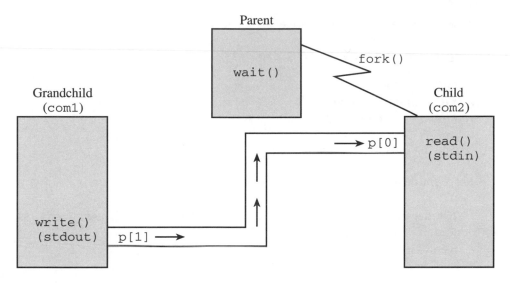

Figure 7.5 *The* join *program.*

```
/* fcntl will now duplicate file descriptor "1" */
dup2(filedes, 1);
    .
    .
    .
/* program will now write its standard output */
/* to the file referred to by filedes */
    .
    .
    .
```

Our next example, join, shows the piping mechanism employed by a shell in simplified form. join takes two parameters, com1 and com2, each of which describes a command to be run. Both parameters are actually arrays of character pointers that will be passed to execvp.

join will run both programs and pipe the standard output of com1 into the standard input of com2. The action of join is shown in Figure 7.5 and can be described in pseudo-code form (excluding error handling) as follows:

process forks, parent waits for child
and child continues

child creates a pipe

child then forks

In child created by second fork (grandchild):
  standard output is coupled to
  write end of pipe using dup2

excess file descriptors are closed

program described by 'com1' is exec'ed

In child of first fork:
standard input is coupled to
read end of pipe using dup2

excess file descriptors are closed

program described by 'com2' is exec'ed

The actual implementation of join is as follows; again, it uses fatal, as introduced in Section 7.1.5:

```
/* join -- join two commands by pipe */

int join(char *com1[], char *com2[])
{
 int p[2], status;

 /* create child to run commands */
 switch(fork()){
 case -1:          /* error */
      fatal("1st fork call in join");
 case 0:           /* child */
      break;
 default:          /* parent */
      wait(&status);
      return (status);
 }

 /* remainder of routine executed by child */

 /* make pipe */
 if(pipe(p) == -1)
      fatal("pipe call in join");

 /* create another process */
 switch(fork()){
 case -1:
      /* error */
      fatal("2nd fork call in join");
 case 0:
      /* the writing process */
      dup2(p[1],1);     /* make std. output go to pipe */

      close(p[0]);      /* save file descriptors */
      close(p[1]);

      execvp(com1[0], com1);
```

```
        /* if execvp returns, error has occurred */
        fatal("1st execvp call in join");
default:
        /* the reading process */
        dup2(p[0], 0);     /* make std. input come from pipe */

        close(p[0]);
        close(p[1]);
        execvp(com2[0], com2);
        fatal("2nd execvp call in join");
    }
}
```

This routine can be invoked along the following lines:

```
#include <stdio.h>

main()
{
 char *one[4] = {"ls", "-l", "/usr/lib", NULL};
 char *two[3] = {"grep", "^d", NULL};
 int ret;

 ret = join(one, two);
 printf("join returned %d\n",ret);
 exit(0);
}
```

Exercise 7.3 How can the technique shown in join be generalized to couple more than two commands in a pipe line?

Exercise 7.4 Incorporate pipes into the smallsh command processor introduced in the previous chapter.

Exercise 7.5 Devise a method where a process creates a child to run a single program, the parent reading the standard output of the child through a pipe. It is worth noting that this idea underlies the popen and pclose routines which form part of the Standard I/O Library. popen and pclose relieve the programmer of much of the clerical detail of coordinating fork, exec, close, dup or dup2. We will discuss them further in Chapter 11.

7.2 FIFOs or named pipes

Pipes are an elegant and powerful inter-process communication mechanism. However, they have several drawbacks.

Firstly, and most seriously, pipes can only be used to connect processes that share a common ancestry, such as a parent process and its child. This drawback becomes apparent when trying to develop a true 'server' program that remains permanently in existence in order to provide a system-wide service. Examples include network control servers and print spoolers. Ideally, client processes should be able to come into being, communicate with an unrelated server process via a pipe and then go away again. Unfortunately, this cannot be done using conventional pipes.

Secondly, pipes cannot be permanent. They have to be created every time they are needed and they are destroyed when the processes accessing them terminate.

To address these deficiencies, a variant of the pipe is available. This inter-process communication mechanism is called the **FIFO** or **named pipe**. As far as read and write are concerned, FIFOs are identical to pipes, acting as a first in/first out communications channel between processes. Indeed, FIFOs and pipes typically share a great deal of common code at kernel level. Unlike a pipe, however, a FIFO is a permanent fixture and is given a UNIX file name. A FIFO also has an owner, a size and associated access permissions. It can be opened, closed and deleted like any other UNIX file, but displays properties identical to pipes when read or written.

Let us take a look at the use of FIFOs at command level before examining the programming interface. The command mknod is used to create a FIFO (guess what the p stands for):

```
$ /etc/mknod channel p
```

Here channel is the name of the FIFO (it could be replaced with any valid UNIX pathname). The second argument p tells mknod to create a FIFO. It is needed since mknod is also used to create device files.

A newly created FIFO can be identified with the ls command in the following way:

```
$ ls -l channel
prw-rw-r--   1    ben    usr     0    Aug 1    21:05    channel
```

The letter p in the first column of the listing indicates that channel is a file of type FIFO. Notice how channel has access permissions (read/write for the owner and the owner's group, read-only for everyone else); an owner and a group owner (ben, usr); a size (0 bytes, that is, currently empty) and a creation date.

This FIFO can be read and written using standard UNIX commands, for example:

```
$ cat < channel
```

If this command was executed just after channel had been created it would 'hang'. This is because, by default, a process opening a FIFO for reading will block until another process attempts to open the FIFO for writing. Similarly, a process attempting to open a FIFO for writing will block until a process attempts to open it for reading. This is entirely sensible, since it saves system resources and makes program coordination simpler. As a consequence, if we wanted to create a reader and a writer for our last example we would have to execute one of the processes in the background (or at least in another window on a GUI interface), for example:

```
$ cat < channel &
102
$ ls -l > channel; wait
total 17
prw-rw-r--   1   ben   usr      0   Aug  1   21:05   channel
-rw-rw-r--   1   ben   usr      0   Aug  1   21:06   f
-rw-rw-r--   1   ben   usr    937   Jul  27  22:30   fifos
-rw-rw-r--   1   ben   usr   7152   Jul  27  22:11   pipes.cont
```

Let us analyse this further. The listing of the directory is initially produced by ls and then written down the FIFO. The waiting cat command then reads data from the FIFO and displays it onto the screen. The process running cat now exits. This is because, when a FIFO is no longer open for writing, a read on it will return 0 just like a normal pipe, which cat takes to mean end of file. The wait command, by the way, causes the shell to wait until cat exits before redisplaying the prompt.

7.2.1 Programming with FIFOs

For the most part, programming with FIFOs is identical to programming with ordinary pipes. The only significant difference is in initialization. Instead of using pipe, a FIFO is created with mkfifo. In older versions of UNIX, you may need to use a more general call named mknod.

Usage

```
#include <sys/types.h>
#include <sys/stat.h>

int mkfifo(const char *pathname, mode_t mode);
```

The mkfifo system call creates a FIFO file named by the first parameter pathname. The FIFO will be given mode permissions. These permissions will be modified by the process' umask value.

Once created, a FIFO must be opened using open. So, for example, the fragment:

```
#include <sys/types.h>
#include <sys/stat.h>
#include <fcntl.h>
   .
   .
```

```
mkfifo("/tmp/fifo", 0666);
   .
   .
   .
fd = open("/tmp/fifo", O_WRONLY);
```

opens a FIFO for writing. The open will block until another process opens the FIFO for reading (of course if the FIFO was already open for reading, our open call will return immediately).

Non-blocking open calls on a FIFO are possible. To achieve this the open call must be made with the O_NONBLOCK flag (which is defined in <fcntl.h>) combined with one of O_RDONLY or O_WRONLY. For example:

```
if((fd = open("/tmp/fifo", O_WRONLY | O_NONBLOCK)) == -1)
 perror("open on fifo");
```

If no process has the FIFO open for reading, then this open will return −1 instead of blocking and errno will contain ENXIO. If, on the other hand, the open was successful, future write calls on the FIFO will also be non-blocking.

It is time for an example. We will introduce two programs that show how a FIFO can be used to implement a message system. They exploit the fact that read and write calls on a FIFO or any other sort of pipe are atomic. If fixed-size messages are passed through a FIFO, individual messages will remain intact when read, even when several processes are concurrently writing the pipe.

We will look first at sendmessage which sends individual messages to a FIFO named fifo. It is called as follows:

$ *sendmessage 'message text 1' 'message text 2'*

Notice how each message is enclosed in quotes and so counts as one long argument. If this is not done, then each word will be treated as a separate message. The code for sendmessage follows:

```
/* sendmessage -- send messages via FIFO */

#include <fcntl.h>
#include <stdio.h>
#include <errno.h>
#define MSGSIZ    63

char *fifo = "fifo";

main(int argc, char **argv)
{
 int fd, j, nwrite;
 char msgbuf[MSGSIZ+1];

 if(argc < 2)
 {
      fprintf(stderr, "Usage: sendmessage msg ... \n");
      exit(1);
 }
```

```
/* open fifo with O_NONBLOCK set */
if((fd = open(fifo, O_WRONLY | O_NONBLOCK)) < 0)
      fatal("fifo open failed");

/* send messages */
for( j = 1; j < argc; j++)
{
      if(strlen(argv[j]) > MSGSIZ)
      {
            fprintf(stderr, "message too long %s\n", argv[j]);
            continue;
      }

      strcpy(msgbuf, argv[j]);

      if((nwrite = write(fd, msgbuf, MSGSIZ+1)) == -1)
            fatal("message write failed");
}
exit(0);
}
```

Again, we make use of our error routine `fatal`. Messages are sent as 64-character chunks, via a non-blocking `write` call. The actual message text is restricted to 63 characters to allow for a trailing null character.

The program that receives the messages by reading the FIFO is called rcvmessage. It does nothing useful, and is intended just to serve as a basic framework.

```
/* rcvmessage -- receive message via fifo */

#include <fcntl.h>
#include <stdio.h>
#include <errno.h>
#define MSGSIZ    63

char *fifo = "fifo";

main(int argc, char **argv)
{
 int fd;
 char msgbuf[MSGSIZ+1];

 /* create fifo, if it doesn't already exist */
 if(mkfifo(fifo, 0666) == -1 )
 {
      if(errno != EEXIST)
            fatal("receiver: mkfifo");
 }

 /* open fifo for reading and writing */
 if((fd = open(fifo, O_RDWR)) < 0)
      fatal("fifo open failed");
```

```
/* receive messages */
for(;;)
{
        if(read(fd, msgbuf, MSGSIZ+1) < 0)
                fatal("message read failed");

/*
 * print out message; in real life
 * something more interesting would
 * be done
 */

        printf("message received:%s\n",msgbuf);
}
}
```

Notice how the FIFO is opened for reading and writing (via the O_RDWR flag). To understand why this is done, suppose the FIFO was opened with just O_RDONLY. The program would first block at the open call. As soon as an invocation of sendmessage opened the FIFO for writing, the open call would return; rcvmessage would then read through each message sent. However, when the FIFO was empty, and the sendmessage process had vanished, read would start to return 0 immediately it was called, because no process would have the FIFO open for writing. The program would therefore enter an unnecessary loop. Using O_RDWR makes sure that at least one process, that is, the invocation of rcvmessage itself, has the FIFO open for writing. As a result, the read call will always block until data is actually written to the FIFO.

The following dialogue shows how these programs can be used. rcvmessage is placed into the background to receive messages from different invocations of sendmessage.

```
$ rcvmessage &
40
$ sendmessage 'message 1' 'message 2'
message received: message 1
message received: message 2
$ sendmessage 'message number 3'
message received: message number 3
```

Exercise 7.6 sendmessage and rcvmessage form the basis of a simple spooling system. The messages sent to rcvmessage could, for example, be the names of files which are to be processed in some way. The problem here is that the current directories of sendmessage and rcvmessage may be different and so relative pathnames will be misinterpreted. How could you solve this problem? Is use of a FIFO alone adequate for, say, a printer spooler on a large system?

Exercise 7.7 If rcvmessage was replaced by a true server program, we would normally want to make sure that only one copy of the server was running at any one time. There are several ways of doing this. One method involves the creation of a lock file. Consider the following routine:

```
#include <errno.h>
#include <fcntl.h>

extern int errno;
char * lck = "/tmp/lockfile";

int makelock(void)
{
    int fd;
    if((fd = open(lck, O_RDWR | O_CREAT | O_EXCL, 0600)) < 0)
    {
        if(errno == EEXIST)
            exit(1);                    /* someone else has got in */
        else
            exit(127);                  /* unexpected error */
    }
    /* lock created if we get here, so return */
    close(fd);
    return (0);
}
```

This uses the fact that the open call will be done atomically. So, if several processes race to execute makelock, one will get there first, create the lock file, and so 'lock' out the rest. Add this routine to sendmessage. Make sure that, when killed with SIGHUP or SIGTERM, sendmessage removes the lock file before exiting. Why do you think we used open rather than creat in makelock?

CHAPTER 8

Advanced inter-process communications

8.1 Introduction

Using the tools provided in Chapters 6 and 7 you can now achieve basic inter-process communication. The more advanced inter-process communication facilities discussed in this chapter will allow you to make use of more sophisticated programming techniques.

The first and most straightforward topic is **record locking**. This is not really a form of direct process communication, more a method of process cooperation. (Indeed, we originally intended to discuss record locking in one of the chapters on the file structure. On reflection it fits more easily here.) It allows a process to temporarily reserve part of a file for its own exclusive use, thus resolving some difficult problems in database management. A word of warning however; the *XSI* only supports *advisory* locking, which means the responsibility lies entirely with a process to check to see if a lock is already set on a file.

The other inter-process communication mechanisms, discussed in this chapter, are rather more exotic. Generically, these advanced features are described as **IPC facilities** (where *IPC* stands for *inter-process communication*). This single descriptive term emphasizes similarities in structure and usage, although there are three distinct types of facility gathered under this heading:

1. *Message passing* The message passing facility allows a process to send and receive messages, a message being in essence an arbitrary sequence of bytes or characters.

2. *Semaphores* Compared with message passing, semaphores provide a rather low-level means for process synchronization, not suited to the transmission of large amounts of information. They have their theoretical origin in work by E.W. Dijkstra (1968).

3. *Shared memory* This IPC facility allows two or more processes to share the data contained in specific memory segments. Usually, of course, the data area of a process is private to itself. It is usually the fastest of the IPC mechanisms.

8.2 Record locking

8.2.1 Motivation

As a first step, it is worth pursuing a simple example to demonstrate why record locking is essential in some situations.

Our example concerns that well-known corporation, *ACME Airlines*, which uses a UNIX system for its booking system. It has two booking offices, called A and B, each of which has its own terminal connected to the airline's computer. The booking clerks use a program called acmebook to access the bookings database, which is implemented as an ordinary UNIX file. This program allows the user to read and update the database. In particular, a booking clerk can decrement by one the number of free seats for a particular flight, signifying that a booking has been made.

Now suppose that on flight ACM501 to London just one free seat remains, and that Ms Jones enters office A at the same time as Mr Smith enters office B. Both ask for a seat on flight ACM501. The following series of events is then entirely possible:

1. The clerk at office A starts acmebook. Let us call the resultant process *PA*.

2. Immediately afterwards, the clerk at office B also starts up acmebook. We shall call this process *PB*.

3. Process *PA* now reads the relevant part of the database using the read system call. It discovers that there is one seat available.

4. Process *PB* reads the database just after *PA*. It too discovers that there is one seat left on ACM501.

5. Process *PA* then sets the free seat count for the flight to zero by using the write system call to change the relevant part of the database. The clerk at office A gives a ticket to Ms Jones.

6. Immediately afterwards, process *PB* also writes to the database, again inserting zero for the free seat count. This time however the value is erroneous; if anything it should be −1. The point to emphasize here is that although *PA* has already updated the database, *PB* has no way of knowing this and presses on as if a seat was still available. As a consequence Mr Smith also receives a ticket and the flight is overbooked.

The problem arises because a UNIX file may be accessed by any number of processes simultaneously. A logical operation which is made up of several calls to lseek, read and write can be performed by two or more processes concurrently and, as we saw in our simple example, this can have disastrous consequences.

One solution is to allow a process to *lock* the part of the file it is working on. The lock, which does not alter the file contents in any way, serves as an indication to other processes that the data in question is in use. It prevents another process from interfering during a series of discrete physical operations which form one logical action or transaction. This type of mechanism is often called **record locking**, where record just refers to an arbitrary subsection of a file. To make things absolutely secure, the locking operation itself must be atomic, so that it cannot overlap with a conflicting locking attempt in another process.

In order for locking to work, it must be performed in some centralized way. Perhaps the best way is to let the kernel take care of locking, although a user process acting as a database agent could, with care, serve the same purpose. Kernel-based record locking can be performed via our old friend fcntl.

Note that the first edition of this book also covered a routine called lockf – an alternative way of locking records. It is still found on many systems – see your local manual for details.

8.2.2 Record locking with fcntl

We have already met the file control system call fcntl. Apart from its more usual functions, fcntl can be used to perform a general form of record locking. It offers two types of lock:

1. *Read locks*   A read lock simply prevents any process from applying the other type of fcntl lock, which is called a write lock. Several processes may read lock the same segment simultaneously. Read locks would, for example, be useful when a programmer wants to prevent data from being updated, but does not want it hidden from scrutiny by other users.

2. *Write locks*   A write lock stops any other process from applying a read or write lock to the file. In other words, only one write lock may exist for a given segment at a time. Write locks could be used, for example, to remove segments from the public gaze while an update is being performed.

Again we must stress that, according to the *XSI*, the locks available via fcntl are advisory only. Processes must therefore explicitly cooperate in order for fcntl locking to be effective.

As a record locking call, fcntl is used as follows.

Usage

```
#include <fcntl.h>

int fcntl(int filedes, int cmd, struct flock *ldata);
```

As usual, the argument filedes must be a valid, open file descriptor. For read locks, filedes must have been opened using O_RDONLY or O_RDWR, so a file descriptor from creat will not do. For write locks, filedes must have been opened using O_WRONLY or O_RDWR.

As we saw in our previous encounters with fcntl, the cmd parameter specifies the required action, via values defined in <fcntl.h>. The following three values relate to record locking:

F_GETLK Get lock description based on data passed via the ldata argument. (The information returned describes the first lock that 'blocks' the lock described in ldata.)

F_SETLK Apply lock to file, return immediately if this is not possible. Also used to remove an active lock.

F_SETLKW Apply lock to file, sleep if lock blocked by a previous lock owned by another process. A process sleeping on an fcntl lock can be interrupted by a signal.

The ldata structure carries the lock description. The struct flock is defined in <fcntl.h> and includes the following members:

```
short  l_type;      /* describes type of lock */
short  l_whence;    /* offset type, like lseek */
off_t  l_start;     /* offset in bytes */
off_t  l_len;       /* segment size in bytes */
pid_t  l_pid;       /* set by F_GETLK command */
```

The three members l_whence, l_start and l_len specify the file segment to be locked, tested or unlocked. l_whence is identical to the third argument of lseek. It takes one of the values SEEK_SET, SEEK_CUR or SEEK_END to indicate that the offset is to be taken from the file's beginning, the current position of the read–write pointer or the end of file. The member l_start gives the start position of the segment, relative to the point indicated by l_whence. l_len is the length of the segment in bytes; a value of zero here denotes a segment from the specified start

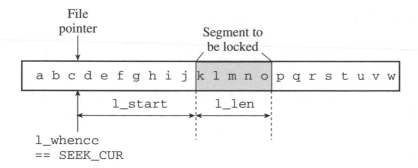

Figure 8.1 *Locking parameters.*

position to the largest possible offset. Figure 8.1 shows how this works more clearly, for the case where l_whence is equal to SEEK_CUR.

l_type gives the type of lock to be applied. It can take one of three values defined in <fcntl.h>:

F_RDLCK   Lock to be applied is a read lock.

F_WRLCK   Lock to be applied is a write lock.

F_UNLCK   Lock on specified segment is to be removed.

l_pid is only relevant when the fcntl command selected is F_GETLK. If a lock exists which blocks the lock described by the other members of the structure, l_pid will be set to the process-id of the process that set it. The other members of the structure will also be reset by the system to give more information on the lock maintained by the other process.

Setting a lock with fcntl

The following example shows how fcntl can be used to set a write lock.

```
#include <unistd.h>
#include <fcntl.h>

    .
    .
    .

struct flock my_lock;

my_lock.l_type = F_WRLCK;
my_lock.l_whence = SEEK_CUR;
my_lock.l_start = 0;
my_lock.l_len = 512;

fcntl(fd, F_SETLKW, &my_lock);
```

This will lock 512 bytes, starting from the current position of the read–write pointer. The locked section is regarded as being 'reserved' for the exclusive use of the process. The lock information itself is placed into a free slot in a system-maintained table of locks.

If all or part of the specified section has already been locked by another process, the calling process will sleep until the whole section becomes available. Sleeping in this way can be interrupted by a signal; in particular, alarm can be invoked to provide a timeout. If the sleeping process is not interrupted, and the section does eventually become free, then the lock will be applied. If an error occurs, for example if fcntl is passed a bad file descriptor or the system lock table is full, then −1 is returned.

The next example program, lockit, opens a file locktest (which must already exist) and locks the first ten bytes with fcntl. It then forks; the child attempts to lock the first five bytes; meanwhile, the parent sleeps for five seconds, then exits. At this point, the system automatically releases the parent's lock.

```
/* lockit -- demonstration of fcntl locking */

#include <fcntl.h>
#include <unistd.h>
#include <stdlib.h>

main()
{
 int fd;
 struct flock my_lock;

 /* set the parameters for the write lock */
 my_lock.l_type = F_WRLCK;
 my_lock.l_whence = SEEK_SET;
 my_lock.l_start = 0;
 my_lock.l_len = 10;

 /* open file */
 fd = open("locktest", O_RDWR);

 /* lock first ten bytes */
 if( fcntl(fd, F_SETLKW, &my_lock) == -1)
 {
      perror("parent: locking");
      exit(1);
 }

 printf("parent: locked record\n");

 switch(fork()){
 case -1:                    /* error */
      perror("fork");
      exit(1);
```

```
case 0:                     /* child */
      my_lock.l_len = 5;
      if( fcntl(fd, F_SETLKW, &my_lock) == -1)
      {
            perror("child: locking");
            exit(1);
      }
      printf("child: locked\n");
      printf("child: exiting\n");
      exit(0);
}

sleep(5);

/* now exit, which releases lock */
printf("parent: exiting\n");
exit(0);
}
```

The actual output produced by lockit will look something like:

```
parent: locked record
parent: exiting
child: locked
child: exiting
```

Notice the order in which the messages are displayed. It shows that the child process could not apply the desired lock until the parent had exited and released its lock, otherwise the "child: locked" message would appear second, not third. This example also shows that the lock made by the parent affected the child, even though the file segments used by each were not identical. In other words, a lock attempt will fail even if the section only partially overlaps an already locked section. The program illustrates several other interesting points: first, lock information is not inherited across fork calls; the child and parent processes in our example are independent as far as locking goes. Second, a call to fcntl does not alter the file's read–write pointer. Throughout the execution of both child and parent, this pointed to the beginning of the file. Third, all locks belonging to a process are removed automatically when the process dies.

Unlocking with fcntl

A segment previously locked by the calling process can be unlocked by setting l_type to F_UNLCK. It will usually be used some time after a previous fcntl request. If there are any other processes waiting to lock the section which has been released, then one of these will be restarted.

If the section to be unlocked happens to lie in the middle of a larger locked section of the file, then the system will create two smaller locks that exclude the section to be unlocked. This means that an extra slot in the system lock table is taken up. As a consequence, an unlock request can fail, somewhat counter-intuitively, because the system lock table is full.

For example, in the previous example of `lockit`, the parent released its lock by exiting from the program. The parent could, however, have explicitly released the lock with the following piece of code.

```
/* now parent releases lock before exiting */
printf("parent: unlocking\n");
my_lock.l_type = F_UNLCK;
if( fcntl(fd, F_SETLK, &my_lock) == -1)
{
      perror("parent: unlocking");
      exit(1);
}
```

The ACME Airlines *problem revisited*

We can now provide a solution to the contention problem we encountered in our *ACME Airlines* example. To ensure the integrity of the database, we simply need to treat the critical section of code in the `acmebook` as follows:

lock relevant database segment with a write lock

update database segment

unlock database segment

Providing no other program bypasses the locking mechanism, the lock request ensures the calling process has exclusive access to the crucial part of the database when it needs it. The unlock request again makes the area available for public use. Any competing copy of `acmebook` that attempts to access the relevant part of the database while it is locked will be put to sleep as soon as it makes its own lock request.

The actual code might look like:

```
/* skeleton of acmebook update routine */

struct flock db_lock;

.
.
.


/* set up the parameters for the lock */
db_lock.l_type = F_WRLCK;
db_lock.l_whence = SEEK_SET;
db_lock.l_start = recstart;
db_lock.l_len = RECSIZE;

.
.
.
```

```
/* lock record, will sleep here if */
/* record already locked */
if( fcntl(fd, F_SETLKW, &db_lock) == -1)
 fatal("lock failed");

/* code to examine and update bookings data */
 .
 .
 .
/* now free record for use by another process */
db_lock.l_type = F_UNLCK;
fcntl(fd, F_SETLK, &db_lock);
```

Testing for a lock

If an F_SETLK is attempted and fails because a lock is already set, fcntl will return
−1 and set errno to either EAGAIN or EACCES (the *XSI* specifies both). If a lock does
exist then the process can determine which process has the lock by calling F_GETLK.
For example,

```
#include <unistd.h>
#include <stdio.h>
#include <errno.h>

 .
 .
 .
if( fcntl(fd, F_SETLK, &alock) == -1)
{
 if(errno == EACCES || errno == EAGAIN)
 {
      fcntl(fd, F_GETLK, &b_lock);
      fprintf(stderr, "record locked by %d\n", b_lock.l_pid);
 }
 else
      perror("unexpected lock error");
}
```

Deadlock

Let us assume that two processes, *PA* and *PB*, are working on the same file.
Suppose that *PA* locks section *SX* of the file and *PB* locks a completely separate
section *SY*. Problems arise if *PA* then attempts to lock *SY* with an F_SETLKW and
PB attempts to lock *SX* with another F_SETLKW. If nothing was done, *PA* would
sleep, waiting for *PB* to release *SY*, while *PB* would also sleep, waiting for *PA* to
release *SX*. Barring some outside intervention, it would seem that the two processes
are doomed to remain sleeping in this deadly embrace forever.

This sort of situation is described as **deadlock** for obvious reasons. Happily,
UNIX prevents it from occurring. If an F_SETLKW request would cause deadlock in
this way, the call fails, −1 is returned and errno is set to EDEADLK. On the negative

side, fcntl can only detect deadlock between two processes, and it is possible to devise a three-way deadlock. Complex applications which use locks should always incorporate a timeout to avoid this situation.

The following example should clarify things. At point /*A*/ the program locks bytes 0 to 9 of the file locktest. The program then forks. The child, at points commented /*B*/ and /*C*/, immediately applies a lock to bytes 10 to 14 and attempts to apply a lock to bytes 0 to 9. Because the parent has already done the latter, the child will then sleep. Meanwhile the parent has executed a 10-second sleep call. Hopefully this is enough to allow the child to perform its two lock calls. When the parent awakens, it attempts, at point /*D*/, to lock bytes 10 to 14, which of course have been locked previously by its child process. This is the point at which deadlock would occur and fcntl should fail.

```
/* deadlock -- demonstrate deadlock error */

#include <fcntl.h>
#include <unistd.h>
#include <stdlib.h>

main()
{
 int fd;
 struct flock first_lock;
 struct flock second_lock;

 first_lock.l_type = F_WRLCK;
 first_lock.l_whence = SEEK_SET;
 first_lock.l_start = 0;
 first_lock.l_len = 10;

 second_lock.l_type = F_WRLCK;
 second_lock.l_whence = SEEK_SET;
 second_lock.l_start = 10;
 second_lock.l_len = 5;

 fd = open("locktest", O_RDWR);

 if( fcntl(fd, F_SETLKW, &first_lock) == -1)              /*A*/
      fatal("A");

 printf("A: lock succeeded (proc %d)\n", getpid());

 switch(fork()){
 case -1:
      /*error*/
      fatal("error on fork");
 case 0:
      /*child*/
      if( fcntl(fd, F_SETLKW, &second_lock) == -1)        /*B*/
           fatal("B");
      printf("B: lock succeeded (proc %d)\n", getpid());
```

```
            if( fcntl(fd, F_SETLKW, &first_lock) == -1)          /*C*/
                  fatal("C");
            printf("C: lock succeeded (proc %d)\n", getpid());
            exit(0);
      default:
            /*parent*/
            printf("parent sleeping\n");
            sleep(10);
            if( fcntl(fd, F_SETLKW, &second_lock) == -1)         /*D*/
                  fatal("D");
            printf("D: lock succeeded (proc %d)\n", getpid());
      }
}
```

When run, this program produces output like:

```
A: lock succeeded (proc 1410)
parent sleeping
B: lock succeeded (proc 1411)
D: Deadlock situation detected/avoided
C: lock succeeded (proc 1411)
```

Here the lock fails at point /*D*/ and perror prints the corresponding system error message. Notice how, once the parent has exited and so has its locks released, the child is able to apply its second lock.

The example makes use of the error routine called fatal which we have used in previous chapters.

Exercise 8.1 Write routines which duplicate the actions of read and write but which fail if a lock on the file section exists. Adapt the read lookalike so that it locks the section it reads (where possible). Each lock should be removed at the next call to the read routine.

Exercise 8.2 Design and implement a limited, record-orientated scheme of read and write locks based on record number. (Hint: you can lock portions of the file near the maximum possible file offset, even when data does not exist there. A portion of the file in this region could be reserved, each byte representing a logical record. Locking here could then be used for flag purposes.)

8.3 Advanced IPC facilities

8.3.1 Introduction and basic concepts

UNIX offers a variety of advanced inter-process communication mechanisms. The presence of these advanced IPC facilities makes UNIX an extremely rich system in the process communication area, and allows a developer to use a variety of approaches when programming a system made up of cooperating tasks. The advanced IPC facilities we will examine next fall into the following categories:

1. Message passing.

2. Semaphores.

3. Shared memory.

The facilities we will discuss are commonly used and originate from UNIX system V. You should note that alternatives have been defined in recent versions of *POSIX*.

IPC facility keys

The programming interface for all three IPC facilities has been made as similar as possible, reflecting a similarity of implementation within the kernel. The most important common feature is the IPC facility **key**. Keys are numbers used to identify an IPC object on a UNIX system in much the same way as a filename identifies a file. In other words, a key allows an IPC resource to be shared between several processes. The object identified can be a message queue, a set of semaphores or a shared memory segment. The actual data type of a key is determined by the implementation-dependent type key_t, which is defined in the system header file <sys/types.h>.

Keys are not filenames and carry less meaning. They should be chosen carefully to avoid clashes between programs, perhaps on the basis of 'project numbers' assigned to the different developments on a particular machine. (One well-known database product once used a hexadecimal key value something like 0xDB: a nice idea but one that could occur to another developer.) UNIX provides a simple library function that maps a file's pathname into a key. The routine is called ftok.

Usage
| ```
#include <sys/ipc.h>

key_t ftok(const char *path, int id);
``` |

The routine returns a key number based on information associated with the file path. The parameter id is also taken into account and provides an extra level of uniqueness; in other words, the same path will produce different keys for different values of id. ftok is rather an awkward routine; for example, if a file is deleted, then replaced by one with the same name, the keys returned will differ. The routine fails, and so returns (key_t) - 1, if the file path does not exist. ftok is probably most useful with applications where IPC functions are specifically used in the manipulation of named files, or when given the name of a file which is an essential, permanent and unchanging part of the application.
```

IPC get operations

A program uses a key to either create an IPC object or gain access to an existing one. Both options are called out by an IPC get operation. The result of a get operation is an integer IPC **facility identifier** which can be used in calls to other IPC routines. If we pursue the file analogy further, the get operation is like a call to either creat or open, and the IPC facility identifier acts a little like a file descriptor. Actually, unlike file descriptors, an IPC facility identifier is unique. Different processes will use the same value for the same IPC object.

As an example, the following statement uses the IPC call msgget to create a new message queue (do not worry about what a message queue actually is; we will discuss that later):

```
mqid = msgget( (key_t)0100, 0644 | IPC_CREAT | IPC_EXCL);
```

Here, the first argument to msgget is the message queue key. If successful, the routine will return a non-negative value in mqid, which acts as the message queue identifier. The corresponding calls for semaphores and shared memory are semget and shmget, respectively.

Other IPC operations

There are two other types of operation that can be performed with IPC facilities. First, there are control operations, which can be used to get status information, or set control values. The actual calls that perform these functions are msgctl, semctl and shmctl. Second, there are more specific operations which perform the interesting work; these are grouped under the heading of IPC operations. A variety of operations are available for each facility and these will be discussed under the appropriate headings. For example, there are two message operations: msgsnd places a message onto a message queue and msgrcv reads a message from a message queue.

Status data structures

When an IPC object is created, the system also creates an **IPC facility status structure** which will contain any administrative information associated with the object. There is one type of status structure for messages, semaphores and shared memory. Each type necessarily contains information that relates only to the specific IPC facility. However, all three types of status structure contain a common permission structure. This permission structure, identified by ipc_perm, includes the following members:

```
uid_t cuid;        /* user-id of creator of IPC object */
gid_t cgid;        /* group-id of creator */
uid_t uid;         /* effective user-id */
gid_t gid;         /* effective group-id */
mode_t umode;      /* permissions */
```

This decides whether a user can 'read' an IPC object (that is, obtain information on the object) or 'write' to it (which means manipulate it). The permissions are constructed in exactly the same way as with files. So the value 0644 for the umode member means that the owner can read and write the associated object, while other users can only read it. Note that it is the effective user- and group-ids (recorded in the members uid and gid) that determine access rights in conjunction with umode. It should also be clear that execute permission has no meaning here. As usual, superuser has carte blanche. Unlike other UNIX constructs, the user's umask value takes no effect when an IPC facility is created.

8.3.2 Message passing

We will start our detailed examination of the IPC facilities by looking at the message passing primitives.

In essence, a message is simply a sequence of characters or bytes (not necessarily null-terminated). Messages are passed between processes by means of **message queues**, which are created or accessed via the msgget primitive. Once a queue is established, a process may, given appropriate queue permissions, place a message onto it with msgsnd. Another process can then read this message with msgrcv, which also removes it from the queue. You might be able to see from this brief description that message passing in the IPC sense is similar to what can be achieved using read and write calls with pipes (as discussed in Section 7.1.2).

The msgget function is defined as follows.

Usage
``#include <sys/msg.h>

int msgget(key_t key, int permflags);``` |

Again, it is best to think of this call as paralleling the action of open or creat. As we saw in Section 8.3.1, the key parameter, essentially just a number, identifies the message queue to the system. If the call is successful, and a new queue is created or an existing one accessed, msgget will return a non-negative integer called the **message queue identifier**.

The permflags parameter determines the exact action performed by msgget. Two constants are of relevance here, both defined in the file <sys/ipc.h>; they can be used alone, or bitwise ORed together:

IPC_CREAT   This tells msgget to create a message queue for the value key if one does not already exist. If we pursue our file metaphor, this flag causes msgget to act along the lines of a creat call, although the message queue will not be 'overwritten' if it already exists. If the IPC_CREAT flag is not set, then, as long as a queue

already exists for that key, the existing message queue identifier is
returned by msgget.

IPC_EXCL   If this and IPC_CREAT are both set, then the call is intended only
to create a message queue. So, when a queue for key already
exists, msgget will fail and return −1. The error variable errno
then contains the value EEXIST.

When a message queue is created, the low-order nine bits of permflags are
used to give the permissions for the message queue, rather like a file mode. These
are stored in the ipc_perm structure which is created along with the queue itself.
We can now return to the example we met in Section 8.3.1:

```
mqid = msgget( (key_t)0100, 0644 | IPC_CREAT | IPC_EXCL);
```

This call is intended to create (and only create) a message queue for the key
value (key_t)100. If the call is successful, the queue will have permissions 0644.
These are interpreted in the same way as file permissions, indicating that the creator
of the queue can send or read messages to and from the queue, while members of
the creator's group and all others can only read from it. If necessary, msgctl can be
used later to alter the permissions and ownerships associated with the queue.

Message queue operations: msgsnd and msgrcv

Once a queue has been created, there are two message queue operation primitives
which can be used to manipulate it, as follows:

Usage

```
#include <sys/msg.h>

int msgsnd(int mqid, const void *message, size_t size,
           int flags);

int msgrcv(int mqid, void *message, size_t size, long msg_type,
           int flags);
```

The first of these, msgsnd, is used to add a message to the queue denoted by
mqid, the value of which will normally have been obtained from msgget.
The message itself is contained, unsurprisingly, in the structure message,
which is declared with a user-supplied template. The form of this template is:

```
struct mymsg{
  long mtype;                /* message type */
  char mtext[SOMEVALUE];     /* message text */
};
```

The mtype member can be used by the programmer to categorize messages, each possible value representing a different potential category. Only positive values are meaningful here; negative and zero values will not work. mtext will hold the text of the message itself (the constant SOMEVALUE is entirely arbitrary). The length of the message to be actually sent is given by the size parameter to msgsnd, and this can range from zero to the smaller of SOMEVALUE or a system-determined maximum.

The flags parameter for msgsnd can take just one meaningful value: IPC_NOWAIT. If IPC_NOWAIT is *not* set, the calling process will sleep if there are insufficient system resources to send the message. In practice, this will occur when the total length of messages on the queue exceeds either a per-queue or a system-wide maximum. If IPC_NOWAIT is set, the call will return immediately if the message cannot be sent. Its return value will then be −1, and errno will be set to EAGAIN, meaning try again.

msgsnd can also fail because of the permissions associated with the message queue. If, for example, the user had neither the effective user-id nor the effective group-id associated with the queue, and the queue permissions are 0660, then a call to msgsnd for that queue will fail. errno will then contain EACCES.

Let us move on to reading messages. msgrcv is used to read a message off the queue identified by mqid, providing the queue's permissions allow the process to do this. The act of reading a message causes it to be removed from the queue.

This time message is used to hold a received message, and the size parameter gives the maximum length that can be held within the structure. If the call is successful, then retval will contain the length of the received message.

The msg_type parameter decides exactly what message is actually received. It selects according to the value of a message's mtype field. If msg_type is zero, the first message on the queue, that is, the earliest sent, is read. If msg_type has a non-zero, positive value then the first message with that value is read. For example, if the queue contains messages with mtype values of 999, 5 and 1, and msgrcv is called with msg_type set to 5, then the message of type 5 is read. Finally, if msg_type has a non-zero, *negative* value, the first message with the lowest mtype number that is less than or equal to msg_type's absolute value is received. This is a cumbersome way of saying a simple thing; staying with our previous example where there are three messages with mtype values of 999, 5 and 1 on the queue, if the msg_type parameter is set to −999 (cast to long of course), and msgrcv is called three times, then the messages will be received in the order 1, 5 and 999.

The last parameter flags again contains control information. Two values, IPC_NOWAIT and MSG_NOERROR, can be set, alone or ORed together. IPC_NOWAIT means much as it did before; if it is not set then the process will sleep if there is not a suitable message on the queue, returning when a message of the appropriate type arrives. If it is set, the call will return immediately, whatever the circumstances.

If MSG_NOERROR is set, a message will be truncated if it is longer than size bytes, otherwise the call to msgrcv would fail. There is unfortunately no way of knowing when truncation has occurred.

You may well have found this section heavy going; the formulation of the IPC facilities goes rather against the UNIX grain in its complexity and style.

However, the message passing routines are in fact simple to use, with many potential applications. We hope that the next example shows this to some extent.

A message passing example: a queue with priorities

In this section we will develop a straightforward message passing application. The aim is to implement a queuing system where each item queued can be given a priority. A server process will then take the items from the queue and, in some unspecified way, process them. The items queued could for example be filenames, and the server process could copy the files to a line printer. It is similar to the FIFO example developed in Section 7.2.1.

Our starting point is a header file called q.h, which contains the following:

```
/* q.h -- header for message facility example */

#include <sys/types.h>
#include <sys/ipc.h>
#include <sys/msg.h>
#include <string.h>
#include <errno.h>

#define QKEY        (key_t)0105 /* identifying key for queue */
#define QPERM       0660        /* permissions for queue */
#define MAXOBN      50          /* maximum length of obj. name */
#define MAXPRIOR    10          /* maximum priority level */

struct q_entry {
 long mtype;
 char mtext[MAXOBN+1];
};
```

The first part of this file just groups together #include statements. The QKEY definition gives the key value that will identify the message queue to the system. QPERM gives the permissions that will be associated with the queue. Since it is defined as 0660, the owner and members of the queue's group will be able to read or write the message queue. As we shall see, MAXOBN and MAXPRIOR will impose limits on the messages that can be placed on the queue. The final part of the include file contains a structure template definition with tag q_entry. We will use structures of this type to hold the messages transmitted and received by our routines.

The first routine we shall investigate is called enter, which places a null-terminated object name onto the queue. It has the following form:

```
/* enter -- place an object into queue */

#include "q.h"

int enter(char *objname, int priority)
{
 int len, s_qid;
 struct q_entry s_entry;   /* structure to hold message */
```

```
/* validate name length, priority level */

if( (len = strlen(objname)) > MAXOBN)
{
     warn("name too long");
     return (-1);
}

if(priority > MAXPRIOR || priority < 0)
{
     warn("invalid priority level");
     return (-1);
}

/* initialize message queue as necessary */

if( (s_qid = init_queue()) == -1)
     return (-1);

/* initialize s_entry */
s_entry.mtype = (long)priority;
strncpy(s_entry.mtext, objname, MAXOBN);

/* send message, waiting if necessary */

if(msgsnd(s_qid, &s_entry, len, 0) == -1)
{
     perror("msgsnd failed");
     return (-1);
}
else
     return (0);
}
```

The first action of `enter` is to check the object name length and the priority level. Notice how the minimum value for `priority` is 1, since a zero value would cause `msgsnd` to fail. `enter` next 'opens' the queue by calling `init_queue`. We will see how this is implemented shortly.

If all is well, the routine constructs the message and attempts to send it with `msgsnd`. Notice how we use a `q_entry` structure called `s_entry` to hold the message. Also notice how the last parameter for `msgsnd` is zero. This means that the system will put the calling process to sleep if the queue is full (because `IPC_NOWAIT` is not set).

`enter` indicates problems by using `warn` or the library function `perror`. For the sake of simplicity, we will implement `warn` as follows:

```
#include <stdio.h>

int warn(char *s)
{
 fprintf(stderr, "warning: %s\n", s);
}
```

In a real-life system, it might well be better to have warn write to an error log file.

Returning to init_queue, the purpose of this function is clear. It initializes, if possible, the message queue identifier, otherwise it returns the message queue identifier already associated with the queue.

```
/* init_queue -- get queue identifier */

#include "q.h"

int init_queue(void)
{
 int queue_id;

 /* attempt to create or open message queue */
 if( (queue_id = msgget(QKEY, IPC_CREAT | QPERM)) == -1)
      perror("msgget failed");

 return (queue_id);
}
```

The next routine is used by the server process to handle items from the queue. We have given it the imaginative name serve. It is a reasonably straightforward inverse of enter.

```
/* serve -- serve object with highest priority on the queue */

#include "q.h"

int serve(void)
{
 int mlen, r_qid;
 struct q_entry r_entry;

 /* initialize message queue as necessary */

 if((r_qid = init_queue()) == -1)
      return (-1);

 /* get and process next message, waiting if necessary */

 for(;;)
 {

      if((mlen = msgrcv(r_qid, &r_entry, MAXOBN,
                    (-1 * MAXPRIOR), MSG_NOERROR)) == -1)
      {
            perror("msgrcv failed");
            return (-1);
      }
```

```
        else
        {
                /* make sure we've a string */
                r_entry.mtext[mlen]='\0';

                /* process object name */
                proc_obj(&r_entry);
        }
    }
}
```

Notice how `msgrcv` is called. Because the negative value (`-1 * MAXPRIOR`) is given as the type parameter, the system will first examine the queue for messages with `mtype` equal to 1, then equal to 2 and so on, up to and including `MAXPRIOR`. To put it another way, the messages with the lowest numbers will have the highest priority. The routine `proc_obj` actually does the work. In the case of a printer system, it might copy a file to the printer device.

The following two simple programs demonstrate the interaction of these routines: `etest` places an item on the queue, while `stest` processes an item (actually it just prints the contents and type of the message).

The `etest` program

```
/* etest -- enter object names on queue */

#include <stdio.h>
#include <stdlib.h>
#include "q.h"

main(int argc, char **argv)
{
  int priority;

  if(argc != 3 )
  {
        fprintf(stderr, "usage: %s objname priority\n", argv[0]);
        exit(1);
  }

  if((priority = atoi(argv[2])) <= 0 || priority > MAXPRIOR)
  {
        warn("invalid priority");
        exit(2);
  }

  if(enter(argv[1], priority) < 0)
  {
        warn("enter failure");
        exit(3);
  }

  exit(0);
}
```

The stest *program*

```
/* stest -- simple server for queue */
#include <stdio.h>
#include "q.h"

main()
{
 pid_t pid;

 switch(pid = fork()){
 case 0:                  /* child */
      serve();
      break;              /* actually, serve never exits */
 case -1:
      warn("fork to start server failed");
      break;
 default:
      printf("server process pid is %d\n", pid);
 }
 exit(pid != -1 ? 0 : 1);
}

int proc_obj(struct q_entry *msg)
{
 printf("\npriority: %ld name: %s\n", msg->mtype, msg->mtext);
}
```

An example of the use of these two simple programs follows. Four messages are entered on the queue with etest, before the server stest is started. Notice the order in which the messages are finally printed:

```
$ etest objname1 3
$ etest objname2 4
$ etest objname3 1
$ etest objname4 9
$ stest
server process pid is 2545
$
priority: 1 name: objname3

priority: 3 name: objname1

priority: 4 name: objname2

priority: 9 name: objname4
```

Exercise 8.3 Adapt enter and serve so that control messages can be sent to the server. Reserve message type one for such messages (what should happen to priority values?). Implement the following options:

1.   Halt server.

2.   Flush all messages from the queue.

3.   Flush messages at a given priority level.

The `msgctl` *system call*

The `msgctl` routine serves three purposes: it allows a process to get status information about a message queue, to change some of the limits associated with a message queue, or to delete a queue from the system altogether.

Usage

`#include <sys/msg.h>`
 	
`int msgctl(int mqid, int command, struct msqid_ds *msq_stat);`

mqid is, of course, a valid message queue identifier. Skipping `command` for the moment, the third parameter `msq_stat` holds the address of a `msqid_ds` structure. This unattractively named structure is defined in `<sys/msg.h>` and includes the following members:

```
struct ipc_perm    msg_perm;    /* ownership/perms */
msgqnum_t          msg_qnum;    /* no. messages on queue */
msglen_t           msg_qbytes;  /* max no. bytes for queue */
pid_t              msg_lspid;   /* pid of last msgsnd */
pid_t              msg_lrpid;   /* pid of last msgrcv */
time_t             msg_stime;   /* last msgsnd time */
time_t             msg_rtime;   /* last msgrcv time */
time_t             msg_ctime;   /* last change time */
```

We have met `ipc_perm` structures before. They hold the ownership and access permissions associated with the message queue. The types `msgqnum_t`, `msglen_t`, `pid_t` and `time_t` are system dependent. The `time_t` variables will hold times as seconds elapsed since 00:00 GMT, 1 January 1970. (The next example will show you how to convert such values into readable strings.)

The `command` parameter to `msgctl` tells the system what operation is to be performed. There are three options available here, all of which apply to all three IPC facilities. They are identified by constants defined in `<sys/ipc.h>`.

IPC_STAT   Tells the system to place status information about the structure into `msq_stat`.

IPC_SET   Used to set the values of control variables for the message queue, according to information held within `msq_stat`. Only the following items can be changed:

```
msq_stat.msg_perm.uid
msq_stat.msg_perm.gid
msq_stat.msg_perm.mode
msq_stat.msg_qbytes
```

An IPC_SET operation will succeed only if executed by superuser or the current owner of the queue as indicated by msq_stat.msg_perm.uid. In addition, only superuser can increase the msg_qbytes limit, which gives the maximum number of characters that may exist on the queue at any one time.

IPC_RMID   This removes the message queue from the system. Again, this can be done only by superuser or the queue owner. If command is set to IPC_RMID then msq_stat is set to NULL.

The following example program show_msg prints out some of the status information associated with a message queue. It is intended to be invoked as:

$ *show_msg keyvalue*

show_msg uses the ctime library routine to convert time_t values to readable form. (ctime and its companion will be discussed in Chapter 12.) The program text follows:

```
/* showmsg -- show message queue details */

#include <sys/types.h>
#include <sys/ipc.h>
#include <sys/msg.h>
#include <stdio.h>
#include <time.h>

void mqstat_print(key_t, int, struct msqid_ds *);

main(int argc, char **argv)
{
 key_t mkey;
 int msq_id;
 struct msqid_ds msq_status;

 if(argc != 2)
 {
      fprintf(stderr, "usage: showmsg keyval\n");
      exit(1);
 }

 /* get message queue identifier */
 mkey = (key_t)atoi(argv[1]);
 if(( msq_id = msgget(mkey, 0)) == -1)
 {
      perror("msgget failed");
      exit(2);
 }
```

```
    /* get status information */
    if(msgctl(msq_id, IPC_STAT, &msq_status) == -1)
    {
          perror("msgctl failed ");
          exit(3);
    }

    /* print out status information */
    mqstat_print(mkey, msq_id, &msq_status);
    exit(0);
}

void mqstat_print(key_t mkey, int mqid, struct msqid_ds *mstat)
{
 printf("\nKey %d, msg_qid %d\n\n", mkey, mqid);

 printf("%d message(s) on queue\n\n", mstat->msg_qnum);

 printf("Last send by proc %d at %s\n", mstat->msg_lspid,
                               ctime(&(mstat->msg_stime)));
 printf("Last recv by proc %d at %s\n", mstat->msg_lrpid,
                               ctime(&(mstat->msg_rtime)));
}
```

Exercise 8.4   Adapt show_msg so that it prints out the ownerships and permissions associated with the message queue.

Exercise 8.5   Write a program msg_chmod that alters the permissions associated with a message queue. Model it on the chmod program. Again, the message queue should be identified via its key value.

8.3.3 Semaphores

The semaphore as a theoretical construct

The semaphore concept was first put forward by the Dutch theoretician E.W. Dijkstra as a solution to the problems of process synchronization. In these terms, a semaphore *sem* can be seen as an integer variable on which the following operations are allowed (note that the *p* and *v* mnemonics come from the Dutch terms for *wait* and *signal*, the latter not to be confused with the old UNIX signal call):

p(sem) or wait(sem)

if (sem != 0)
  decrement sem by one
else
  wait until sem becomes non-zero, then decrement

v(sem) or signal(sem)

> *increment sem by one*
> *if (queue of waiting processes not empty)*
>   *restart first process in wait queue*

The test and set part of both operations must be indivisible, which means that only one process can ever change *sem* at any one time.

Formally, the nice thing about semaphores is the fact that the statement:

> *(semaphore's initial value*
> *+ number of v operations*
> *− number of completed p operations) >= 0*

is always true. This is the **semaphore invariant**. Computer scientists love such invariant conditions since they make programs amenable to systematic, rigorous proofs.

Semaphores can be used in a variety of ways. Most simply, they can be used to ensure **mutual exclusion**, where only one process can execute a particular region of code at any one time. Consider the following program skeleton:

> *p(sem);*
>
> *something interesting . . .*
>
> *v(sem);*

Let us assume further that the initial value of *sem* is one. From the semaphore invariant, we can see that:

> *(number of completed p operations −*
> *number of completed v operations) <= initial value of semaphore*

or:

> *(number of completed p operations −*
> *number of completed v operations) <= 1*

In other words, only one process can execute the group of statements between these particular *p* and *v* operations at any one time. Such an area of program is often called a **critical section**.

The UNIX implementation of semaphores is based upon these ideas, although the actual facilities offered are rather more general (and possibly overly complex). The first routines we shall examine are `semget` and `semctl`.

The `semget` *system call*

Usage

`#include <sys/sem.h>`
 	
`int semget(key_t key, int nsems, int permflags);`

The `semget` call is analogous to `msgget`. The extra parameter `nsems` gives the number of semaphores required in the semaphore set; this raises an important point – the UNIX semaphore operations are geared to work with sets of semaphores, not single objects. Figure 8.2 shows a semaphore set. As we shall see, this complicates the interface to the remaining semaphore routines.

The return value from a successful `semget` call is a **semaphore set identifier**, which acts much like a message queue identifier. This is represented in Figure 8.2 by `semid`. Following normal C usage, an index into a semaphore set can run from 0 to `nsems-1`.

Associated with each semaphore in the set are the following values:

semval   The semaphore value, always a positive integer. This must be set via the semaphore system calls; that is, the semaphore is not directly accessible as a data object to a program.

sempid   This is the pid of the process that last acted on the semaphore.

semcnt   Number of processes that are 'waiting' for the semaphore to reach a value greater than its current value.

semzcnt   Number of processes that are 'waiting' for the semaphore to reach the value zero.

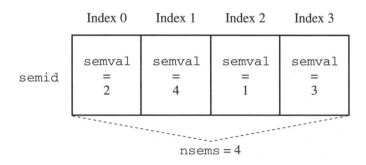

Figure 8.2 *A set of semaphores.*

The `semctl` *system call*

Usage
| ```
#include <sys/sem.h>
int semctl(int semid, int sem_num, int command,
           union semun ctl_arg);
``` |

As you can see from its definition, the `semctl` function is considerably more complicated than `msgctl`. The `semid` parameter must be a valid semaphore identifier, returned from a call to `semget`. The `command` parameter has much the same meaning as in `msgctl`, giving the exact function required. These fall into three categories: standard IPC functions (such as `IPC_STAT`), functions which affect only a single semaphore, and functions which affect the whole semaphore set. All the available functions are shown in Table 8.1.

The `sem_num` parameter is used with the second group of `semctl` options to identify a particular semaphore. The final parameter `ctl_arg` is a union defined as follows:

```
union semun{
  int val;
  struct semid_ds *buf;
  unsigned short *array;
};
```

Table 8.1 `semctl` *function codes*

Standard IPC functions
(note that the `semid_ds` structure is defined in `<sys/sem.h>`)

`IPC_STAT`	Place status information into `ctl_arg.stat`
`IPC_SET`	Set ownerships/permissions information from `ctl_arg.stat`
`IPC_RMID`	Remove semaphore set from system

Single semaphore operations
(these apply to semaphore `sem_num`, values returned by `semctl`)

`GETVAL`	Return value of semaphore (that is, `semval`)
`SETVAL`	Set value of semaphore to `ctl_arg.val`
`GETPID`	Return value of `sempid`
`GETNCNT`	Return `semncnt` (see above)
`GETZCNT`	Return `semzcnt` (see above)

All semaphore operations

`GETALL`	Place all `semvals` into `ctl_arg.array`
`SETALL`	Set all `semvals` according to `ctl_arg.array`
```

Each member of the union represents a different type of value to be set for each of the three types of semctl function. For example, if semval is SETVAL then ctl_arg.val will be used.

One important use of semctl is to set the initial values of semaphores, since semget does not allow a process to do this. The following example function can be used by a program to either create a single semaphore, or simply obtain the semaphore set identifier associated with it. If the semaphore is indeed created, it is assigned an initial value of one with semctl.

```
/* initsem -- semaphore initialization */

#include "pv.h"

int initsem(key_t semkey)
{
 int status = 0, semid;

 if((semid = semget(semkey, 1, SEMPERM|IPC_CREAT|IPC_EXCL)) == -1)
 {
      if(errno == EEXIST)
            semid = semget(semkey, 1, 0);
 }
 else          /* if created ... */
 {
      semun arg;
      arg.val = 1;
      status = semctl(semid, 0, SETVAL, arg);
 }

 if(semid == -1 || status == -1)
 {
      perror("initsem failed");
      return (-1);
 }
 /* all okay */
 return (semid);
}
```

The include file pv.h contains the following:

```
/* semaphore example header file */

#include <sys/types.h>
#include <sys/ipc.h>
#include <sys/sem.h>

#include <errno.h>

#define SEMPERM    0600
#define TRUE       1
#define FALSE      0
```

```
typedef union _semun {
     int val;
     struct semid_ds *buf;
     ushort *array;
} semun;
```

We shall use `initsem` as part of an example in the next section.

Semaphore operations: the `semop` call

`semop` is the call that actually performs the fundamental semaphore operations.

Usage

`#include <sys/sem.h>`
 	
 `int semop(int semid, struct sembuf *op_array, size_t num_ops);`

`semid` is the semaphore set identifier, which will probably have been obtained from a previous call to `semget`. The `op_array` parameter is an array of `sembuf` structures, the structure `sembuf` being defined in `<sys/sem.h>`. The `num_ops` parameter is the number of `sembuf` structures in the array. Each `sembuf` structure holds a specification of an operation to perform on a semaphore.

Again, the stress is on actions on sets of semaphores, the `semop` function allowing a group of operations to be performed atomically. This means that if one of the operations cannot be done, then none will be done. Unless otherwise specified the process will then normally block until it can do all the operations at once.

Let us dissect the `sembuf` structure further. It includes the following members:

```
unsigned short    sem_num;
          short    sem_op;
          short    sem_flg;
```

`sem_num` contains the index of a semaphore in the set. If, for example, the set contains only one member, then `sem_num` must be zero. `sem_op` contains a signed integer which is what really tells the `semop` function what to do. There are three cases:

Case 1: sem_op *value negative*

This is a generalized form of the semaphore `p()` command we discussed earlier. In pseudo-code, we can summarize the action of `semop` as follows (note that *ABS* is used to represent a variable's absolute value):

```
if( semval  >=  ABS(sem_op) )
{
 set semval to semval – ABS(sem_op)
}
else
{
 if( (sem_flg & IPC_NOWAIT) )
        return –1 immediately
 else
 {
        wait until semval reaches or exceeds ABS(sem_op)
        then subtract ABS(sem_op) as above
 }
}
```

The basic idea is that the `semop` function first tests the value of the `semval` associated with semaphore `sem_num`. If the `semval` is large enough, it is decremented immediately. If not, the process normally waits until `semval` becomes large enough. However, if the `IPC_NOWAIT` flag is set in `sem_flg`, `sem_op` returns −1 immediately and places `EAGAIN` into `errno`.

Case 2: `sem_op` ***value positive***
This matches the traditional `v()` operation. The value of `sem_op` is simply added to the corresponding `semval`. Other processes waiting on the new value of the semaphore will be woken up.

Case 3: `sem_op` ***value zero***
In this case `sem_op` will wait until the semaphore value becomes zero, but `semval` is not altered. If `IPC_NOWAIT` is set in `sem_flg`, and `semval` is not already zero, then `semop` returns an error immediately.

The `SEM_UNDO` *flag*

This is another flag that can be set in the `sem_flg` member of a `sembuf` structure. It tells the system to automatically 'undo' the operation when the process exits. To keep track of what could be a series of such operations, the system maintains an integer called the *semadj* value for the semaphore. It is important to understand that *semadj* values are allocated on a per-process basis, and so different processes will have different *semadj* values for the same semaphore. When a `semop` operation is applied, and `SEM_UNDO` is set, the value of `sem_num` is simply subtracted from the *semadj* value. Here, the sign of `sem_num` is significant; the *semadj* value decreases when `sem_num` is positive, and increases when `sem_num` is negative. When a process exits, the system adds all its *semadj* values to their matching semaphores, and so negates the effect of any `semop` calls. In general, `SEM_UNDO` should be used, unless the values set by a process can retain a meaning beyond the boundaries of that process' existence.

A semaphore example

We will now continue the example we started with the `initsem` routine. It centres around the two routines `p()` and `v()`, which are implementations of the traditional semaphore operations. First, let us look at `p()`:

```
/* p.c -- semaphore p operation */

#include "pv.h"

int p(int semid)
{
 struct sembuf p_buf;

 p_buf.sem_num = 0;
 p_buf.sem_op = -1;
 p_buf.sem_flg = SEM_UNDO;

 if(semop(semid, &p_buf, 1) == -1)
 {
      perror("p(semid) failed");
      exit(1);
 }
 return (0);
}
```

Notice how we use the `SEM_UNDO` flag. The code for `v()` follows:

```
/* v.c -- semaphore v operation */

#include "pv.h"

int v(int semid)
{
 struct sembuf v_buf;

 v_buf.sem_num = 0;
 v_buf.sem_op = 1;
 v_buf.sem_flg = SEM_UNDO;

 if(semop(semid, &v_buf, 1) == -1)
 {
      perror("v(semid) failed");
      exit(1);
 }
 return (0);
}
```

We can demonstrate the use of these relatively simple routines to perform mutual exclusion. Consider the following program:

```
/* testsem -- test semaphore routines */

#include "pv.h"

void handlesem(key_t skey);
```

```
main()
{
 key_t semkey = 0x200;
 int i;

 for(i = 0; i < 3; i++)
 {
      if(fork() == 0)
            handlesem(semkey);
 }
}

void handlesem(key_t skey)
{
 int semid;
 pid_t pid = getpid();

 if((semid = initsem(skey)) < 0)
      exit(1);

 printf("\nprocess %d before critical section\n",pid);

 p(semid);

 printf("process %d in critical section\n", pid);

 /* in real life do something interesting */
 sleep(10);

 printf("process %d leaving critical section\n", pid);

 v(semid);

 printf("process %d exiting\n", pid);
 exit(0);
}
```

testsem spawns three child processes which use p() and v() to stop more than one of them performing a critical section at the same time. Running testsem on one machine produced the following results:

```
process 799 before critical section
process 799 in critical section
process 800 before critical section
process 801 before critical section
process 799 leaving critical section
process 801 in critical section
process 799 exiting
process 801 leaving critical section
process 801 exiting
process 800 in critical section
process 800 leaving critical section
process 800 exiting
```

8.3.4 Shared memory

The shared memory operations allow two or more processes to share a segment of physical memory (normally, of course, the data areas of any two programs are entirely separate). They normally provide the most efficient of all the IPC mechanisms.

For a piece of memory to be shared it must first be created with the shmget system call. Once the memory exists a process can attach itself to the memory with shmat, and use it for its own mysterious purposes. Once the memory is no longer needed the process can detach itself, with shmdt.

The shmget *system call*

Shared memory segments are created with the shmget call.

Usage
| ```
#include <sys/shm.h>

int shmget(key_t key, size_t size, int permflags);
``` |

This call closely corresponds to msgget and semget. The most interesting parameter is size which gives the required minimum size (in bytes) of the memory segment. key is the key value that identifies the segment. permflags gives the permissions for the memory segment and, as with msgget and semget, these can be ORed with IPC_CREAT and IPC_EXCL.

Shared memory operations: shmat *and* shmdt

The memory segment created by shmget is part of physical memory, and not the process' *logical* data space. To use it, the process (and any cooperating process) must explicitly attach the memory segment to its logical data space using the shmat call:

Usage
| ```
#include <sys/shm.h>

void *shmat(int shmid, const void *daddr, int shmflags);
``` |

shmat associates the memory segment identified by shmid (which will have come from a shmget call) with a valid address for the calling process. The address is the value returned by shmat (in C, such data addresses are usually represented by a pointer to void).

daddr gives the programmer some control over the address selected by the call. If it is NULL, the segment is attached at the first available address as chosen by the system. This, of course, is the most straightforward case to program. If daddr is not NULL, the segment will be attached at, or near, the address held within it, the exact action depending on flags held in the shmflags argument. This presents many more difficulties than a NULL value, since you will have to know about the layout of your program in memory.

shmflag is constructed from the two flags SHM_RDONLY and SHM_RND which are defined in the header file <sys/shm.h>. SHM_RDONLY requests that the segment is attached for reading only. SHM_RND – when available – affects the way shmat treats a non-zero value for daddr. If it is set, the call will round daddr to a page boundary in memory. If not, shmat will use the exact value of daddr.

If an error occurs, the return from shmat will contain the rather nasty value:

```
(void *)-1
```

There is one other operation call, shmdt. It is the inverse of shmat and detaches a shared memory segment from the process' logical address space (meaning that the process can no longer use it!). It is called straightforwardly:

```
retval = shmdt(memptr);
```

retval is an integer and is 0 on success, −1 on error.

The shmctl *system call*

Usage
#include <sys/shm.h>   int shmctl(int shmid, int command, struct shmid_ds *shm_stat);

This exactly parallels msgctl, and command can take, among other options, the values IPC_STAT, IPC_SET and IPC_RMID. We will use it, with command set to IPC_RMID, in the next example.

A shared memory example: shmcopy

In this section we will construct a simple example program shmcopy to demonstrate a practical use of shared memory. shmcopy just copies its standard input to its standard output, but gets round the UNIX property that all read and write calls block until they complete. Each invocation of shmcopy results in two processes, a reader and a writer, that share two buffers implemented as shared memory segments. While the reader process reads data into the first buffer, the writer will write the contents of the second buffer, and vice versa. Since reading and writing are being performed simultaneously, data throughput should be increased. This approach is used, for example, in programs that need to drive tape streamers at speed.

To coordinate the two processes, and so prevent the writer writing a buffer before the reader has filled it, we will use two binary semaphores. Almost all shared memory programs will need to use semaphores in one form or another for synchronization, the shared memory facilities providing no synchronization features of their own.

shmcopy uses the following header file share_ex.h:

```
/* header file for shared memory example */

#include <stdio.h>
#include <signal.h>
#include <sys/types.h>
#include <sys/ipc.h>
#include <sys/shm.h>
#include <sys/sem.h>

#define SHMKEY1     (key_t)0x10 /* shared mem key */
#define SHMKEY2     (key_t)0x15 /* shared mem key */
#define SEMKEY      (key_t)0x20 /* semaphore key */

/* buffer size for reads and writes */
#define SIZ 5*BUFSIZ

/* will hold data and read count */
struct databuf {
 int d_nread;
 char d_buf[SIZ];
};

typedef union _semun {
      int val;
      struct semid_ds *buf;
      ushort *array;
} semun;
```

Remember that BUFSIZ is defined in <stdio.h>, and gives the system's disk blocking factor. The template databuf shows the structure we will impose on each shared memory segment. In particular, the member d_nread will enable the reader process to pass the number of characters read to the writer via the memory segments.

The next file contains routines for initializing the two shared memory segments and semaphore set. It also contains the routine remobj, which deletes the various IPC objects at the end of program execution. Notice in particular the way shmat is called to attach the shared memory segments to the process' address space.

```
/* initialization routines */

#include "share_ex.h"

#define IFLAGS      (IPC_CREAT | IPC_EXCL)
#define ERR         ((struct databuf *)-1)
```

```
static int shmid1, shmid2, semid;

void getseg(struct databuf **p1, struct databuf **p2)
{
 /* create shared memory segment */
 if((shmid1 = shmget(SHMKEY1, sizeof(struct databuf),
                                0600 | IFLAGS)) == -1)
       fatal("shmget");
 if((shmid2 = shmget(SHMKEY2, sizeof(struct databuf),
                                0600 | IFLAGS)) == -1)
       fatal("shmget");

 /* attach shared memory segments */
 if((*p1 = (struct databuf *)shmat(shmid1,0,0)) == ERR)
       fatal("shmat");
 if((*p2 = (struct databuf *)shmat(shmid2,0,0)) == ERR)
       fatal("shmat");
}

int getsem(void)          /* get semaphore set */
{
 semun x;
 x.val = 0;

 /* create two semaphore set */
 if((semid = semget(SEMKEY, 2, 0600 | IFLAGS)) == -1)
       fatal("semget");

 /* set initial values */
 if(semctl(semid, 0, SETVAL, x) == -1)
       fatal("semctl");
 if(semctl(semid, 1, SETVAL, x) == -1)
       fatal("semctl");
 return(semid);
}

/* remove shared memory identifiers + sem set id */
void remobj(void)
{
 if(shmctl(shmid1, IPC_RMID, NULL) == -1)
       fatal("shmctl");
 if(shmctl(shmid2, IPC_RMID, NULL) == -1)
       fatal("shmctl");
 if(semctl(semid, IPC_RMID, NULL) == -1)
       fatal("semctl");
}
```

Errors in these routines are handled with fatal, which we have used in previous examples. It simply calls perror, then exit.

The main function for shmcopy follows. It is very simple, just calling the initialization routines, then creating the reading (parent) and writing (child) processes. Notice how it is the writing process that calls remobj when the program finishes.

```
/* shmcopy -- main function */

#include "share_ex.h"

main()
{
 int semid;
 pid_t pid;
 struct databuf *buf1, *buf2;

 /* initialize semaphore set */
 semid = getsem();

 /* create and attach shared memory segments */
 getseg(&buf1, &buf2);

 switch(pid = fork()){
 case -1:
       fatal("fork");
 case 0: /* child */
       writer(semid, buf1, buf2);
       remobj();
       break;
 default: /* parent */
       reader(semid, buf1, buf2);
       break;
 }

 exit(0);
}
```

main creates the **IPC** objects before the `fork`. Note that the addresses that identify the shared memory segments (held in `buf1` and `buf2`) will be meaningful in both processes.

reader, which takes its input from standard input, that is, file descriptor 0, is the first interesting routine. It is passed the semaphore set identifier in `semid`, and the addresses of the two shared memory segments in `buf1` and `buf2`.

```
/* reader -- handle reading of file */

#include "share_ex.h"

/* these define p() and v() for two semaphores */
struct sembuf p1 = {0,-1,0}, p2 = {1,-1,0};
struct sembuf v1 = {0,1,0}, v2 = {1,1,0};

void reader(int semid, struct databuf *buf1,
                       struct databuf *buf2)
{
 for(;;)
 {
       /* read into buffer buf1 */
       buf1->d_nread = read(0, buf1->d_buf, SIZ);
```

```
      /* synchronization point */
      semop(semid, &v1, 1);
      semop(semid, &p2, 1);

      /* test here to avoid writer sleeping */
      if(buf1->d_nread <=0)
            return;

      buf2->d_nread = read(0, buf2->d_buf, SIZ);

      semop(semid, &v1, 1);
      semop(semid, &p2, 1);

      if(buf2->d_nread <=0)
            return;
 }
}
```

The `sembuf` structures here just define `p()` and `v()` operations for a two-semaphore set. However, this time they are not used for locking a critical section of code. Instead they are used to synchronize the reader and writer. `reader` uses v2 to signal that a read has been completed, and waits, by calling `semop` with p1, for the `writer` to signal that a write has been completed. This will become clearer when we describe the `writer` routine. Other techniques are possible, involving either four binary semaphores, or semaphores that can take more than two values.

The final routine called by `shmcopy` is `writer`:

```
/* writer -- handle writing */

#include "share_ex.h"

extern struct sembuf p1, p2; /* defined in reader.c */
extern struct sembuf v1, v2; /* defined in reader.c */

void writer(int semid, struct databuf *buf1,
                       struct databuf *buf2)
{
 for(;;)
 {
      semop(semid, &p1, 1);
      semop(semid, &v2, 1);

      if(buf1->d_nread <= 0)
            return;

      write(1, buf1->d_buf, buf1->d_nread);

      semop(semid, &p1, 1);
      semop(semid, &v2, 1);

      if(buf2->d_nread <= 0)
            return;

      write(1, buf2->d_buf, buf2->d_nread);
 }
}
```

Again, notice the use of the semaphore set to coordinate reader and writer. This time writer uses v2 to signal and waits on p1. It is also important to note that the values for buf1->d_nread and buf2->d_nread are set by the reading process.

When compiled, shmcopy can be used with a command such as

$ *shmcp < big > /tmp/big*

Exercise 8.6 Improve the error handling and reporting of shmcopy (especially for calls to read and write). Make shmcopy accept filenames as arguments in a cat like manner. What are the consequences of interrupting shmcopy? Can you improve things?

Exercise 8.7 Devise a message passing system that uses shared memory. Benchmark and compare with the IPC message passing routines.

8.3.5 The ipcs and ipcrm commands

There are two shell level commands provided for use with IPC facilities. The first is ipcs, which prints out information on the current status of IPC facilities. A simple example is:

$ *ipcs*

```
IPC status from /dev/kmem as of Wed Feb 26 18:31:31 1998
T    ID    KEY           MODE        OWNER     GROUP
Message Queues:
Shared Memory:
Semaphores:
s    10    0x00000200    --ra-------  keith     users
```

The other command is ipcrm, which is used to remove IPC facilities from the system (providing the user is the owner of the facility, or superuser). For example:

$ *ipcrm -s 0*

removes the semaphore associated with identifier 0, and:

$ *ipcrm -S 200*

removes the semaphore associated with key value 200.

For more details of the options available, see your system manual.

CHAPTER 9

The terminal

9.1 Introduction

Whenever a program and a user interact via a terminal, there is a lot more going on than might at first meet the eye. For example, if a program writes a string to a terminal device, that string is first processed by a section of the kernel we shall call the **terminal driver**. Depending on the value of certain state flags held by the system, the string might simply be passed on verbatim, or altered in some way by the driver. One common alteration is the replacement of line-feed or newline by the two-character sequence carriage-return, newline. This ensures that each line always begins on the left-hand side of the terminal screen or open window.

Similarly, the terminal driver will, in normal circumstances, allow the user to edit mistakes in an input line with the current erase and kill characters. The erase character will delete the last character typed, while the kill character will erase up to the beginning of the line. Only when the user is happy with the line, and presses the *Return* key, will the terminal driver pass it to the program.

This is not the end of the story. For example, once an output string reaches the terminal, the terminal hardware may either display the string directly or interpret it as an **escape-sequence** sent for screen control. The final result might therefore be an English message, or a cleared screen.

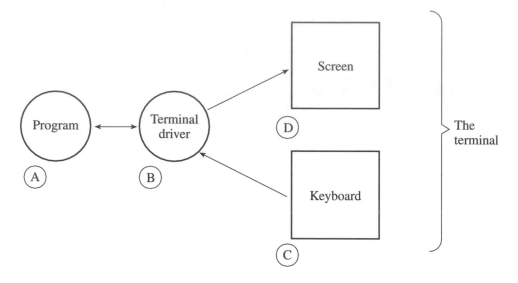

Figure 9.1 *The link between a UNIX process and a terminal.*

Figure 9.1 shows the various components of a link between computer and terminal more clearly.

It consists of four elements:

- *The program (A)* This generates output character sequences and interprets input character sequences. It might interact with the terminal using system calls such as read or write, a higher-level library such as *Standard I/O*, or a special library package designed for screen control. Ultimately of course, all I/O will be via read and write, since higher-level libraries must eventually call these fundamental primitives.

- *The terminal driver (B)* The terminal driver's main function is to transfer data from the program to the peripheral device, and vice versa. Within the UNIX kernel itself, a terminal typically consists of two major software components, the **device driver** and a **line discipline**.

   The device driver is a low-level piece of software written to interface to the specific hardware that allows the computer to communicate with its terminal. Indeed, systems will typically require device drivers to deal with more than one type of hardware. Built on this low-level layer are facilities which ensure that the basic features the device driver supports appear general, whatever the hardware.

   Aside from just this fundamental transmission function, the terminal driver will perform a degree of logical processing of input and output data, mapping one sequence of characters to another. This is handled by the line discipline component. It can also provide a variety of functions to aid the end user, such as input line editing. The exact processing and mappings performed depend upon state flags held by the line discipline for each terminal port. These can be set by a group of system calls, as we shall explore in later sections.

- *Keyboard and screen (C and D)*   These two elements represent the terminal itself and emphasize its dual nature. Node (C) stands for the terminal keyboard and acts as a source of input. Node (D) represents the terminal's screen and acts as a sink for output. However, a program can gain access to the terminal both as an input source and an output sink via just one terminal name, and ultimately a single file descriptor. To make this possible, the line discipline maintains an input and an output queue of characters for each terminal. This arrangement is shown in Figure 9.2.

So far, we have assumed that the peripheral device connected to a terminal line is a standard VDU. However, the peripheral device could equally well be a serial line-printer, a plotter, an entry point to a network, or even another computer. Nevertheless, whatever the nature of the peripheral device, it can act both as a source and a sink for input and output streams of characters, respectively.

This chapter will concentrate on nodes (A) and (B) in the diagram. In other words, we will examine the interaction between the program and the terminal driver at system call level. We will not consider the entirely separate issue of screen handling since the terminal driver plays no part in constructing the appropriate escape sequences for screen control.

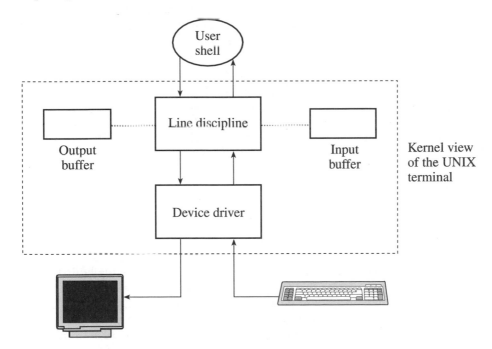

Figure 9.2 *An implementation of the terminal.*

Before proceeding we should add two caveats. First, we will only consider 'normal' terminal environments, not the complexities of window-based environments found under X-Windows or MS-Windows. They present their own special problems, which we will not consider. Second, terminal handling under UNIX is historically an area notorious for inconsistencies. The *XSI* does however provide a standard set of interface system calls. It is on these we will focus.

9.2 The UNIX terminal

As you might expect from Chapter 4, terminals are identified by device files (and, because of the nature of terminals, they are treated as character devices). As a consequence terminals, or more precisely terminal ports, can typically be accessed via filenames in the dev directory. Typical terminal names include:

```
/dev/console
/dev/tty01
/dev/tty02
/dev/tty03
...
```

tty is a synonym for terminal, much used in UNIX.

Because of the generality of the UNIX file concept, terminals can be accessed using the standard system call primitives such as read and write. File permissions retain their usual meanings, and so control access to terminals on the system. To ensure that this arrangement behaves sensibly, the system changes the ownership of a terminal when a user logs in, all users owning the terminal they are working on.

A process will not normally need to explicitly open a terminal file to interact with its user. This is because its standard input and standard output, unless redirected, will be connected to the user's terminal. So, assuming standard output is not assigned to a file, the following code fragment results in data being written to the terminal screen:

```
#define FD_STDOUT 1
.
.
.
write(FD_STDOUT, mybuffer, somesize);
```

In a traditional UNIX environment login terminals are actually first opened during system startup, under the control of the process supervisor program init. The terminal file descriptors are passed down to init's children, and ultimately each user's shell process will inherit three file descriptors connected to the user's terminal. These are, of course, the shell's standard input, standard output and standard error. They in turn are passed to any programs started from within the shell.

9.2.1 Control terminals

In normal circumstances, the terminal associated with a process through its standard file descriptors is the **control terminal** for that process and its session. A control terminal is an important process attribute that determines the handling of interrupts generated at the keyboard. For example, if a user hits the current interrupt key then all processes that recognize the terminal as their control terminal will receive the signal SIGINT. Control terminals, like other process attributes, are inherited across fork calls. (More specifically, a terminal becomes a control terminal for a session when the session leader opens it. This is providing the terminal is not already associated with a session and the session leader has not already acquired a control terminal. As a corollary, a process can break its relationship with its control terminal by changing its session with setsid. We saw this, rather prematurely, in Chapter 5. You should now also be able to gain an insight into how init arranges things.)

In cases when a process must gain access to its control terminal, whatever the state of its standard file descriptors, the filename:

```
/dev/tty
```

can be used. It is always interpreted as meaning the process' current control terminal. Consequently, the actual terminal this file identifies varies from process to process.

9.2.2 Data transmission

The fundamental task of the terminal driver is to transmit characters between the process and the terminal device. This, in fact, is a complicated requirement, since the user may type characters at any time, even while output is occurring. To understand the situation, go back to Figure 9.1 and imagine data passing along the paths (C) to (B) and (B) to (D) simultaneously. Remember that the program represented at node (A) in the diagram can only issue a single read or write request at any one time.

To manage two simultaneous streams of characters, while only one is being processed by a user program, the line discipline stores both input and output data in internal buffers. Input data is passed to the user program when it issues a read request. Input characters can be lost when either the buffers maintained by the kernel become completely full, or the number of characters associated with the terminal exceeds a system-specific maximum, represented by the constant MAX_INPUT, defined in <limits.h>. A typical figure for this limit is 255, generous enough to make loss of data rare in normal use. However, there is no way of determining when data has been lost; the system simply throws the extra characters away unannounced.

The situation with output is somewhat simpler. Each write to a terminal places characters into an output queue. If this queue ever becomes full, a successive write will 'block' (that is, hang) until the output queue drains to a suitable level.

9.2.3 Echoing and type-ahead

Because terminals are used for interaction between human beings and computer programs, the UNIX terminal driver provides a large number of additional facilities to make things easier for mortals.

Perhaps the most basic of these additional facilities is character echoing. After all, it helps to see an 'A' appear on the screen when you type 'A' on the keyboard. Terminals attached to UNIX systems normally work in **full-duplex** mode, which means that character echoing is the responsibility of the UNIX system, not the terminal. Consequently, when a character is typed it is first transmitted by the terminal to the UNIX system. When it is received, the line discipline immediately places a copy into the output queue for that terminal. It is then 'echoed' on the terminal screen. Returning again to Figure 9.1, it means that a character is sent first along the path (C) to (B), then immediately echoed along the path (B) to (D). All this may occur before the program (A) is ready to read the character. It leads to the interesting UNIX phenomenon of input echoing in the middle of output when a user types at the same time a program is writing to the screen. In other systems, the echoing of input may be suppressed until the program is ready to read it.

9.2.4 Canonical mode, line editing and special characters

A terminal can be set to a variety of modes according to the type of program attached to it and these modes will be handled by the correct line discipline. For example a screen editor will want maximum control and so will place the terminal into a 'raw' state, where the line discipline simply passes characters to the program as they arrive, without any processing.

However, UNIX would not be the programming environment it is if all programs had to deal with the minutiae of terminal control. So the standard terminal line discipline provides a mode of operation specifically tailored to simple, line-oriented, interactive use. This is described as **canonical mode**, and is used by the shell, the ed editor and similar programs.

In canonical mode, the terminal driver performs special actions when certain keys are pressed. Many of these actions are concerned with line-editing. As a corollary, input is only made available to a program in the form of complete lines when the terminal is in its canonical state (more of this later).

The most familiar editing key provided in canonical mode is the erase character. Pressing this causes the previous character on a line to be rubbed out. For example, the command line:

> $ whp < erase > o

followed by newline will result in the terminal driver sending the string *who* to the shell. If the terminal is correctly set, the '*p*' should also be physically erased from the screen.

The `erase` character can be set by the user to any ASCII value. The most common character used for this purpose is ASCII `backspace`.

The simplest way to change things at shell level is to use the `stty` command. For example:

$ *stty erase "^h"*

sets the `erase` character to *Ctrl-H*, which is another name for backspace. Note that you can usually type the string "*^h*", rather than the *Ctrl-H* character itself.

What follows is a systematic description of the other characters that have special meanings to the shell in canonical mode, as defined in the *XSI*. Unless otherwise stated, their exact values can be set by the user or system administrator.

kill　　　This results in all characters up to the beginning of the line being erased. So the input sequence:

　　　$ *echo < kill > who*

followed by a newline results in the command *who* being executed. The default value for *kill* is *Ctrl-?*. Common alternatives include *Ctrl-X* and *Ctrl-U*. The *kill* character can be reset with the shell command:

　　　$ *stty kill < new_char >*

intr　　　The interrupt character. If the user types this, the signal `SIGINT` is sent to the program reading from the terminal, and all other processes that recognize the terminal as their control terminal. A program like the shell is sensible enough to trap the signal, since the default action on receipt of `SIGINT` is program termination. One default value for the *intr* character under is ASCII *delete*, sometimes referred to as *DEL*. A common alternative is *Ctrl-C*. To change the current value of *intr* at shell level use:

　　　$ *stty intr < new_char >*

Refer back to Chapter 6 for more details of signal handling.

quit　　　This character, if typed by the user, causes the signal `SIGQUIT` to be sent to the process group associated with the terminal. Again, the shell will trap the signal leaving the user program to take appropriate action. As we saw in Chapter 6, the normal consequence is a core dump, where the contents of the program's memory space are written to disk and program execution is ungracefully terminated with the message Quit - core dumped. The normal *quit* character is ASCII *FS*, or *Ctrl-*. It can be changed with:

　　　$ *stty quit < new_char >*

eof   This is the character used to mark the end of an input stream from the terminal (to do so, it must be typed on a new line by itself). It is, for example, the character used to force logout. One standard initial setting is ASCII *eot*, otherwise known as *Ctrl-D*. It can be changed with:

$ *stty eof < new_char >*

nl   This is the normal line delimiter. It always has the value ASCII *line-feed*, which is the C *newline* character. It cannot be set or changed by the user. On terminals which send *carriage-return* instead of *line-feed*, the line discipline can be set to map carriage returns into line-feeds.

eol   This is an additional line delimiter which acts like *nl*. It is not normally used and has a default value of ASCII *NULL*.

stop   This normally has the value *Ctrl-S* and in some implementations cannot be altered by the user. It is used to temporarily suspend the output being written to the terminal. It is particularly useful when using an old-fashioned VDU terminal, since it can be used to suspend output before it vanishes for ever off the top of the terminal screen.

start   This normally has the value *Ctrl-Q*. Again, whether it can be altered by the user is implementation dependent. It is used to restart output which has been halted by a previous *Ctrl-S*. If no *Ctrl-S* has been typed, then *Ctrl-Q* is ignored.

susp   This character, if typed by the user, causes the signal SIGTSTP to be sent to the process group associated with the terminal. This has the effect of suspending the current foreground process group and placing it into the background. The normal *suspend* character is *Ctrl-Z*. Again, it can be changed with:

$ *stty susp < new-char >*

In entering commands the *erase*, *kill* and *eof* characters may be 'escaped' by immediately preceding them with a backslash (\) character. When this is done the function associated with the escaped character in question is not performed and it is sent to the reading program. For example, the line:

aa\ < erase > b < erase > c

results in *aa\ < erase > c* being sent to the program currently reading from the terminal.

9.3 The program's view

So far, we have studied the facilities offered by the terminal driver in terms of the user interface. Now, we will consider things from the viewpoint of a program using the terminal.

9.3.1 The `open` system call

`open` can be used to open a terminal line discipline in much the same way as an ordinary disk file. For example:

```
fd = open("/dev/tty0a", O_RDWR);
```

However, an attempt to open a terminal will not return until a connection has been established. For terminals with modem control this means that the open will not return until the modem control signals are correctly set up and 'carrier-detect' is valid, which can take time or fail to happen at all.

The following routine uses `alarm` (introduced in Chapter 6) to force a timeout if open fails to return after a reasonable period:

```
/* ttyopen - open with timeout */

#include <stdio.h>
#include <signal.h>

#define TIMEOUT    10
#define FALSE      0
#define TRUE       1

static int timeout = FALSE;
static char *termname;

static void settimeout(void)
{
 fprintf(stderr, "timeout on opening %s\n", termname);
 timeout = TRUE;
}

int ttyopen(char *filename, int flags)
{
 int fd = -1;
 static struct sigaction act, oact;

 termname = filename;

 /* set timeout flag */
 timeout = FALSE;
```

```
/* set SIGALRM action */
act.sa_handler = settimeout;
sigfillset(&(act.sa_mask));
sigaction(SIGALRM, &act, &oact);

alarm(TIMEOUT);

fd = open(filename, flags);

/* reset things */
alarm(0);
sigaction(SIGALRM, &oact, &act);

return (timeout ? -1 : 0);
}
```

9.3.2 The read system call

Out of all the file access primitives, it is the read system call that is most affected when used with a terminal device file, rather than an ordinary disk file. This is particularly so when the terminal is in canonical mode, the mode intended for normal interactive use. In this state, the line becomes the fundamental unit of input. Consequently, characters cannot be read from a line by a program until the user types the *Return* key, which is interpreted by the system as meaning newline. Equally importantly, a call to read will always return after a newline, even if the number of characters on the line is less than the number of characters requested in the read call. If just a *Return* is typed and an empty line is sent to the system, the corresponding read call will return a value of 1, since the newline is itself made available to the program. A return value of zero can still therefore be used to detect end of file (that is, the *eof* character has been typed).

We first saw this kind of interaction between read and the terminal driver in the io example way back in Chapter 2. However, the topic really deserves a more detailed explanation, so consider the statement:

```
nread = read(0, buffer, 256);
```

If the process' standard input is being taken from a regular file, the interpretation of this call is straightforward; while more than 256 characters remain in the file, the call to read will return exactly 256 characters in buffer. Since the relationship between read and a terminal is a little more complicated, we will use Figure 9.3, which shows a brief interaction between program and user, to make things clearer.

The diagram illustrates a possible sequence of actions when the read call above is applied to a terminal. At each step there are two boxes shown. The top box shows the current state of the input line as the terminal driver sees things; the lower, labelled Read buffer, shows the data currently available to be read by a process. We should stress that the diagram shows a logical picture only, taken from the

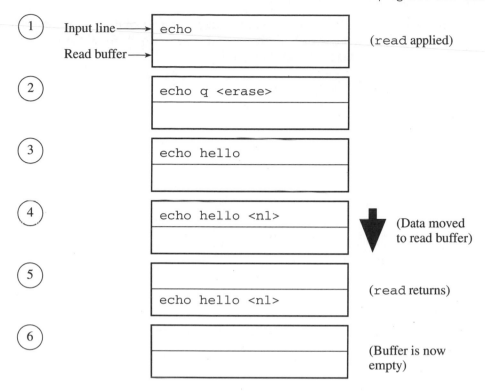

Figure 9.3 *Stages in reading from a terminal in canonical mode.*

viewpoint of a user process. However, the most common implementation of a terminal driver also uses a two-buffer or queue arrangement which is not much more complicated than the scheme presented in the diagram.

Step 1 represents the situation when the program makes the read call. The user has at this point already typed the string *echo*, but since no newline has yet been entered, there is no data in the read buffer, and the execution of the process is suspended.

At step 2 the user has typed *q*, then changed his or her mind, and pressed the current *erase* key to remove the character for the input line. This part of the diagram emphasizes how editing can be performed on the input line without involving the program which is performing the read.

At step 3 the input line is complete except for the final newline. The part of the diagram marked as step 4 shows the instant at which newline is entered, and the terminal driver transfers the input line, including the terminating newline, into the read buffer. This leads to step 5, where the entire input line has become available for reading. Within the process that made the read call, the call returns, giving a value of 11 for nread. Step 6 shows the situation just after the call has been satisfied in this way; both the input line and read buffer are temporarily empty.

The next example reinforces the above discussion. It centres on the entirely trivial program read_demo, which has just one distinguishing feature: the small size of the buffer it uses to take bites at standard input.

```
/* read_demo -- read/terminal driver interaction */

#include <sys/types.h>

#define SMALLSZ 10

main(int argc, char **argv)
{
 ssize_t nread;
 char smallbuf[SMALLSZ+1];

 while((nread = read(0, smallbuf, SMALLSZ)) > 0)
 {
      smallbuf[nread] = '\0';
      printf("nread:%d %s\n", nread, smallbuf);
 }
}
```

If this program is presented with the following keyboard input:

1
1234
This is a much longer line.
<EOF>

the following dialogue would be produced:

1
nread:2 1

1234
nread:5 1234

This is a much longer line.
nread:10 This is a
nread:10 much longe
nread:8 r line.

Notice how the longest line requires several consecutive reads to absorb it. Also note that figures for nread include the trailing newline at the end of each line. Again, we have not explicitly shown these for clarity.

What happens if the terminal is not in canonical mode? In this case, a program must set additional state variables associated with the terminal in order to fully control input. This is done via a set of system calls, which we shall discuss in detail later.

Exercise 9.1   Try the read_demo example with the same input redirected from a file.

9.3.3 The write **system call**

This is, as far as terminal interaction goes, a much simpler beast. The only point of significance is that a write will block if the output queue for the terminal is full. Program execution will resume only when the number of characters in the queue drains below some threshold level.

9.3.4 ttyname **and** isatty

We will now introduce two useful utilities which we can make use of in later examples. ttyname returns the name of a terminal device associated with an open terminal file descriptor, while isatty returns 1 (that is, *true* in C terms) if a file descriptor describes a terminal device, 0 (*false*) otherwise.

Usage

```
#include <unistd.h>

char* ttyname(int filedes);

int isatty(int filedes);
```

In both cases filedes is the open file descriptor. If filedes does not represent a terminal, ttyname returns NULL. Otherwise the return value from ttyname points to a static data area which is overwritten by each call to ttyname.

The following example routine what_tty prints out the terminal associated with a file descriptor, if possible:

```
/* what_tty -- print tty name */

void what_tty(int fd)
{
  if(isatty(fd))
        printf("fd %d =>> %s\n", fd, ttyname(fd));
  else
        printf("fd %d =>> not a terminal!\n", fd);
}
```

Exercise 9.2   Adapt the ttyopen routine from the last section so that it will only return a file descriptor for a terminal special file, not a disk file or any other file type. Use isatty to perform the checking. Are there other ways to achieve this?

9.3.5 Changing terminal characteristics: the `termios` structure

At shell level, the user can invoke the `stty` command to alter the characteristics of the terminal line discipline. A program can do much the same thing by using `termios` structures in conjunction with the relevant functions. Note that older systems used the `ioctl` (the name stands for I/O control) system call, as documented in the first edition of this book. The `ioctl` call is a little too general purpose and has now been broken up into these more specific calls. These calls all taken together provide a general programming interface to all UNIX asynchronous communication ports, whatever the nature of the underlying hardware.

An occurrence of a `termios` structure can be thought of as representing a possible state for a terminal, corresponding to state flags held by the system for each terminal device. The precise definition of a `termios` structure will be discussed shortly. `termios` structures can be filled out with the current terminal settings by using the `tcgetattr` call. This is defined as follows:

Usage

```
#include <termios.h>
int tcgetattr(int ttyfd, struct termios *tsaved);
```

This particular function saves the present state of the terminal associated with `ttyfd` in the `termios` structure `tsaved`. `ttyfd` must be a file descriptor that describes a terminal. Similarly:

Usage

```
#include <termios.h>
int tcsetattr(int ttyfd, int actions,
              const struct termios *tnew);
```

---

will set the line discipline represented by `ttyfd` to the new state represented by `tnew`. It is `tcsetattr`'s second parameter, `actions`, that specifies how and when the new terminal attributes should be set. There are three possible actions, which are defined in `<termios.h>`:

`TCSANOW`	The effect is instantaneous, which can cause problems if the terminal driver is simultaneously writing to the terminal and you alter the output flags in `tnew`.
`TCSADRAIN`	This performs the same function as `TCSANOW`. However, it waits for the current output queue to empty before setting the new parameters. Consequently, this value should normally be used when altering parameters concerned with output to the terminal.
`TCSAFLUSH`	This is similar to `TCSADRAIN`, it waits for the output queue to empty, then flushes the input queue, before setting the line discipline parameters to the values held in `tnew`.

The following two functions make use of these calls. `tsave` saves the current parameters associated with the process' control terminal, and `tback` restores the last set of saved parameters. A Boolean variable `saved` is used to stop `tback` setting a terminal state when `tsave` has not been used.

```c
#include <stdio.h>
#include <termios.h>

#define SUCCESS    0
#define ERROR      (-1)

/* tsaved will hold terminal parameters */
static struct termios tsaved;

/* TRUE if parameters saved */
static int saved = 0;

int tsave(void)
{
  if(isatty(0) && tcgetattr(0,&tsaved) >= 0)
  {
       saved = 1;
       return (SUCCESS);
  }
  return (ERROR);
}

int tback(void)             /* restore terminal state */
{
  if( !isatty(0) || !saved)
       return (ERROR);

  return tcsetattr(0, TCSAFLUSH, &tsaved);
}
```

These two routines can be used to bracket a section of code that temporarily alters the terminal state, as follows:

```c
#include <stdio.h>

main()
{
  if(tsave() == -1)
  {
       fprintf(stderr, "couldn't save terminal parameters\n");
       exit(1);
  }

  /* do the interesting part */

  tback();
  exit(0);
}
```

Definition of termios

Now let us explore termios structures in detail. The structure template for termios structures is found in the include file <termios.h> and includes the following members:

```
tcflag_t    c_iflag;        /* input modes */
tcflag_t    c_oflag;        /* output modes */
tcflag_t    c_cflag;        /* control modes */
tcflag_t    c_lflag;        /* line disc. modes */
cc_t        c_cc[NCCS];     /* control chars */
```

It is easiest to examine this structure by starting with its last member cc_c.

The c_cc *array*

The line-editing characters we examined in Section 9.2.4 are actually contained in the array c_cc. Their relative positions are given by constants defined in <termios.h>. All of the values defined in the *XSI* are shown in Table 9.1. The size of the array is determined by the constant NCCS also defined in <termios.h>.

The following program fragment shows how to alter the value of the quit character for the terminal associated with standard input (file descriptor 0):

```
struct termios tdes;

/* get initial terminal characteristics */
tcgetattr(0, &tdes);

tdes.c_cc[VQUIT] = \031; /* CTRL-Y */

/* reset terminal */
tcsetattr(0, TCSAFLUSH, &tdes);
```

Table 9.1 *Control character codes*

Constant	Meaning
VINTR	Interrupt key
VQUIT	Quit key
VERASE	Erase character
VKILL	Kill (line erase) character
VEOF	End of file character
VEOL	Optional end of line marker
VSTART	Start character
VSTOP	Stop character
VSUSP	Suspend character

This example serves to illustrate the safest approach to changing the state of a terminal. First, get the terminal's current state. Second, alter only those parameters you are interested in, without touching anything else. Third, change the terminal state with the modified `termios` structure. As we have seen, it is also worth saving the original value to reset the terminal before exiting, otherwise there may be surprises for later programs.

The `c_cflag` field

The `c_cflag` field defines the hardware control of the terminal. Normally, a process should leave the `c_cflag` field for its control terminal well alone. It becomes useful in applications such as communications packages, or when a program opens an extra terminal line such as a printer port. Values for `c_cflag` are constructed by ORing constants defined in `<termios.h>`. In general, each constant represents a single bit within the flag field which can be set on or off. There are a large number of such constants which we will not discuss in full (consult your local manual for complete details). However, there are four functions which allow you to get and set both the input and output speed without having to worry about the bit twiddling.

Usage

```
#include <termios.h>

/* set input speed */
int cfsetispeed(struct termios *tdes, speed_t speed);

/* set output speed */
int cfsetospeed(struct termios *tdes, speed_t speed);

/* get input speed */
speed_t cfgetispeed(const struct termios *tdes);

/* get output speed */
speed_t cfgetospeed(const struct termios *tdes);
```

The following example sets the terminal speed to 9600 baud. `B9600` is defined in `<termios.h>`.

```
struct termios tdes;

/* get initial terminal characteristics */
tcgetattr(0, &tdes);

/* change the input and output speed */
cfsetispeed(&tdes, B9600);
cfsetospeed(&tdes, B9600);
```

Of course, this will have no effect until `tcsetattr` is called, as follows:

```
tcsetattr(0, TCSAFLUSH, &tdes);
```

The next example enables parity generation and detection by setting bits directly:

```
tdes.c_cflag |= (PARENB | PARODD);
tcsetattr(0, TCSAFLUSH, &tdes);
```

Here, it is the `PARENB` flag that enables parity checking. The `PARODD` flag indicates that the parity desired is odd. If `PARODD` is turned off with `PARENB` set, then even parity is assumed. (The term **parity** describes the use of check bits in data transmission. There is one such check bit per character, which is possible because the ASCII character set takes up only seven bits out of the eight used to hold a byte on most machines. The value of the check bit can be used to make the total number of bits set per byte either odd or even. Alternatively, the programmer can choose to ignore parity altogether.)

The `c_iflag` *field*

The `c_iflag` field within a `termios` structure describes basic terminal input control. Again we will not examine all the possible settings, but will study a selection of those that are used most often in practice.

Three of the flags associated with this field are concerned with the treatment of carriage return. These can be useful with terminals that send a sequence involving carriage return to mark end of line. (UNIX of course expects ASCII line-feed or newline as its end of line character.) The flags in question are:

INLCR   Map, that is, translate, newline to carriage return.

IGNCR   Ignore carriage return.

ICRNL   Map carriage return to newline.

Three other `c_iflag` fields are concerned with flow control:

IXON   Allow start/stop control over output.

IXANY   Allow any character to restart output.

IXOFF   Allow start/stop control over input.

The `IXON` flag gives the user control over output. If set, then the user can stop output with *Ctrl-S*. *Ctrl-Q* will restart the output. If `IXANY` is also set any character can be pressed to restart suspended output, although *Ctrl-S* must in general be used to halt it. If the `IXOFF` flag is set, the system itself will transmit a stop character (*Ctrl-S* as usual) to the terminal when its input buffer is nearly full. *Ctrl-Q* will be sent to restart input once the system is ready to accept data again.

The c_oflag *field*

The c_oflag field specifies the system's treatment of output. The most important flag here is OPOST. If this is not set, then output characters are transmitted without alteration. If it is, characters are post-processed as indicated by the remaining flags set within c_oflag. Some of these are concerned about the processing of carriage return in output to the terminal:

ONLCR Map newline to carriage return, newline.

OCRNL Map carriage return to newline.

ONOCR No carriage return output at column 0.

ONLRET Newline to perform carriage return function.

If ONLCR is set, newlines are mapped to the sequence carriage-return, newline. This ensures that each line begins on the left-hand side of the screen. Conversely, if OCRNL is set, then carriage returns are translated into newlines. The flag ONLRET tells the terminal driver that newlines themselves will perform the carriage return function for the type of terminal being used. If ONOCR is set then no carriage return will be sent if a line of zero length is output.

Almost all the other flags for the c_oflag member are concerned with delays in transmission associated with specific characters such as newline, tab, form-feed, etc. These delays allow for mechanical or screen movements which take up a finite time. Again, see your local manual for details.

The c_lflag *field*

Perhaps the most interesting member of the termios structure for the programmer is the c_lflag member. It is used by the current line discipline to control terminal functions. The available flags are:

ICANON Canonical, line-oriented input.

ISIG Enable interrupt processing.

IEXTEN Enable extended (implementation-dependent) input character processing.

ECHO Enable basic echoing of input.

ECHOE Echo erase as backspace-space-backspace.

ECHOK Echo newline after kill.

ECHONL Echo newline.

NOFLSH Disable flush after interrupt.

TOSTOP Send SIGTTOU for background output.

If ICANON is set, then canonical processing is performed. As we saw above, this enables use of the line-editing characters and the assembly of input in lines before they can be read. If ICANON is not set, the terminal is in a 'raw' mode usually associated with screen-oriented software and communications packages. Calls to read will now be satisfied directly from the input queue. In other words, the basic unit of input becomes the single character rather than the logical line. Programs can choose to read data a character at a time (useful for screen editors), or in large blocks of fixed size (useful for communications software). However, the programmer must now specify two additional parameters in order to fully control the behaviour of read. These are VMIN, the minimum number of characters to be received before a read returns, and VTIME, a timeout period for a read. Both parameters are stored in the c_cc array. This is an important topic, which we study in full detail in the next section. For now, just note that the following example shows how to turn the ICANON flag off:

```
#include <termios.h>

struct termios tdes;
.
.
.
tcgetattr(0, &tdes);

tdes.c_lflag &= ~ICANON;

tcsetattr(0, TCSAFLUSH, &tdes);
```

If the ISIG flag is set, the processing of the interrupt keys *intr* and *quit* is enabled. Normally, of course, this allows a user to abort a running program. If ISIG is not set, no checking is done and the *intr* and *quit* characters are passed without alteration to the reading program.

If ECHO is set, then you will not be surprised to learn that characters will be echoed as they are typed. Turning this flag off is useful for password-checking routines, programs that use keys for special functions such as cursor movement and the like.

If ECHOE is set, and ECHO is on, then the erase character will be echoed as the sequence backspace−space−backspace. This physically rubs out the last character on a terminal with a screen, giving the user positive feedback that the character has actually been erased. If ECHOE is set when ECHO is not, erase is instead echoed as space−backspace, and so rubs out the character under the cursor on a CRT/VDU-type terminal.

If ECHONL is set, newline will always be echoed even if other echoing is turned off, a useful feature with terminals that do their own, local echoing (in what is often referred to as **half-duplex** mode).

The last flag worth discussing in this group is NOFLSH which suppresses the normal flushing of both input and output queues when the intr or quit keys are pressed, and flushing of the input queue when the susp key is pressed.

Exercise 9.3 Write a program `ttystate` that prints out the current state of the terminal associated with standard input. Output should be in terms of the names of pre-processor constants introduced in this section (for example `ICANON` and `ECHOE`). Use your system's UNIX manual to obtain a full list of the available names.

Exercise 9.4 Write a program `ttyset` that takes the output of `ttystate` and sets the terminal associated with its standard output to the state described. Are `ttystate` and `ttyset` in any way useful, singularly or as a pair?

9.3.6 The `MIN` and `TIME` parameters

The `MIN` and `TIME` parameters have meaning only when the `ICANON` flag is turned off. They are intended to fine-tune a program's control over data input. `MIN` gives the minimum number of characters that the terminal driver must receive before a call to `read` from the terminal returns. `TIME` specifies a timeout value that allows an additional degree of control. The actual timeout period is measured in tenths of a second.

The `MIN` and `TIME` values are held in the `c_cc` array of the `termios` structure that describes the terminal state. Their position in the array is defined by the constants `VMIN` and `VTIME` from `<termios.h>`. The following program fragment shows how to set them:

```
#include <termios.h>

struct termios tdes;
int ttyfd;

/* get current state */
tcgetattr(ttyfd, &tdes);

tdes.c_lflag &= ~ICANON;      /* turn off canonical mode */
tdes.c_cc[VMIN] = 64;         /* in characters */
tdes.c_cc[VTIME] = 2;         /* tenths of a second */

tcsetattr(0, TCSAFLUSH, &tdes);
```

`VMIN` and `VTIME` typically have the same values as `VEOF` and `VEOL`. This means that `MIN` and `TIME` occupy the same storage positions as the `eof` and `eol` characters. The moral here is that, when switching from canonical to non-canonical mode, be sure to give `MIN` and `TIME` values. Otherwise strange behaviour may result. (In particular, if *Ctrl-D* is your *eof* character, you may find your program reading input in blocks of four characters. Why?) A similar argument applies in the reverse direction.

There are four possible MIN and TIME combinations:

1. MIN *and* TIME *are both zero*   Here, a read will always return immediately. If characters are present within the input queue for that terminal (remember input may arrive at any time) they will be placed in the process' buffer. So, if a program puts its control terminal into a 'raw' state with ICANON off, and MIN and TIME are both equal to zero, the statement:

    ```
    nread = read(0, buffer, SOMESZ);
    ```

    will return any number of characters from zero up to SOMESZ depending on how many characters are waiting in the queue when the call is made.

2. MIN *greater than zero,* TIME *zero*   The timer plays no role here. A call to read will be satisfied only when there are MIN characters waiting to be read. This occurs even if the read call requested less than MIN characters.

    The most trivial setting in this category has MIN equal to one, with TIME zero. This causes read to return each time the system receives a character on the terminal line. This may be useful when simply reading from a terminal keyboard, although keys which send multiple character sequences present a problem.

3. MIN *zero,* TIME *greater than zero*   In this case, MIN plays no role. The timer is started as soon as the read call is made. The read returns as soon as the first character is received. If the timer expires (when TIME tenths of a second elapse) the read returns zero characters.

4. *Both* MIN *and* TIME *greater than zero*   This is perhaps the most useful and flexible case. The timer is now activated when the first character is received, rather than when the read call is made. If MIN characters are received before the timeout period elapses, the read call returns. If the timeout point is reached, just the characters currently in the input queue will be returned to the user program. This mode of operation is useful when input arrives in bursts sent over a short period of time. It simplifies programming and also reduces the number of system calls that might otherwise need to be made. It would be useful, for example, in dealing with function keys that send a series of characters when pressed.

9.3.7 Other terminal system calls

The additional terminal system calls provide the programmer with some degree of control over the input and output queues maintained by the terminal driver. They have the following usage.

Usage

```
#include <termios.h>

int tcflush(int ttyfd, int queue);

int tcdrain(int ttyfd);

int tcflow(int ttyfd, int actions);

int tcsendbrk(int ttyfd, int duration);
```

The `tcflush` call flushes the specified queue. If `queue` is set to `TCIFLUSH` (defined in `<termios.h>`) the input queue is flushed. In other words, all characters in the input queue are discarded. If `queue` is `TCOFLUSH` the output queue is flushed. If `queue` is `TCIOFLUSH` both input and output queues are flushed.

The `tcdrain` call will cause a process to pause until all the current output is written to `ttyfd`.

The `tcflow` call provides start/stop control over the terminal driver. When `actions` is `TCOOFF` output is suspended. It can be restarted by making a new call with the value of `actions` set to `TCOON`. The `tcflow` call can also be used to send a `STOP` or `START` character to the terminal device by setting `actions` to `TCIOFF` or `TCION`, respectively.

The `tcsendbrk` call is used to send a break, which corresponds to zero bits for a specified duration. If `duration` is 0 then the bits will be sent for at least a quarter of a second and not more than half a second. If `duration` is not 0 then it will send the bits for an implementation-dependent time.

9.3.8 The hangup signal

In Chapter 6 we saw that the hangup signal `SIGHUP` is sent to the members of a session when the session leader exits (providing it has a control terminal). It also has another use, intended for environments where the connection between computer and terminal can be broken and the carrier signal associated with the terminal line can 'drop'. This can occur, for example, when terminals are connected over phone lines, or with certain local area networks. In such circumstances, the terminal driver should send `SIGHUP` to all processes that recognize the terminal as their control terminal. Unless trapped, this signal will cause program termination. (Unlike `SIGINT`, `SIGHUP` will normally halt a shell. In effect, a user is automatically logged out when his or her connection to the system is broken – a nice security feature.)

Normally a programmer should leave `SIGHUP` alone – it serves a good purpose. However, you might want to trap it in order to perform some clean-up operations:

```
#include <signal.h>

void hup_action();
static struct sigaction act;
   .
   .
   .

act.sa_handler=hup_action;
sigaction(SIGHUP, &act, NULL);
```

This approach is used in some editors which save your edited file and send you mail before exiting. If SIGHUP is ignored altogether (setting act.sa_handler to SIG_IGN) and the terminal is hung up, future read calls on the terminal will return 0 to simulate end of file.

9.4 Pseudo terminals

Another common use of the line discipline structure is to create a **pseudo terminal** for network access. A pseudo terminal can be used to provide a means of connecting a terminal on one machine to a shell on another. An example is shown in Figure 9.4. Here the user is connected to machine A (the client), but is using a shell on machine B (the server). The arrows in the diagram show the direction of an input key stroke. We have simplified the diagram by ignoring detail about the networking protocol stacks on both the client and the server.

When a user connects to a shell on another machine (typically through the rlogin command) the local terminal connection has to be modified. As data is read from the local terminal, it is passed, unchanged by the line discipline, to the rlogin process running on the local machine. The line discipline, on the local machine, is therefore set to work in a raw bypass mode. The following code should act as a reminder of how to do this:

```
#include <termio.h>

struct termios attr;
   .
   .
   .
/* get the current line discipline */
tcgetattr(0, &attr);

/* read after every single character, with no timeout */
attr.c_cc[VMIN] = 1;
attr.c_cc[VTIME] = 0;
attr.c_lflag &= ~(ISIG|ECHO|ICANON);

/* set the new line discipline */
tcsetattr(0, TCSAFLUSH, &attr);
```

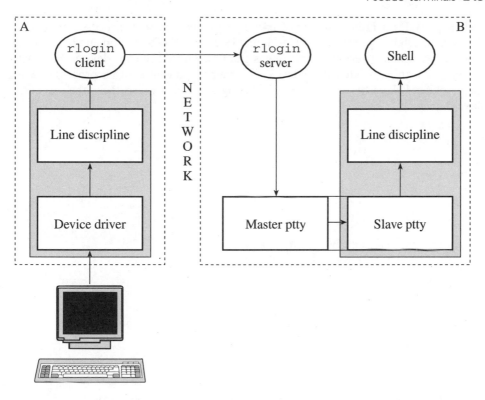

Figure 9.4 *Remote login between two UNIX systems.*

The `rlogin` client process then passes the unchanged data across the network.

When the server machine (B) receives the initial login request it `forks` and execs a new shell. The new shell has no controlling terminal associated with it and therefore a pseudo terminal is constructed which mimics a normal terminal device driver. The pseudo terminal, usually called a **pseudo tty**, acts in a very similar manner to a bidirectional pipe and simply allows two different processes to transfer data. In our example it connects the shell process to the appropriate network process. A pseudo tty is a pair of devices known as the master device and the slave device. The network process opens, and then reads and writes to the master device and the shell process opens, and then reads and writes to the slave device (via the line discipline). Any write to the master device appears as input to the slave device and vice versa. The net effect is that the user on the client (A) seems to be directly using the shell which is actually running on the server (B). Similarly as data is written by the shell on the server, it is processed by the line discipline on the server (acting in canonical mode) and then passed unchanged to the client terminal, without being modified by the line discipline on the client.

Although the means by which pseudo ttys are initialized has improved with newer versions of UNIX and the *XSI*, it is still somewhat cumbersome! The UNIX system provides a finite number of pseudo ttys and the shell process has to open the next available pseudo tty. This is achieved on SVR4 by opening the device /dev/ptmx which determines and opens the first unused master device. All master devices have an associated slave device. In order to prevent another process opening the associated slave device, the act of opening /dev/ptmx also locks the associated slave device.

```
#include <fcntl.h>

int mfd;
.
.
.


/* open the pseudo tty -
 * obtain the file descriptor of the master ptty */
if( (mfd = open("/dev/ptmx", O_RDWR)) == -1)
{
      perror("Opening the master ptty");
      exit(1);
}
.
.
.
```

Before opening and 'unlocking' the slave device it is necessary to ensure that only a process with the appropriate permissions should be able to read and write to it. The grantpt function changes the mode and ownership of the slave device to those of the effective user ID of the associated master device. The unlockpt function simply unlocks an internal state flag associated with the slave device (that is, makes it available). Finally, we need to open the slave device. However, at this stage we do not know its name. The ptsname function returns the name of the slave device associated with the specified master device. They will typically have names like /dev/pts/pttyXX. The following code fragment puts these together:

```
#include <fcntl.h>

int mfd, sfd;
char *slavenm;
.
.
.


/* open the master device as before */
if( (mfd = open("/dev/ptmx", O_RDWR)) == -1)
{
 perror("Opening the master ptty");
 exit(1);
}
```

```
/* change the permissions of the slave ptty */
if(grantpt(mfd)== -1)
{
      perror("Unable to grant access to ptty");
      exit(1);
}

/* unlock the slave device associated with mfd */
if(unlockpt(mfd)== -1)
{
      perror("Unable to unlock the ptty");
      exit(1);
}

/* retrieve the name of the slave ptty and then open it */
if( (slavenm = ptsname(mfd)) == NULL )
{
      perror("No slave name");
      exit(1);
}
if( (sfd = open(slavenm, O_RDWR)) == -1)
{
      perror("Opening slave ptty");
      exit(1);
}
```

Now that we have gained access to the pseudo terminal device driver we have to construct the associated line discipline. Until now we have viewed the line discipline as a complete entity whereas in reality it is made up of a number of internal kernel modules known as a **STREAM**. A standard pseudo terminal line discipline STREAM is made up of three modules: ldterm (the line discipline terminal module), ptem (the pseudo terminal emulation module) and the slave end of the pseudo tty. Together they act like a real terminal. This configuration is shown in Figure 9.5.

To construct this STREAM we have to 'push' the additional modules onto the slave device. This is achieved using the multi-purpose function ioctl. For example:

```
/*
 * The stropts.h header file contains the STREAMS interface and
 * defines the macro I_PUSH used as the second argument to
 * ioctl()
 */
#include <stropts.h>
.
.
.


/* open the master and slave devices as before */

/* push the two modules onto the slave device */
ioctl(sfd, I_PUSH, "ptem");
ioctl(sfd, I_PUSH, "ldterm");
```

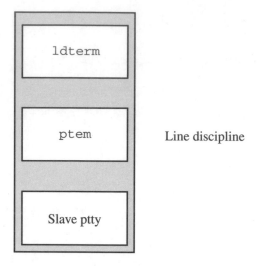

Line discipline

Figure 9.5 *STREAM for a pseudo terminal device.*

Now let us turn to a major example, called tscript, which uses the concept of a pseudo tty on a *single* machine to capture keystrokes from an interactive shell session without impacting the execution of that session. It is similar to the UNIX command script. The approach is extendible across a network.

9.5 A terminal handling example: tscript

The overall design is structured as follows. When the tscript program runs, it forks and execs a shell for the user. All data written to the terminal by the shell is then captured in a file by tscript, without the knowledge of the shell, which continues to behave as if it has complete control over the line discipline and therefore the terminal. The logical arrangement of the tscript program is shown in Figure 9.6.

The main elements of this arrangement are:

tscript   The first process to be started. Once the pseudo tty and line disciplines are initialized it uses fork and exec to create the shell. tscript now plays two roles. The first is to read from the real terminal and write any data into the master device of the pseudo tty. (All data written to the master pseudo tty passes straight through to the slave pseudo tty.) Its second role is to read output from the shell, via the pseudo tty, and copy it to both the real terminal and to an output file.

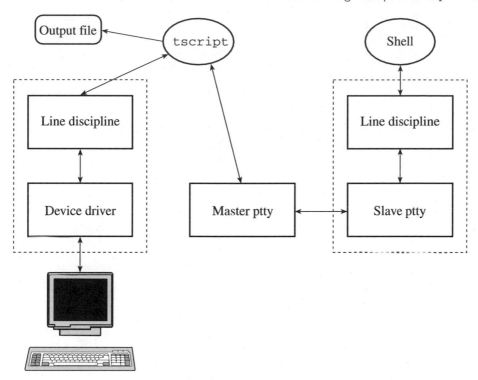

Figure 9.6 *The use of pseudo ttys for the* `tscript` *program.*

shell   Before the `shell` process is run, the line discipline STREAM modules are pushed onto the slave. The shell's standard input, standard output and standard error are then duplicated to be the slave pseudo tty device.

    A header file, `"tscript.h"`, is used throughout our example. Its contents are as follows:

```
/* tscript.h - header file for the tscript example */

#include <stropts.h>
#include <sys/types.h>
#include <sys/wait.h>
#include <sys/stream.h>
#include <sys/ptms.h>
#include <unistd.h>
#include <stdio.h>
#include <stdlib.h>
#include <fcntl.h>
#include <termio.h>
#include <signal.h>
```

```
/* internal functions */
void   catch_child(int);
void   runshell(int);
void   script(int);
int    pttyopen(int *,int *);

extern struct termios dattr;
```

The main tscript program is shown below. The first task of the program is to set up a signal handler for SIGCHLD and then open the pseudo tty. The program then creates the shell process. Finally the script routine is called which sits and reads input from the keyboard, which it passes to the master pseudo tty, or input from the master pseudo tty which it writes to the output file as well as passing to standard output.

```
/* tscript - terminal handling */

#include "tscript.h"
struct termios dattr;

main()
{
 struct sigaction  act;
 int               mfd, sfd;
 char              buf[512];

 /* save the current terminal settings */
 tcgetattr(0, &dattr);

 /* open the pseudo tty */
 if (pttyopen(&mfd, &sfd) == -1)
 {
      perror("opening pseudo tty");
      exit(1);
 }

 /* set up the action to be taken on receipt of SIGCHLD */
 act.sa_handler = catch_child;
 sigfillset(&(act.sa_mask));
 sigaction(SIGCHLD, &act, NULL);

 /* create the shell process */
 switch(fork()){
 case -1:    /* error */
      perror("fork failed on shell");
      exit(2);
 case 0:     /* child */
      close(mfd);
      runshell(sfd);

 default:    /* parent */
      close(sfd);
      script(mfd);
 }

}
```

The above calls four routines. The first is `catch_child`. This is a signal handler associated with the signal `SIGCHLD`. When `SIGCHLD` is received, `catch_child` resets the terminal attributes and then terminates.

```
void catch_child(int signo)
{
 tcsetattr(0, TCSAFLUSH, &dattr);
 exit(0);
}
```

The second routine, `pttyopen`, opens the pseudo tty.

```
int pttyopen(int *masterfd, int *slavefd)
{
  char *slavenm;

 /* open the pseudo tty -
  * obtain the file descriptor of the master ptty */
 if( (*masterfd = open("/dev/ptmx", O_RDWR)) == -1)
      return (-1);

 /* change the permissions of the slave ptty */
 if(grantpt(*masterfd)== -1)
 {
      close(*masterfd);
      return (-1);
 }

 /* unlock the slave device associated with mfd */
 if(unlockpt(*masterfd)== -1)
 {
      close(*masterfd);
      return(-1);
 }

 /* retrieve the name of the slave ptty and then open it */
 if( (slavenm = ptsname(*masterfd)) == NULL )
 {
      close(*masterfd);
      return (-1);
 }

 if( (*slavefd = open(slavenm, O_RDWR)) == -1)
 {
      close(*masterfd);
      return(-1);
 }

 /* construct the line discipline */
 if( ioctl(*slavefd, I_PUSH, "ptem") == -1)
 {
      close(*masterfd);
      close(*slavefd);
      return (-1);
 }
```

```
if( ioctl(*slavefd, I_PUSH, "ldterm") == -1)
{
     close(*masterfd);
     close(*slavefd);
     return (-1);
}

 return (1);
}
```

`runshell` is next. It performs the following tasks:

- Calls `setpgrp` so that the shell runs in its own process group. This allows the shell to have full control over signal handling, particularly with respect to job control.

- Invokes the `dup2` system call in order to set `stdin`, `stdout` and `stderr` to reference the slave file descriptor. This is a critical step.

- `execs` the shell, which runs until terminated by the user.

```
void runshell(int sfd)
{
 setpgrp();

 dup2(sfd, 0);
 dup2(sfd, 1);
 dup2(sfd, 2);

 execl("/bin/sh", "sh", "-i", (char *)0);

}
```

The first task of the actual `script` routine is to change the line discipline so that it functions in raw mode. This is achieved by retrieving the current attributes, changing them accordingly and calling `tcsetattr`. Next `script` opens the file `output`. The routine then uses the `select` system call (as discussed in Chapter 7) to poll for input on either standard input or the master pseudo tty. If information is received on standard input then `script` passes it unchanged to the master pseudo tty device. If however input is received on the master pseudo tty `script` writes the information to both the user's terminal and the `output` file.

```
void script(int mfd)
{
   int          nread, ofile;
   fd_set       set, master;
   struct       termios attr;
   char         buf[512];

   /* change the line discipline to raw mode */
   tcgetattr(0, &attr);
```

```
attr.c_cc[VMIN] = 1;
attr.c_cc[VTIME] = 0;
attr.c_lflag &= ~(ISIG|ECHO|ICANON);
tcsetattr(0, TCSAFLUSH, &attr);

/* open the output file */
ofile = open("output",O_CREAT|O_WRONLY|O_TRUNC,0666);

/* set the bit masks for the select system call */
FD_ZERO(&master);
FD_SET(0, &master);
FD_SET(mfd, &master);

/* select is called with no timeout,
 * it will block until an event occurs */
while(set=master, select(mfd+1, &set, NULL, NULL, NULL) > 0)
{
    /* check standard input */
    if(FD_ISSET(0, &set))
    {
        nread = read(0, buf, 512);
        write(mfd, buf, nread);
    }

    /* check the master device */
    if(FD_ISSET(mfd, &set))
    {
        nread = read(mfd, buf, 512);
        write(ofile, buf, nread);
        write(1, buf, nread);
    }

}
}
```

The following output shows how the `tscript` program is run. The comments, indicated by #, show which shell is being run.

```
$ ./tscript

$ ls -l tscript            # we are now running the new shell
-rwxr-xr-x    1 spate    fcf        6984 Jan 22 21:57 tscript

$ head -2 /etc/passwd      # running in the new shell
root:x:0:1:0000-Admin(0000):/:/bin/ksh
daemon:x:1:1:0000-Admin(0000):/:

$ exit                     # exit the new shell

$ cat output               # we are back at the original shell prompt
-rwxr-xr-x    1 spate    fcf        6984 Jan 22 21:57 tscript
root:x:0:1:0000-Admin(0000):/:/bin/ksh
daemon:x:1:1:0000-Admin(0000):/:
```

Exercise 9.5   Add proper error handling to the program and the option for the user to specify an alternative filename to be used as the output file. If no name is specified, use the name `output` by default.

Exercise 9.6   The equivalent standard UNIX program `script` allows an option -a which appends output to the `output` file. Implement a similar option.

CHAPTER 10

Sockets

10.1 Introduction

In previous chapters we have discussed a number of inter-process communication (IPC) mechanisms which can be used within a UNIX system. However, in the modern computing environment, users and developers are now confronted with a networked environment designed on a client/server basis. This configuration allows systems to share information and resources, such as files, disk space, processors and peripherals. A networked client/server environment inevitably means that processes will need to pass information and cooperate with each other where one process occurs on the client machine and the other on the server.

Due to its history, UNIX networking has grown in two directions. The Berkeley UNIX developers produced their famous and much used socket interface in the early 1980s while the System V developers released their Transport Level Interface (TLI) in 1986. The network programming section of the X/Open documentation is often called the *XTI*. The socket interface and the TLI are both supported in the *XTI*. The base concepts for both implementations are the same but the TLI uses many more structures and its implementation is far more complicated than the socket interface. Therefore it is the well-known and well-tried socket interface that we will be concentrating on in this chapter. Sockets provide a simple programming interface which is consistent for processes on the same machine or across different machines. In short, the aim of the socket is to provide a means of IPC that is sufficiently generic to allow bidirectional messages between two processes regardless of whether those processes reside on the same or different machines.

Our aim in this chapter is to give you something of a whirlwind tour of the basic concepts and facilities. It you want to go further, find a more detailed text (for example Stevens (1992)) or, even better, a friendly network programming expert.

Finally, you should note that you will normally need to link against special libraries (by adding *-lxnet* or other flags to the *cc* command line). See your local manual for details.

10.2 Types of connection

Processes which need to send information across a network can choose one of two ways to communicate. The **connection oriented model** or **virtual circuit** can be used by a process which needs to send an unformatted, uninterrupted stream of characters to the same constant destination; for example, a remote login connection where a client system has a virtual connection to a server. However, in some cases (for example, where the server wishes to send a broadcast message to its clients, and is not necessarily concerned that the clients receive the message) a process can use the **connectionless oriented model**. Here the process sends the message to a specified network address; it may then send the next message to a different address. It is often good to think about these in terms of metaphors. A connection oriented model is like the phone network. A connectionless model is like sending messages in a letter via the postal service. So, in the latter case, you can never be absolutely sure your message arrived and if you want a reply you have to supply your address with the letter. The connection model is good when you need genuine system to system interaction with a defined ordering of messages and acknowledgements. The connectionless model is more efficient and good for circumstances such as sending broadcasts to many machines.

For any communication to take place between processes on different machines, the client and the server need to be connected: at the hardware level by networking equipment such as cables, cards and devices such as routers, and at the software level by a standard set of networking protocols. A protocol is simply a set of rules, in this case a set of rules for sending messages between machines. A UNIX system therefore needs a set of rules for both the connection and connectionless oriented models. For the connection oriented model we use the Transmission Control Protocol, commonly known as TCP, and for the connectionless oriented model the User Datagram Protocol (UDP). A datagram is another term for a message packet.

10.3 Addressing

When processes are communicating across a network there must be a mechanism by which each process knows the **network address** of the machine that the other process resides on. The address essentially gives the physical location of a machine on a network. Addresses are generally layered, representing the different levels of a network. We are going to focus on what is necessary for programming with sockets.

10.3.1 Internet addressing

Across the world's networks there is an almost universally accepted addressing standard – internet (IP) addressing.

An IP address consists of four decimal numbers separated by periods. For example:

197.124.10.1

These four numbers carry sufficient information to specify the location of the destination network as well as the actual host machine on that network, hence the term *internet* – that is, a network spanning networks.

UNIX networking system calls cannot deal with the IP address in the four decimal number format. At the programming level IP addresses are stored in an in_addr_t type. Programmers need not concern themselves with the internal representation of this type, since there is a routine to convert the four figure decimal number to an in_addr_t type, which is called inet_addr.

Usage

```
#include <arpa/inet.h>

in_addr_t inet_addr(const char *ip_address);
```

---

inet_addr takes an IP address in the form of a string like "1.2.3.4" and returns the internet address in the appropriate type. If the call fails because the IP address string is not in the correct format, the return value will be (in_addr_t) - 1. For example:

```
in_addr_t server;

server = inet_addr("197.124.10.1");
```

If a process wishes to refer to its own machine address in later calls then the header file <netinet/in.h> defines the constant INADDR_ANY as a shorthand of the local host address in an in_addr_t format.

10.3.2 Ports

As well as knowing which machine to access, there must also be a way for the client program to connect to the correct server process. To this end a server process sits and listens for connections on a specified **port number**. Therefore a client process will ask for a connection to a particular machine *and* a specific port. To continue the previous postal analogy this would be the equivalent of putting the flat or room number as well as the address on the envelope.

Some numbers are well-known port numbers and are understood, by convention, to offer a particular service, for example ftp or rlogin. These numbers are laid down in the file /etc/services. In general, a port number less than 1024 is reserved for UNIX system processes. Anything above can be used for user processes.

10.4 Socket interface

To hold address and port information, standard structures are provided. A generic socket address structure is defined in the header file <sys/socket.h> as:

```
struct sockaddr{
 sa_family_t sa_family;   /* address family */
 char        sa_data[];   /* socket address */
};
```

This is described as a **generic socket** because in reality different types of sockets are used depending on whether the socket is used as a means of inter-process communication (IPC) on the same UNIX machine, or as an end point for communicating processes across a network. A specific form of socket for network communications is shown below:

```
#include <netinet/in.h>.

struct sockaddr_in{
 sa_family_t     sin_family;  /* internet address family */
 in_port_t       sin_port;    /* port number */
 struct in_addr  sin_addr;    /* holds the IP address */
 unsigned char   sin_zero[8]; /* filling */
};
```

10.4.1 Creation of a transport end point

In all forms of communication both the client and server must establish their own **transport end points**. These are the handles used to establish a link between processes across a network. Creation of these is achieved with the `socket` system call.

Usage

```
#include <sys/socket.h>

int socket(int domain, int type, int protocol);
```

`domain` tells the call where the socket is to be used. For example AF_INET specifies the internet domain for networking. Another domain, which may be of interest to the reader, is AF_UNIX, which is used if the processes are on the same machine.

The `type` of the socket to be created specifies whether it is to be used in a connection or connectionless mode. SOCK_STREAM specifies a connection oriented link, SOCK_DGRAM a connectionless link. The final parameter, `protocol`, specifies which protocol should be used by this socket. This will normally be set to 0, in which case, by default, a SOCK_STREAM socket will use TCP and a SOCK_DGRAM socket will use UDP – both standard UNIX protocols.

The `socket` system call normally returns a non-negative integer which is the socket file descriptor, which enables sockets to be treated using the familiar UNIX file model.

10.5 Programming the connection oriented model

It is now time to start the all-important example. To demonstrate some of the major socket-based system calls we will concentrate on an example where a client sends its server a stream of lower-case characters. The server converts them to upper case and sends them back to the client. In the later stages of this chapter we will demonstrate the same example in a connectionless communication mode.

Firstly, here is the code in outline form, for the server process:

```
/* server process */

/* include the necessary header files */
#include <ctype.h>
#include <sys/types.h>
#include <sys/socket.h>
#include <netinet/in.h>

main()
{
  int sockfd;
```

```
/* set up the transport end point */
if ( (sockfd = socket(AF_INET, SOCK_STREAM, 0)) == -1)
{
        perror("socket call failed");
        exit(1);
}


 /*
    "bind" server address to the end point

    start listening for incoming connections

    loop
       accept a connection
       spawn a child to deal with the connection
       if child
             send and receive information with the client
 */


}
```

The template for the client process is as follows:

```
/* client process */

/* include the necessary header files */
#include <ctype.h>
#include <sys/types.h>
#include <sys/socket.h>
#include <netinet/in.h>

main()
{
 int sockfd;

 /* set up the transport end point */
 if ( (sockfd = socket(AF_INET, SOCK_STREAM, 0)) == -1)
 {
        perror("socket call failed");
        exit (1);
 }

 /* connect the socket to the server's address
    send and receive information from the server */


}
```

We will now start filling in the gaps, starting with the server logic.

10.5.1 Binding

The bind system call associates the true network address of a machine with a socket identifier.

Usage

```
#include <sys/types.h>
#include <sys/socket.h>

int bind(int sockfd, const struct sockaddr *address,
         size_t add_len);
```

The first parameter, sockfd, is the socket file descriptor originally returned by the socket system call. The second parameter is here specified as a pointer to a generic socket structure. However, because we are sending information across the network in our example, we will actually provide the address of the relevant struct sockaddr_in which contains the addressing information for our server. The final parameter holds the size of the actual socket structure used. If the bind call is successful then it returns 0. On error, the bind call returns −1, which may happen if a socket already exists for the address. The errno will then contain EADDRINUSE.

10.5.2 Listening

After binding and before any client system can connect to the newly created server endpoint, the server must set itself up to wait for connections. It does this with listen.

Usage

```
#include <sys/socket.h>

int listen(int sockfd, int queue_size);
```

The sockfd parameter is as above. The server can queue up to queue_size incoming connection requests. (The *XTI* specifies a portable maximum of five such requests.)

10.5.3 Accepting

When the server receives a connect request from a client it has to create an entirely new socket to handle the *specific* communication. The first socket is used only to establish communication. Creation of the second socket is done using accept.

Usage

```
#include <sys/types.h>
#include <sys/socket.h>

int accept(int sockfd, struct sockaddr *address,
           size_t *add_len);
```

The `accept` system call is passed the listening socket descriptor returned from the original `socket` system call. On completion, the return value is the new socket id to be used for the communication. The `address` parameter is filled out with the information about the client. However, because this is a connection oriented communication the server very rarely needs to know the address of the client, and therefore `address` can be replaced with `NULL`. If `address` is not `NULL` then the variable pointed to by `add_len` should initially contain the length of the address structure described by `address`. On the return of the `accept` call, `*add_len` will hold the number of bytes actually copied.

With `bind`, `listen` and `accept` explained, the server code now becomes:

```
/* server process */

#include <ctype.h>
#include <sys/types.h>
#include <sys/socket.h>
#include <netinet/in.h>

#define SIZE sizeof(struct sockaddr_in)

int newsockfd;

main()
{
 int sockfd;

 /* initialize the internet socket with a port number of 7000
  * and the local address, specified as INADDR_ANY */
 struct sockaddr_in server = {AF_INET, 7000, INADDR_ANY};

 /* set up the transport end point */
 if ( (sockfd = socket(AF_INET, SOCK_STREAM, 0)) == -1)
 {
      perror("socket call failed");
      exit(1);
 }

 /* bind an address to the end point */
 if ( bind(sockfd, (struct sockaddr *)&server, SIZE) == -1)
 {
      perror("bind call failed");
      exit(1);
 }
```

```
/* start listening for incoming connections */
if ( listen(sockfd, 5) == -1 )
{
      perror("listen call failed");
      exit(1);
}

for ( ; ;)
{

      /* accept a connection */
      if ( (newsockfd = accept(sockfd, NULL, NULL)) == -1)
      {
            perror("accept call failed");
            continue;
      }

/*
spawn a child to deal with the connection
if child
      send and receive information with the client
 */

}

}
```

A key point here is the use of INADDR_ANY to represent the local machine.

We now have a server process capable of listening and accepting incoming connections. Let us now see how a client could ask for such a connection.

10.5.4 Connecting in the client

To ask for a connection to a server process and machine the client uses the aptly named connect system call.

Usage

```
#include <sys/types.h>
#include <sys/socket.h>

int connect(int csockfd, const struct sockaddr *address,
            size_t add_len);
```

The first parameter, csockfd, is the file descriptor for the associated client socket. This has no relationship to the socket id on the server. The address parameter is a pointer to the stucture containing the address of the server and, again, add_len is the length of the specific address structure being used.

Continuing our example, the client code can now be expanded to:

```
/* client process */

#include <ctype.h>
#include <sys/types.h>
#include <sys/socket.h>
#include <netinet/in.h>

#define SIZE sizeof(struct sockaddr_in)

main()
{
 int sockfd;
 struct sockaddr_in server = {AF_INET, 7000};

 /* convert and store the server's IP address */
 server.sin_addr.s_addr = inet_addr("206.45.10.2");

 /* set up the transport end point */
 if ( (sockfd = socket(AF_INET, SOCK_STREAM, 0)) == -1)
 {
      perror("socket call failed");
      exit (1);
 }

 /* connect the socket to the server's address */
 if ( connect(sockfd, (struct sockaddr *)&server, SIZE) == -1)
 {
      perror("connect call failed");
      exit(1);
 }

 /* send and receive information with the server */

}
```

It is here we need to know the network address of the server machine as used in the `inet_addr` call. The file `/etc/hosts` is usually a good place to start looking for addresses for your network.

10.5.5 Sending and receiving data

If all has gone well a circuit between client and server can now be established. As the sockets are set up to be of type SOCK_STREAM both the client and server will have a (different) file descriptor which can be used for either reading or writing. In most circumstances the `read` and `write` system calls can be used in the normal way. However, there are two new system calls which can be used if extra options need to be set about the way the data will be sent across the network. `send` and `recv` are as simple to use as `read` and `write`. In fact, if their fourth argument is set to 0 they behave identically.

Usage

```
#include <sys/types.h>
#include <sys/socket.h>

ssize_t recv(int sockfd, void *buffer, size_t length,
             int flags);

ssize_t send(int sockfd, const void *buffer, size_t length,
             int flags);
```

The recv call specifies the file descriptor to read the data from, the buffer into which the data should be put, and the length of the buffer. As with read, recv returns the amount of data read.

The flags parameter affects the way in which the data can be received. The possible values are:

MSG_PEEK   The process can look at the data without actually 'receiving' it.

MSG_OOB   Normal data is bypassed and the process only receives 'out of band' data, for example, an interrupt signal.

MSG_WAITALL The recv call will only return when the full amount of data is available.

send behaves just like write if the flags parameter is set to 0. It sends the message contained in buffer to sockfd, the local socket. The length parameter specifies the length of buffer. As with recv the flags parameter affects the way that messages are sent. The possible values are:

MSG_OOB   Send 'out of band' data.

MSG_DONTROUTE The message will be sent ignoring any routing conditions of the underlying protocol. Normally this means that the message will be sent via the most direct route rather than the quickest (the quickest could be more circuitous depending on the current load of the network).

We can now use these calls to convert the message received from lower to upper case in the server process:

```
/* server process */
    .
    .
    .
```

```
main()
{

/* socket initialization as shown previously */
.
.
.
char c;

for (;;)
{

        /* accept a connection */
        if ( (newsockfd = accept(sockfd, NULL, NULL)) == -1)
        {
                perror("accept call failed");
                continue;
        }

        /* spawn a child to deal with the connection */
        if ( fork() == 0)
        {
                /* receive data */
                while (recv(newsockfd, &c, 1, 0) > 0)
                {
                        /* convert to upper case and send back */
                        c = toupper(c);
                        send(newsockfd, &c, 1, 0);
                }
        }

}
}
```

Remember the `fork` call enables our server to serve multiple clients. The client code will contain:

```
/* client process */
.
.
.

main()
{
 int sockfd;
 char c, rc;

 /* socket initialization and connection request
  * as shown previously */
 .
 .
 .
```

```
/* send and receive information with the server */
for(rc = '\n';;)
{
    if (rc == '\n')
        printf("Input a lower case character\n");
    c = getchar();
    send(sockfd, &c, 1, 0);
    recv(sockfd, &rc, 1, 0);
    printf("%c", rc);
}
}
```

10.5.6 Closing the connection

It is very important to deal sensibly with unexpected death of the process at the other end of a socket. Since a socket is a two-way communication mechanism, it is not possible to predict whether a process will be trying to read or trying to write when the break in communication occurs. Both possibilities must be dealt with.

If a process attempts to write or send data to a socket which has become disconnected it will receive the SIGPIPE signal, which should be dealt with in the normal manner; that is, through a proper signal handler.

If read or recv returns zero this indicates end of file and therefore the connection. Thus the return value from read or recv should always be checked and dealt with accordingly.

The close system call can be used on a socket. If the SOCK_STREAM type is being used the kernel guarantees that all data sent to the socket will be sent to the receiving process. This may cause the close operation to be blocked until all outstanding data has been delivered. (If the type is SOCK_DGRAM then the socket is closed immediately.)

So finally we can now have a more complete client server example by adding signal handling to the server process and the close statement to both programs. In our example, this is not hugely relevant given the simplicity of the processing. However, in a real client/server environment these techniques will assure robust handling of exceptions.

```
/* server process */

#include <ctype.h>
#include <sys/types.h>
#include <sys/socket.h>
#include <netinet/in.h>
#include <signal.h>

#define SIZE sizeof(struct sockaddr_in)

void catcher(int sig);
int newsockfd;
```

```
main()
{
 int sockfd;
 char c;
 struct sockaddr_in server = {AF_INET, 7000, INADDR_ANY};
 static struct sigaction act;

 act.sa_handler = catcher;
 sigfillset(&(act.sa_mask));
 sigaction(SIGPIPE, &act, NULL);

 /* set up the transport end point */
 if ( (sockfd = socket(AF_INET, SOCK_STREAM, 0)) == -1)
 {
      perror("socket call failed");
      exit(1);
 }

 /* bind an address to the end point */
 if ( bind(sockfd, (struct sockaddr *)&server, SIZE) == -1)
 {
      perror("bind call failed");
      exit(1);
 }

 /* start listening for incoming connections */
 if ( listen(sockfd, 5) == -1 )
 {
      perror("listen call failed");
      exit(1);
 }

 for (;;)
 {

      /* accept a connection */
      if ( (newsockfd = accept(sockfd, NULL, NULL)) == -1)
      {
           perror("accept call failed");
           continue;
      }

      /* spawn a child to deal with the connection */
      if ( fork() == 0)
      {
           while (recv(newsockfd, &c, 1, 0) > 0)
           {
                c = toupper(c);
                send(newsockfd, &c,1, 0)
           }
           /* when client is no longer sending information
              the socket can be closed and the child process
              terminated */
           close(newsockfd);
           exit (0);
      }
```

```
        /* parent doesn't need the newsockfd */
        close(newsockfd);

    }

}

void catcher(int sig)
{
 close(newsockfd);
 exit (0);
}
```

And for the client:

```
/* client process */

#include <ctype.h>
#include <sys/types.h>
#include <sys/socket.h>
#include <netinet/in.h>

#define SIZE sizeof(struct sockaddr_in)

main()
{
 int sockfd;
 char c, rc;
 struct sockaddr_in server = {AF_INET, 7000};

 /* convert and store the server's IP address */
 server.sin_addr.s_addr = inet_addr("197.45.10.2");

 /* set up the transport end point */
 if ( (sockfd = socket(AF_INET, SOCK_STREAM, 0)) == -1)
 {
      perror("socket call failed");
      exit (1);
 }

 /* connect the socket to the server's address */
 if ( connect(sockfd, (struct sockaddr *)&server, SIZE) == -1)
 {
      perror("connect call failed");
      exit(1);
 }

 /* send and receive information with the server */
 for(rc = '\n'jj)
 {
      if (rc == '\n')
          printf("Input a lower case character\n");
      c = getchar();
      send(sockfd, &c, 1, 0);
```

```
        if(recv(sockfd, &rc, 1, 0)>0)
                printf("%c", rc);
        else
        {
                printf("server has died\n");
                close(sockfd);
                exit(1);
        }
  }


  }
```

Exercise 10.1 Run the code given and start up more than one client. What happens when all the client processes terminate?

Exercise 10.2 Adapt the code so that when all the client processes have terminated the server will timeout after a suitable period of time if no more new connections have been requested.

Exercise 10.3 Adapt the code so that the two communicating processes reside on the same machine. This time the socket will have to be of the AF_UNIX type.

10.6 Programming the connectionless oriented model

Now let us rewrite the example using the connectionless model. The main difference will be the fact that in connectionless mode the packets transmitted between the client and the server will arrive at their destination in an indeterminate order. From a programming viewpoint, in a connectionless model a process wishing to send or receive messages across a network must create its own local socket and bind its own network address to that socket. The process can now effectively use this socket as a gateway out on to the network. To send a message the process must know the destination address; this could be a 'broadcast address' covering many machines.

10.6.1 Sending and receiving messages

The only new system calls for the connectionless model are sendto and recvfrom.

The sockfd parameter in both calls specifies the locally bound socket through which messages will be sent and received.

Usage

```
ssize_t recvfrom(int sockfd, void *message, size_t length,
                 int flags, struct sockaddr *send_addr,
                 size_t *add_len);

ssize_t sendto(int sockfd, const void *message, size_t length,
               int flags, const struct sockaddr *dest_addr,
               size_t dest_len);
```

The recvfrom call works in exactly the same way as recv if send_addr is set to NULL. The message pointer is the buffer into which the received message will be placed and length is the number of bytes to be read into message. The flags parameter takes identical values to those in the recv call. The last two parameters are those which help with the connectionless form of communication. The send_addr structure will be filled with the address information of the machine which sent the message. This means that the receiving process can send a reply if it so wishes. The final parameter is a pointer to a size_t integer which, on completion of the call, will be filled out with the length of the address.

The sendto call is the opposite of recvfrom. This time the dest_addr parameter specifies the address of the peer for the message to be sent to, and dest_len specifies the length of the address.

The following reproduces our example as a connectionless oriented model.

```
/* server */

#include <ctype.h>
#include <sys/types.h>
#include <sys/socket.h>
#include <netinet/in.h>

#define SIZE sizeof(struct sockaddr_in)

main()
{
 int sockfd;
 char c;

 /* the local server port */
 struct sockaddr_in server = {AF_INET, 7000, INADDR_ANY};

 /* the structure to put in process2's address */
 struct sockaddr_in client;
 int client_len = SIZE;

 /* set up the transport end point */
 if ( (sockfd = socket(AF_INET, SOCK_DGRAM, 0)) == -1)
 {
      perror("socket call failed");
      exit(1);
 }
```

```
/* bind the local address to the end point */
if ( bind(sockfd, (struct sockaddr *)&server,SIZE)==-1)
{
     perror("bind call failed");
     exit(1);
}

/* sit in a continual loop waiting for messages */
for( ; ;)
{

     /* receives the message and stores the address of the
        client */
     if(recvfrom(sockfd, &c, 1, 0,
                 &client, &client_len)==-1)
     {
          perror("server: receiving");
          continue;
     }

     c = toupper(c);

     /* sends the message back to where it came from */
     if( sendto(sockfd, &c, 1, 0, &client, client_len) == -1)
     {
          perror("server: sending");
          continue;
     }

 }
}
```

And for the client:

```
/* client process */

#include <ctype.h>
#include <sys/types.h>
#include <sys/socket.h>
#include <netinet/in.h>

#define SIZE sizeof(struct sockaddr_in)

main()
{
 int sockfd;
 char c;

 /* the local port on the client */
 struct sockaddr_in client = {AF_INET, INADDR_ANY, INADDR_ANY};

 /* the remote address of the server */
 struct sockaddr_in server = {AF_INET, 7000};
 /* convert and store the server's IP address */
 server.sin_addr.s_addr = inet_addr("197.45.10.2");
```

```
/* set up the transport end point */
if ( (sockfd = socket(AF_INET, SOCK_DGRAM, 0)) == -1)
{
      perror("socket call failed");
      exit(1);
}

/* bind the local address to the end point */
if ( bind(sockfd, (struct sockaddr *)&client, SIZE) == -1)
{
      perror("bind call failed");
      exit(1);
}

/* read a character from the keyboard */
while( read(0, &c, 1) != 0)
{

      /* send the character to the server */
      if( sendto(sockfd, &c, 1, 0, &server, SIZE) == -1)
      {
            perror("client: sending");
            continue;
      }

      /* receive the message back */
      if(recv(sockfd, &c, 1, 0)== -1)
      {
            perror("client: receiving");
            continue;
      }

      write(1, &c, 1);

}
}
```

Exercise 10.4   Run the code with a number of clients. How can the server select which client to receive from?

10.7 The differences between the two models

It is worth reflecting on the differences between the two examples from a programming viewpoint.

In both models the server has to create a socket and bind its local address to that socket. In the connection model the server must then start to listen for incoming connections. This second step is not necessary in the connectionless scenario because the client will do more of the work.

From a client perspective, in the connection model, the client just connects to the server. In the connectionless model, the client must create a socket and bind its local address to that socket.

Finally, different system calls are normally used to transmit data. The send and recv system calls can be used in both models. However, the sendto and recvfrom calls are normally used in the connectionless model so that the server can retrieve information about the sender of the message and reply appropriately.

CHAPTER 11

The Standard I/O Library

11.1 Introduction

In the final chapters of the book we will examine some of the standard subroutine libraries provided by UNIX (and, with varying degrees of completeness, by a host of C compiler systems in other environments).

We will start by studying the extremely important *Standard I/O Library*, which forms a major part of the C library provided with all UNIX systems. We briefly introduced Standard I/O in Chapter 2, and you have already met a few of its constituent routines, for example: `getchar` and `printf`.

The main aim behind the Standard I/O Library is the provision of efficient, extensive and portable file access facilities. The routines that make up the library achieve efficiency by providing an automatic buffering mechanism, invisible to the user, which minimizes both the number of actual file accesses and the number of low-level system calls made. The library is extensive because it offers many more facilities, such as formatted output and data conversion, than the file access primitives `read` and `write`. Standard I/O routines are portable because they are not tied to any specific features of the UNIX system and, indeed, have become part of the UNIX-independent ANSI standard for the C Language. Any C compiler worth its salt will offer access to a full implementation of the Standard I/O Library, whatever the host operating system.

11.2 `FILE` **structures**

Standard I/O routines identify files by a pointer to a structure of type `FILE`. When a call to most Standard I/O routines is made, one of the parameters passed is a pointer to such a `FILE` structure which indicates which input or output file is to be used. A pointer to a `FILE` structure can therefore be compared to the integer file descriptors used with `read`, `write`, etc.

The definition of `FILE` is found in the standard header file `<stdio.h>`. It must be stressed that a programmer will only very rarely be concerned with the actual implementation of the `FILE` type. Indeed, its definition varies from system to system.

All data read or written to a file passes through the `FILE`'s character buffer. For example, an output routine from the Standard I/O Library will fill the buffer character by character. If the buffer becomes full, an internal Standard I/O routine will write its contents to the file using the `write` system call. This is invisible to the user program. The size of the buffer is `BUFSIZE` bytes. `BUFSIZE` is defined in `<stdio.h>`, and, as we saw in Chapter 2, it normally gives the disk blocking factor for the host environment. Typical values include 512 and 1024, or greater.

Similarly, an input routine will pull data out of the buffer associated with the `FILE` structure. If the buffer is emptied, another buffer-full will be read from the file, using the `read` system call. Again, this remains invisible to the user program.

The Standard I/O Library's buffering mechanism ensures that data is always read from or written to an external file in standard-size chunks. As a result, the numbers of file accesses and internal system calls are kept to an optimum level. However, since this buffering is performed internally by the Standard I/O routines themselves, a programmer can use routines from the library that logically read or write any number of bytes, even just one at a time. A program can therefore be written to reflect the structure of the problem, and efficiency matters largely left to the library. As we will also see, the standard library routines provide simple to use formatting features. For these reasons, Standard I/O is the preferred file access method for many applications.

11.3 Opening and closing file streams: `fopen` **and** `fclose`

Usage

`#include <stdio.h>`
 	
 `FILE * fopen(const char *filename, const char *type);`
 	
 `int fclose(FILE *stream);`

`fopen` and `fclose` are the Standard I/O Library's equivalents of `open` and `close`. The `fopen` routine opens the file identified by `filename` and associates a pointer to a `FILE` structure with it. If successful, `fopen` returns a pointer to a `FILE` structure to identify the open file (the `FILE` structure actually pointed to is a member of an internally maintained table). `fclose` closes the file identified by `stream`, and if it is being used for output flushes any data remaining in the internal buffer.

If `fopen` fails then it will return the constant `NULL`, which stands for a null pointer and is defined in `<stdio.h>`. Under these circumstances, the external integer `errno` will, as for `open`, contain a code indicating the cause of the error.

The second parameter to `fopen` points to a string which determines the mode of access. It can take the following basic values:

r   Open `filename` for reading only. (If the file does not exist the call will fail and `fopen` will return `NULL`.)

w   Create or truncate `filename`, and open it for writing only.

a   Open `filename` for writing only; any data written will be automatically appended to the end of the file. If the file does not exist then create it for writing.

A file can also be opened for update, which in this context means a program can both read and write to the file. In other words, a program can mix input and output operations for the same file, without reopening it. However, this is more restrictive than the read/write mode supported by `read` and `write`, due to the Standard I/O Library's buffering mechanism. In particular, output cannot be followed by input unless an intervening call to one of the two Standard I/O routines `fseek` or `rewind` is made. These routines adjust the internally maintained read–write pointer and are discussed below. Similarly, input cannot be followed by output without a call first to fseek or rewind, or an input routine which positions the program at end of file. Update mode is indicated by an additional '+' symbol on the type argument passed to fopen. All three of the strings we met above can be modified in this way:

r+   Open filename for reading and writing. Again, fopen will fail if the file does not exist.

w+   Create or truncate filename, and open it for reading and writing.

a+   Open for reading and writing. Data will be appended to the file end as it is written. If the file does not exist then it will be created for writing.

In some environments, a 'b' also needs to be added to r, w or a for access to binary, rather than text, files. For example: rb.

When fopen creates a file it will usually give it a permissions setting of 0666. This enables all users to read and write the file. These default permissions can be changed by setting the process' umask value to a non-zero value. (We introduced the umask system call in Chapter 3.)

The following skeleton program demonstrates the use of fopen and its relationship to fclose. It will cause the file indata to be opened for reading providing it exists, and the file outdata to be either truncated or created. fatal is the error routine we introduced in previous chapters. It will simply pass its string argument to perror, then call exit to terminate execution.

```
#include <stdio.h>

char *inname = "indata";
char *outname = "outdata";

main()
{
 FILE *inf, *outf;

 if( (inf = fopen(inname, "r")) == NULL)
      fatal("Could not open input file");

 if( (outf = fopen(outname, "w")) == NULL)
      fatal("Could not open output file");

 /* Do something interesting ..... */

 fclose(inf);
 fclose(outf);

 exit(0);
}
```

Actually, neither fclose call is needed in this particular context. The file descriptors associated with inf and outf will be automatically closed when the process exits, and `exit` will automatically 'flush' the data remaining in the buffer associated with `outf`, writing it to the file `outdata`.

A routine closely allied to `fclose` is `fflush`:

Usage

```
#include <stdio.h>

int fflush(FILE *stream);
```

This causes the output buffer associated with `stream` to be flushed; in other words, data in the buffer is written to the file immediately, regardless of whether the file buffer is full or not. It ensures that the external file matches the process' view of reality. (Remember, as far as the process is concerned, the data within the buffer has already been written to the file. The buffering mechanism is transparent.) Any *input* data is discarded.

`stream` remains open after the call to `fflush`. Like `fclose`, `fflush` will return the constant EOF on error, zero on success. (EOF is defined in `<stdio.h>` as −1. It actually stands for end of file, but can also be used for indicating errors.)

11.4 Single-character I/O: `getc` and `putc`

Usage

```
#include <stdio.h>

int getc(FILE *inf);

int putc(int c, FILE *outf);
```

The simplest input and output routines provided by the Standard I/O Library are `getc` and `putc`. The routine `getc` returns the next character from the input stream `inf`. `putc` places a character, here denoted by `c`, onto the output stream `outf`.

For both routines the character `c` is defined, perhaps counterintuitively, as `int` rather than `char`. This enables the routine to be used for 16 bit wide character sets. It also enables `getc` to return the constant EOF which, because it takes the value −1, lies outside the possible range of values for an `unsigned char` variable. EOF is used by `getc` to indicate either that it has reached end of file or that an error has occurred. `putc` can also return EOF, if an error occurs.

The following example is a new version of the `copyfile` routine we introduced in Chapter 2; instead of using `read` and `write`, we have used `getc` and `putc`:

```
#include <stdio.h>

/* copy file f1 to f2 using Standard I/O */

int copyfile(const char *f1, const char *f2)
{
 FILE *inf, *outf;
 int c;

 if( (inf = fopen(f1, "r")) == NULL)
      return (-1);

 if( (outf = fopen(f2, "w")) == NULL)
 {
      fclose(inf);
      return (-2);
 }

 while( (c = getc(inf) ) != EOF)
      putc(c, outf);

 fclose(inf);
 fclose(outf);
 return (0);
}
```

The basic form of the inner while loop is probably the closest thing the C language has to a cliché. Again, note how the variable c is defined as int rather than char.

Before moving on, a word of warning: getc and putc may not be functions. They may be macros defined in <stdio.h>, which are then expanded in line. Because they may be macros, getc and putc will not behave sensibly if they are given arguments with side effects. In particular, the expressions getc(*f++) and putc(c, *f++) will not produce the right results. Of course, the macro implementation ensures efficiency by eliminating unnecessary function calls. However, purists will be glad to know that fgetc and fputc are true functions, which do the same as their (almost) namesakes. They are rarely used, but are useful if function names need to be passed as parameters to other functions.

Exercise 11.1 In Exercises 2.4 and 2.5 we described a program called count which displayed the number of characters, words and lines in an input file. (Remember that a word is defined as either a single non-alphanumeric character or any contiguous sequence of alphanumeric characters.) Rewrite count using getc.

Exercise 11.2 Using getc, write a program which records the distribution of characters in a file; that is, a program which records the number of times each separate character appears in the file. One way of doing this would be to declare an array of long integers to act as counts, then use the integer value of each input character as an index into the array. In this case, make sure your program behaves sensibly, even if the char type is by default signed on your machine (which means input bytes could take negative integer values). Using printf and putc, make your program display a simple histogram of the distribution it finds.

11.5 Pushing characters back onto a file stream: ungetc

Usage

```
#include <stdio.h>

int ungetc(int c, FILE *stream);
```

ungetc inserts the character c back onto stream. This is a logical operation only. The input file itself will not be altered. If ungetc is successful, the character contained in c will be the next character read by getc. Only one character of pushback is guaranteed. If the attempt to insert c fails, ungetc returns EOF. An attempt to push back EOF itself will always fail. This is not usually a problem, however, since calling getc successively after end of file has been reached will result in EOF being returned on each occasion.

Typically, ungetc is used to restore an input stream to its original state after one character too many has been read to test a condition. The following routine getword exploits this simple technique to return a string which contains either a contiguous sequence of alphanumeric characters or a single non-alphanumeric character. End of file is denoted by a return value of NULL. The routine getword takes a FILE pointer as argument. It uses two test macros from the standard header file <ctype.h>. The first is isspace, which determines whether a character is a white-space character, such as space itself, tab or newline. The second is isalnum, which tests whether a character is alphanumeric; that is, a number or a letter.

```
#include <stdio.h>

/* for isspace and isalnum definitions */
#include <ctype.h>

#define MAXTOK      256

static char inbuf[MAXTOK+1];

char *getword(FILE *inf)
{
  int c, count = 0;
```

```
/* strip white space */
do{
      c = getc(inf);
} while( isspace(c) );

if(c == EOF)
      return (NULL);

if( !isalnum(c)) /* is character non-alphanumeric */
      inbuf[count++] = c;
else
{
      /* assemble "word" */
      do{
            if(count < MAXTOK)
                  inbuf[count++] = c;

            c = getc(inf);

      } while( isalnum(c));
      ungetc(c, inf);           /* push back character */
}

inbuf[count] = '\0';            /* make sure string returned */
return (inbuf);
}
```

If presented with the following input:

```
This is
the
 input data!!!
```

getword would return the following sequence of strings:

```
This
is
the
input
data
!
!
!
```

Exercise 11.3 Make getword understand numbers which might include a leading minus or plus sign and a decimal point.

11.6 Standard input, standard output and standard error

The Standard I/O Library offers three FILE structures connected to standard input, standard output and standard error. (As we warned some way back, do not be confused by the terminology. The Standard I/O Library and standard input are two entirely different things.) These standard FILE structures do not need to be opened, and are identified by the following FILE pointers:

stdin   Corresponds to standard input.

stdout   Corresponds to standard output.

stderr   Corresponds to standard error.

The following statement will get the next character from stdin, which, like file descriptor 0, defaults to the terminal keyboard:

```
inchar = getc(stdin);
```

Because stdin and stdout are used so much, two abbreviated forms of getc and putc are provided, namely getchar and putchar. getchar returns the next character from stdin, and putchar places a character onto stdout. Neither function takes a FILE pointer as argument.

The following program io2 uses getchar and putchar to copy its standard input to its standard output:

```
/* io2 -- copy stdin to stdout */

#include <stdio.h>

main()
{
  int c;

  while( (c = getchar() ) != EOF)
        putchar(c);
}
```

When compiled, io2 behaves more or less like the earlier io example from Chapter 2.

Like getc and putc, getchar and putchar may be defined as macros. In fact, getchar() will usually expand to getc(stdin) and putchar(c) will similarly expand to putc(c, stdout).

stderr is intended for error messages. Because of this special function, output to stderr is normally unbuffered. In other words, a character sent to stderr will immediately be written to the file or device currently attached to standard error. If you are fond of embedding temporary trace statements in your code for test purposes then it is advisable to write to stderr. Output to stdout is buffered and may be displayed one or two steps behind reality. (Alternatively, `fflush(stdout)` can be used to flush all messages held in the `stdout` buffer.)

Exercise 11.4 Using the standard `time` command, compare the performance of `io2` with the program `io` developed in Chapter 2. Adapt the original version of `io` so that it uses `read` and `write` to input, then output, a single character at a time. How do the performances of this and `io2` compare?

Exercise 11.5 Rewrite `io2` so that it more closely resembles the `cat` command. In particular, make it print out the contents of any files named in its command line arguments. Its input should default to `stdin` when no arguments are given.

11.7 Standard I/O status routines

A number of simple routines are provided for enquiring about the status of a FILE structure. In particular, they allow a program to determine whether a Standard I/O input routine such as `getc` has returned EOF because end of file really has been reached, or because an error has occurred. The available routines are listed in the following usage description:

Usage
`#include <stdio.h>`
`int ferror(FILE *stream);`
`int feof(FILE *stream);`
`void clearerr(FILE *stream);`
`int fileno(FILE *stream);`

`ferror` is a Boolean function that returns non-zero (that is, *true* as far as a C program is concerned) if an error has occurred on `stream` due to a previous input or output request. The error could have arisen due to a call to a file access primitive (`read`, `write`, etc.) failing within a Standard I/O routine. Conversely, if `ferror` returns zero (corresponding to *false*), no error has occurred. `ferror` can be used as follows:

```
if(ferror(stream))
{
 /* handle error */
 ...
}
```

```
else
{
 /* non-error branch */
 ...
}
```

 feof is a Boolean function that returns non-zero when an end of file condition has previously occurred on stream. A return value of zero indicates simply that EOF has not been reached.

 clearerr is used to reset both the error and end of file indicators to zero on stream. This ensures that future calls to ferror and feof for that file will return 0 unless some other exception has occurred in the meantime. For obvious reasons, clearerr is not a routine to be used lightly.

 fileno is the odd one out, since it is not concerned with error handling. It returns the integer file descriptor embedded in the FILE structure pointed to by stream. This is useful when you need to pass a file descriptor, instead of a FILE pointer, to a routine, However, do not use fileno to mix calls to the file access primitives and Standard I/O routines. Chaos will be the almost inevitable result.

 The following example, egetc, uses ferror to distinguish between an error and genuine end of file when a Standard I/O routine returns EOF:

```
/* egetc -  gotc with error checking */

#include <stdio.h>

int egetc(FILE *stream)
{
 int c;

 c = getc(stream);

 if(c == EOF)
 {
      if(ferror(stream))
      {
            fprintf(stderr, "fatal error: input error \n");
            exit(1);
      }
      else
            fprintf(stderr, "warning: EOF\n");
 }

 return (c);
}
```

 Note that all the functions described in this section are typically implemented as macros, and the usual caveats apply.

11.8 Input and output by line

Closely allied to the single-character I/O routines are a number of simple routines for reading and writing lines of data (a line being a simple sequence of characters terminated by a newline). These routines are suitable for interactive programs which read from the keyboard and write to the terminal screen. The basic line input routines are gets and fgets.

Usage

```
#include <stdio.h>

char * gets(char *buf);

char * fgets(char *buf, int nsize, FILE *inf);
```

---

gets reads a sequence of characters from standard input (stdin), placing each character into a buffer pointed to by buf. Characters are read until a newline or end of file is encountered. The newline character is then discarded and a null character is placed into buf to give a well-formed string. If successful, gets will return a pointer to buf. If an error occurs, or end of file is encountered and no characters have been read, NULL is returned instead.

fgets is a generalized version of gets. It reads characters from inf into the buffer buf until nsize-1 characters have been read, or a newline or end of file has been encountered. With fgets, newline characters are not discarded and are placed at the end of the buffer (this helps the calling function determine the condition that caused fgets to return). Like gets, fgets returns a pointer to buf if successful or NULL otherwise.

gets is a rather primitive routine. Because it does not know the length of the buffer passed to it, an unexpectedly long line can cause a gross internal error. fgets (in conjunction with stdin) should, for safety, be used instead.

The following routine, yesno, uses fgets in this manner to get a yes or no response from the user; it also calls isspace to skip white space in the answer:

```
/* yesno -- get yes or no response from user */

#include <stdio.h>
#include <ctype.h>

#define YES        1
#define NO         0
#define ANSWSZ     80

static char *pdefault = "Type 'y' for YES, 'n' for NO";
static char *error = "Unexpected response";

int yesno(char *prompt)
{
  char buf[ANSWSZ], *p_use, *p;
```

```
/* if prompt not NULL use it. Otherwise use pdefaults */
p_use = (prompt != NULL) ? prompt : pdefault;

/* loop until correct response */

for(;;)
{
        /* print prompt */
        printf("%s > ", p_use);

        if( fgets(buf, ANSWSZ, stdin) == NULL )
                return EOF;

        /* strip leading white space */
        for(p = buf; isspace(*p); p++)
                ;

        switch(*p){
                case 'Y':
                case 'y':
                        return (YES);
                case 'N':
                case 'n':
                        return (NO);
                default:
                        printf("\n%s\n", error);
        }
  }
}
```

The example assumes stdin is linked to a terminal. How could you make it safer?

The inverse routines for gets and fgets are puts and fputs, respectively.

Usage

```
#include <stdio.h>

int puts(const char *string);

int fputs(const char *string, FILE *outf);
```

---

puts writes the characters in string to standard output (stdout), excluding the terminating null character. fputs writes string to the file denoted by outf. To ensure compatibility with older versions of the system, puts appends a newline character while fputs does not. Both functions return EOF on error.

The following call to puts causes the message Hello, world to be printed on standard output. A newline is automatically added:

```
puts("Hello, world");
```

11.9 Binary input and output: `fread` and `fwrite`

Usage
| ```
#include <stdio.h>

size_t fread(void *buffer, size_t size, size_t nitems,
          FILE *inf);

size_t fwrite(const void *buffer, size_t size, size_t nitems,
          FILE *outf);
``` |

These two highly useful routines are provided for binary input and output. `fread` reads `nitems` objects of data from the input file corresponding to `inf`. The bytes read will be placed in the array `buffer`. Each object read is represented as a sequence of bytes which is `size` in length. The return value in `result` gives the number of objects successfully read.

`fwrite` is the exact inverse of `fread`. It will write the data contained in `buffer` to the output file denoted by `outf`. This `buffer` is considered as consisting of `nitems` objects which are `size` bytes long. The return value gives the number of records actually written.

These routines are typically used to transfer the contents of arbitrary C data structures to and from binary files. In such circumstances, the `size` parameter is then replaced by a call to `sizeof`, which gives the byte size of the structure.

The next example indicates how this works. It centres on a structure template `dict_elem`. An occurrence of this structure can be used to represent part of a record within a simple database system. To use database terminology, a `dict_elem` structure is intended to describe a database field or attribute. We have placed the definition of `dict_elem` in a header file called `dict.h`, which looks like:

```
/* dict.h -- header for data dictionary routines */

#include <stdio.h>

/* dict_elem -- data dictionary element */
/* describes a field in a database record */

struct dict_elem{
  char  d_name[15];       /* name of dictionary member */
  int   d_start;          /* starting position in record */
  int   d_length;         /* length of field */
  int   d_type;           /* denotes type of data */
};

#define ERROR      (-1)
#define SUCCESS    0
```
```

Without going into too much detail about the meaning of the structure, we will introduce two routines `writedict` and `readdict`, which write and read an array of `dict_elem` structures, respectively. The files these two routines create can be thought of as simple data dictionaries for records within the database system.

`writedict` takes two parameters, a name for the output file and the address of an array of `dict_elem` structures. This list is assumed to terminate at the first structure in the array in which the `d_length` member is equal to zero:

```c
#include "dict.h"

int writedict(const char *dictname, struct dict_elem *elist)
{
 int j;
 FILE *outf;

 /* open output file */
 if( (outf = fopen(dictname, "w")) == NULL)
      return ERROR;

 /* calculate length of array */
 for( j = 0; elist[j].d_length != 0; j++)
      ;

 /* write out list of dict_elem structures */
 if( fwrite((void *)elist, sizeof(struct dict_elem), j, outf) < j)
 {
      fclose(outf);
      return ERROR;
 }

 fclose(outf);
 return SUCCESS;
}
```

Notice how the address of the array `elist` is cast to a void pointer with `(void *)`. The use of `sizeof(struct dict_elem)` is another important aspect used to tell `fwrite` how big the `dict_elem` structure is in bytes.

The `readdict` routine uses `fread` to recover a list of structures from a file. It takes three parameters: `indictname`, which points to the name of the dictionary file, `inlist` which points to an array of `dict_elem` structures into which the list held on disk will be led, and `maxlength` which indicates the length of this array.

```c
struct dict_elem *readdict(const char *indictname,
                           struct dict_elem *inlist,
                           int maxlength)
{
 int i;
 FILE *inf;

 /* open input file */
 if( (inf = fopen(indictname, "r")) == NULL)
      return NULL;
```

```
/* read in dict_elem structures from file */
for( i = 0; i < maxlength - 1; i++)
        if( fread((void *)&inlist[i], sizeof(struct dict_elem),
                1, inf) < 1)
                break;

fclose(inf);

/* mark end of list */
inlist[i].d_length = 0;

/* return beginning of inlist */
return inlist;
}
```

Again, note the use of a cast and `sizeof`.

We should add an important caveat to this discussion. The binary data written to a file with `fwrite` reflects the internal storage of data within the system's memory. Since this is machine dependent, due to issues such as byte ordering and padding, data written on one machine may not be readable on another, unless considerable care is taken to put the information into a machine-independent format. Also, addresses stored in pointers should not be read or written for obvious reasons.

One final point: we could have used `read` and `write` directly to achieve much the same result. For example:

```
write(fd, (void *)ptr, sizeof(struct dict_elem));
```

The main advantage of the Standard I/O version is, again, efficiency. Data will ultimately be read and written in large blocks, whatever the size of the `dict_elem` structure.

Exercise 11.6 The present versions of `writedict` and `readdict` manipulate dictionary files that can really describe only one record type. Adapt them so that information on several record types can be held in the same file. In other words, allow a dictionary file to contain several independent, named lists of `dict_elem` structures. (Hint: include a 'header' structure at the top of the file that contains information on the numbers of record and field types.)

11.10 Random file access: `fseek,` `rewind` **and** `ftell`

The Standard I/O Library provides routines for random access which allow the programmer to reposition a file pointer in a file stream, or find out its current position. These routines are: `fseek`, `rewind` and `ftell`. They can be used only on files which support random access (which excludes terminals, for example).

Usage

```
#include <stdio.h>

int fseek(FILE *stream, long offset, int direction);

void rewind(FILE *stream);

long ftell(FILE *stream);
```

---

fseek parallels its low-level counterpart lseek and sets the file pointer within the file associated with stream. It therefore redefines the position of the next input or output operation. The parameter direction determines the starting point from which the new position in the file is to be calculated. If it is given the value SEEK_SET (typical value 0), the start of file is used; if it is SEEK_CUR (typical value 1), the current position is used; if it is SEEK_END (typical value 2) the end of file is used. offset gives the number of bytes to be added to this starting position. As with lseek, this value can be any valid long integer, including negative ones. Under normal circumstances fseek returns zero. A non-zero value indicates error.

rewind(stream) is a simple shorthand for:

```
fseek(stream, 0L, SEEK_SET);
```

In other words, it resets the read–write pointer to the beginning of the file.

ftell returns the program's current logical position within the file stream. This is given in terms of the number of bytes from the start of the file, counting from zero.

11.11 Formatted output: the printf **family**

Usage

```
#include <stdio.h>

/* NB parameters arg1 .. have arbitrary type */

int printf(const char *fmt, arg1, arg2 ... argn);

int fprintf(FILE *outf, const char *fmt, arg1, arg2 ... argn);

int sprintf(char *string, const char *fmt, arg1, arg2 ... argn);
```

These routines each take a format string fmt and a variable number of arguments of arbitrary type (denoted here by arg1, arg2, etc.) to produce an output string. This string will contain the information held in the parameters arg1 to argn using the format specified in fmt. With printf this string is then copied onto stdout. With fprintf it is copied to the file identified by outf. As for sprintf, it is not really an output function at all. The 'output' string created by sprintf is instead copied into the character array pointed to by the pointer string. For programming convenience, sprintf will also automatically add a terminating null character.

The format string argument fmt is a similar construct to the formats found in the ancient Fortran language. It contains a mixture of ordinary characters, which are copied verbatim, and a series of **conversion specifications**. These are sub-strings which always begin with the percentage sign '%' (if you need to print out the percentage sign itself, you must represent it by two percentage signs '%%').

There should be one such conversion specification for each of the arguments arg1, arg2, etc. Each conversion specification tells printf and its relatives the type of the corresponding argument, and how it is to be mapped to an output sequence of ASCII characters.

Before discussing the general form of these specifications, the following example demonstrates the use of a printf format for two simple cases. In the first there are no arguments apart from the fmt string itself. In the second there is one additional argument: the integer iarg.

```
int iarg = 34;
    .
    .
    .
printf("Hello, world!\n");
printf("The variable iarg has the value %d\n", iarg);
```

Because there are no arguments for conversion in the first call, there are no conversion specifications embedded in the format string. The statement therefore simply results in the message:

```
Hello, world!
```

being displayed on standard output, followed by a newline (remember, the symbol \n within a string is interpreted by C as standing for newline). In the second printf statement, there is one additional argument iarg and therefore one conversion specification within the format string, namely %d. This tells printf that the additional argument is an integer which is to be printed in decimal form (hence the use of the letter d). The output from this statement will therefore be:

```
The variable iarg has the value 34
```

The various forms of conversion specification possible include:

Integer conversions

%d   As we have seen, this is the standard conversion code for a signed integer. If the value is negative, a minus sign will be added automatically.

%u Argument is an `unsigned int`, to be printed in decimal form.

%o Argument is an integer, to be printed in unsigned octal form.

%x Argument is an integer, to be printed in unsigned hexadecimal form. The characters a, b, c, d, e, f will be used for the additional hexadecimal digits. If the specification %X is given instead, then A, B, C, D, E, F will be substituted.

%ld Argument is a `long`, signed integer, to be printed in decimal form. The programmer can also use %lo, %lu, %lx, %lX.

Floating-point conversion

%f Argument is of type `float` or `double`, to be printed in standard decimal form.

%e Argument is of type `float` or `double`, to be printed in exponential form, which is conventional in scientific applications. The letter e will be used to introduce the exponent. If the specification %E is given, upper case E will be used instead.

%g This is a mixture of the %e and %f specifications. It indicates that the argument it matches is either `float` or `double`. Floating-point or exponential notation (as for %e) will be used according to the size of the number. If %G is given instead, then the %E style will be used when appropriate.

String and character control

%c Argument is of type `char`, to be output exactly as it is, even if it is a 'non-printing' character. The numeric value held in a character can be displayed using an integer conversion code. This is useful if the character has no meaningful representation on your terminal.

%s The corresponding argument is taken to be a string (that is, a character pointer). The contents of this string will be transferred verbatim to the output stream. The string must, of course, be null-terminated.

The next example routine `warnuser` demonstrates use of the %c and %s conversions. It uses `fprintf` to print a warning message on standard error via the file stream `stderr`. If `stderr` corresponds to a terminal, the routine also attempts to ring the bell three times by sending *Ctrl-G* (ASCII *BEL*, which has value 0x07 in hexadecimal). The routine makes use of `isatty`, which determines whether a file descriptor corresponds to a terminal, and `fileno`, which returns the file descriptor associated with a file stream. `isatty` is a standard UNIX function we introduced in Chapter 9, while `fileno` is a part of the Standard I/O Library itself, described in Section 11.7.

```
/* warnuser -- ring bell, print message */

#include <stdio.h>

/* this works for most common terminals */
const char bel = 0x07;

void warnuser(const char *string)
{
 /* is it a terminal?? */
 if(isatty(fileno(stderr)))
       fprintf(stderr, "%c%c%c", bel, bel, bel);

 fprintf(stderr, "warning: %s\n", string);
}
```

Specifying width and precision

Conversion specifications can also include information about the minimum character **width** of a field in which an argument is printed, and the **precision** for that field. In the case of an integer argument, precision is taken to mean the minimum number of digits to appear. In the case of a float or double argument, the precision gives the number of digits to appear after the decimal point. With a string argument, it gives the maximum number of characters that can be taken from the string.

The width and precision information in a conversion specification appear immediately after the percentage sign, separated by a decimal point. For example:

```
%10.5d
```

means: *print the corresponding* int *argument in a field 10 characters wide; if the argument has fewer than five digits, pad it with leading zeros.* The specification:

```
%.5f
```

means: *print the corresponding* float *or* double *argument with five decimal places.* This particular example emphasizes that the precision part can occur on its own. Similarly, just the width can be given. So the specification:

```
%10s
```

means: *print the corresponding string in a field which is a minimum of 10 characters in length.*

All of the above examples will produce output which is right-justified within the specified character field. To ensure output is left-justified, a minus sign must appear immediately after the percentage symbol. So, the conversion specification:

```
%-30s
```

means that the corresponding string argument will be printed on the left-hand side of a field at least 30 characters across.

On occasion, the width part of a conversion specification cannot be calculated until the program is actually running. To get around this, the width specification can be replaced with an asterisk (*). printf will then expect the asterisk to be matched by an integer giving the desired field width. So:

```
int width, iarg;
.
.
.
printf("%*d", width, iarg);
```

will cause the integer iarg to be printed in a field width characters wide.

An economy pack example

The number of permutations of different formats is obviously immense, so to save space we have crammed several examples in the next, entirely unrealistic, example program. The function atan is the standard arctangent function from the UNIX maths library. (For this reason, if you try this example you must normally give the flag -lm, or similar, to cc in order to load the maths library during linking.)

```
/* cram -- economy pack printf demonstration */

#include <stdio.h>
#include <math.h>

main()
{
 char *weekday = "Sunday";
 char *month = "September";
 char *string = "Hello, world";

 int i = 11058;
 int day = 15, hour = 16, minute = 25;

 /* print a date */
 printf("Date is %s, %d %s, %d:%.2d\n",
         weekday, day, month, hour, minute);

 /* print newline again */
 putchar('\n');

 /* show width, precision interaction for string */
 printf(">>%s<<\n", string);
 printf(">>%30s<<\n", string);
 printf(">>%-30s<<\n", string);
 printf(">>%30.5s<<\n", string);
 printf(">>%-30.5s<<\n", string);

 putchar('\n');
```

```
/* print i in variety of styles */
printf("%d, %u, %o, %x, %X\n", i, i, i, i, i);

/* print pi to 5 decimal places */
printf("PI is %.5f\n", 4*atan(1.0));
}
```

This produces the following output:

```
Date is Sunday, 15 September, 16:25

>>Hello, world<<
>>                     Hello, world<<
>>Hello, world                    <<
>>                           Hello<<
>>Hello                           <<

11058, 11058, 25462, 2b32, 2B32
PI is 3.14159
```

Special symbols

Output conversion specifications can be complicated still further by some additional symbols. One such is hash or sharp, that is, #. It must occur immediately before the width part of a specification. For unsigned integer conversions involving the o, x, and X conversion codes, it causes one of 0, 0x or 0X to be automatically prepended to the output number as appropriate. So, the code fragment:

```
int arg = 0xFF;
printf("In octal, %#o\n", arg);
```

produces the output:

```
In octal, 0377
```

With floating-point conversions, a # will force a decimal point to be printed, even with zero precision.

The plus sign (+) can also be introduced in conversion specifications to force a + symbol to be printed when the number is positive. (This only has meaning for signed integers or floating-point numbers.) It occupies rather a peculiar place in the conversion specification, coming immediately after the minus sign that indicates left-justification, or the percentage symbol if no minus sign is present. The following lines of code:

```
float farg = 57.88;
printf("Value of farg is %-+10.2f\n", farg);
```

produce:

```
Value of farg is +57.88
```

Notice the combination of the minus and plus symbols. The + symbol could also be replaced with a space. In this case, printf would print out a space where a plus sign would appear. This enables negative and positive numbers to be properly aligned.

The sprintf *routine*

Before moving on, there is one point to make about sprintf. It is simply this: do not think of sprintf as an output routine. It provides, in fact, the most flexible string manipulation and general conversion facilities in the C libraries. The following code fragment indicates how it might be used:

```
/* genkey -- generate key for use in database */
/*          key will always be 20 chars long */

#include <stdio.h>
#include <string.h>

char * genkey(char *buf, const char *suppcode, long orderno)
{
 /* is suppcode valid? */
 if(strlen(suppcode) != 10)
        return (NULL);

 sprintf(buf, "%s_%.9ld", suppcode, orderno);

 return (buf);
}
```

The following call to genkey:

```
printf("%s\n", genkey(buf, "abcdefghij", 12));
```

will produce this string:

```
abcdefghij_000000012
```

11.12 Formatted input: the scanf **family**

Usage

```
#include <stdio.h>

/* NB: ptr1 .. ptrn are all pointers.
 * The type of the variable they point
 * to is arbitrary.
 */
```

```
int scanf(const char *fmt, ptr1, ptr2, ... ptrn);

int fscanf(FILE *inf, const char *fmt, ptr1, ptr2 ... ptrn);

int sscanf(const char *string, const char *fmt, ptr1, ptr2 ... ptrn);
```

These routines are the inverse of the routines in the printf family. They all accept input from a file (or string in the case of sscanf), decode this according to format information carried in the string fmt, and place the resulting data into the variables indicated by the pointers ptr1 to ptrn. The file pointer is advanced by the number of characters processed.

scanf will always read from stdin. The routine fscanf reads from the file denoted by inf. The routine sscanf is the black sheep of the family and decodes a string pointed to by string rather than accept input from a file. Because it acts on a string held in memory, sscanf is particularly useful when an input string has to be read more than once.

The format string fmt is similar in structure to the format strings used by printf. For example, the following statement reads the next integer on standard input:

```
int inarg;

scanf("%d", &inarg);
```

The most important thing to note here is that scanf is given the address of inarg. This is because C is only able to pass parameters by value, and never by reference. Therefore, if we want scanf to alter a variable that lives in the calling routine, we must pass it a pointer which contains the address of that variable. It is all too easy to forget the ampersand, and this can cause a memory fault. Enthusiastic novices should also resist the temptation to over-compensate by placing ampersands before existing pointers or addresses, such as the name of character arrays.

In general a scanf format string can contain:

1. *White-space characters*; that is, blanks, tabs, newlines and form-feeds. Usually, this matches all white space from the current position in the input stream, up until the first non-white-space character.

2. *Ordinary, non-white-space characters.* These must match exactly the corresponding characters in the input stream.

3. *Conversion specifications.* As we mentioned earlier, these are in general very similar to the specifications used with printf.

The next example shows the use of scanf with several variables of different types:

```
/* demo program for scanf */

#include <stdio.h>

main()
{
 int i1, i2;
 float flt;
 char str1[10], str2[10];

 scanf("%2d %2d %f %s %s", &i1, &i2, &flt, str1, str2);
 .
 .
 .
}
```

The first two conversion specifications within the format string tell scanf to look for two integers (in decimal format). Because a field width of two is given in each case, the first integer will be assumed to be held in the next two characters read, while the second will lie in the two positions after that (in general, a field width denotes the maximum number of characters that a value can occupy). The %f specification denotes a variable of type float. %s indicates that a string, delimited by white-space characters, is expected. So, if this program was to be presented with the input sequence

11 12 34.07
keith ben

the result would be as follows:

i1 would be set to 11

i2 would be set to 12

flt would be set to 34.07

The string str1 would contain "keith"

The string str2 would contain "ben"

Both strings would be null-terminated. Note that str1 and str2 must have been defined large enough to hold the expected input strings and the terminating null. It is not good enough to pass a non-initialized character pointer to scanf.

With the conversion specification %s, the string in question is expected to be delimited by white-space characters. To read white-space and other characters the %c conversion code should be used. For example, the statement:

```
scanf ("%10c", s1);
```

will read in the next 10 characters from the input stream, whatever they are, and place them into the character array s1. Because the c conversion code matches white space, the specification %1s should be used to get the next non-space character. For example:

```
/* read in 2 chars, starting at 1st non-space char */
scanf("%1s%1c", &c1, &c2);
```

Another way of specifying string data, and one that has no equivalent in the format strings used with printf, is the scan-set. This is a sequence of characters placed between square brackets: [and]. The input field is taken to be the longest sequence of characters that matches characters in the scan-set (and in this case white space is not skipped unless it is part of the scan-set). For example, the statement:

```
scanf("%[ab12]%s", str1, str2);
```

will, when presented with the input string:

```
2bbaa1other
```

place 2bbaa1 into the string str1 and other into the string str2.

There are several useful conventions used in the construction of scan-sets, conventions that should be familiar to users of grep and ed. For example, a range of characters is denoted by a substring like *first-last*. So, [a-d] is equivalent to [abcd]. If the dash (-) is to appear as part of the scan-set itself, it must be the first or last character. Similarly, if the right square bracket] is to appear, then it must be the first character after the opening [. If the circumflex (^) appears as the first character in the scan-set, then the scan-set is redefined as all the characters *not* in the present scan-set.

For assignments to long integers and floating-point variables of type double, an l (ell) must follow the percentage symbol in the corresponding conversion specification. This enables scanf to determine the size of the parameter it is dealing with. The following program fragment shows how to read variables of both types from the input stream:

```
long l;
double d;

scanf("%ld %lf", &l, &d);
```

One other situation that will often occur is when the input stream contains more data than the programmer is interested in. To deal with this, a conversion specification can contain an asterisk (*) immediately after the leading percentage symbol. This indicates assignment suppression. In effect, an input field which matches the specification is ignored. The call:

```
scanf("%d %*s %*d %s", &ivar, string);
```

with the input line:

131 cat 132 mat

will cause `scanf` to assign `131` to `ivar`, skip the next two fields, then place `mat` into `string`.

Finally, what of the return value for members of the `scanf` family? They will normally return the number of successfully matched and assigned items. This return value can be zero when an early conflict occurs between a format string and the actual input. If the input runs out before a successful match of a conversion conflict, then `EOF` is returned.

Exercise 11.7 Write a program that takes its arguments, which should be decimal integers, and displays them in hexadecimal and octal form.

Exercise 11.8 Write `savematrix`, which should save an integer matrix of arbitrary dimensions in a file in readable form, and `readmatrix`, which recovers a matrix from file. Use only `fprintf` and `fscanf` to do the work. Ensure that the amount of white space (blanks, tabs, etc.) within the file is kept to a minimum. Hint: use the variable width symbol (`*`) when writing the file.

11.13 Running programs with the Standard I/O Library

The Standard I/O Library provides a small number of routines for running one program from another. The most basic of these is a routine we have met before: `system`, which is now properly regarded as a general purpose routine.

Usage
`#include <stdlib.h>`
`int system(const char *comstring);`

`system` runs the command contained in `comstring`. It does this by first creating a child process. This in turn calls `exec` to run a standard UNIX shell with `comstring` as input. The `system` routine in the first process invokes `wait` to ensure that it only continues execution after the command has finished. The eventual return value `retval` gives the exit status of the shell, from which the success or failure of the command can be determined. If either of the calls to `fork` or `exec` fails, then `retval` will contain −1.

Because the shell is invoked as intermediary, `comstring` can be any command that could be typed at a terminal. This enables the programmer to take advantage of facilities such as file name expansion, I/O redirection and so on. The following statement uses system to create a subdirectory with the mkdir program:

```
if( (retval = system("mkdir workdir")) != 0)
    fprintf(stderr, "system returned %d\n", retval);
```

Some points of detail. Firstly, system in the *calling* process will ignore the signals SIGINT and SIGQUIT. This allows the user to safely interrupt a command without disturbing the parent process. Secondly, the command run by system will inherit some open file descriptors from the calling process. In particular, the command will take its standard input from the same source as the parent process. If this is a file, then it can pose problems when system is used to run an interactive program, since the program will take its input from the file. The following program fragment shows one possible solution to this problem. In it, fcntl is used to ensure that standard input, identified by file descriptor 0, corresponds to the processes controlling terminal /dev/tty. The example calls the fatal function we introduced earlier.

```
#include <stdio.h>
#include <fcntl.h>
    .
    .
    .
int newfd, oldfd;
    .
    .
    .
/* dup. current file descriptor for std input */
if( (oldfd = fcntl(0, F_DUPFD, 0)) == -1)
    fatal("fcntl failed");

/* open controlling terminal */
if( (newfd = open("/dev/tty", O_RDONLY)) == -1)
    fatal("open failed");

/* close standard input */
close(0);

/* create a new standard input */
if( (fcntl(newfd, F_DUPFD, 0) != 0)
    fatal("fcntl problem");

close(newfd);

/* start up interactive editor */
if(system("ed newfile") == -1)
    fatal("system failed");

/* restore old standard input */
close(0);
```

```
if(fcntl(oldfd, F_DUPFD, 0) != 0)
    fatal("fcntl problem");
close(oldfd);
    .
    .
    .
```

system has one major disadvantage. It does not allow a program to directly access the output generated by the command it runs. To do this, the programmer can make use of two more routines from the Standard I/O Library: popen and pclose.

Usage
#include <stdio.h> FILE * popen(const char *comstring, const char *type); int pclose(FILE *strm);

Like system, the popen routine creates a child shell process to run the command pointed to by comstring. Unlike system, it also creates a pipe between the calling process and the command. It then returns the FILE structure associated with the pipe. If type is "w", the program is able to write to the standard input of the command via the FILE structure. If type is "r" instead, the program will be able to read the command's standard output. In this way popen provides a simple, clean method of communicating with another program.

pclose should always be used to close a stream that has been opened by popen. It will wait for the command to terminate, then returns its exit status.

The following example routine, getlist, uses popen and the ls command to obtain a directory listing. Each filename is then placed into a two-dimensional character array, the address of which has been passed to getlist as a parameter.

```
/* getlist -- routine for getting filenames from directory */

#include <stdio.h>
#include <string.h>

#define    MAXLEN     255    /* maximum filename length */
#define    MAXCMD     100    /* maximum length of command */
#define    ERROR      (-1)
#define    SUCCESS    0

int getlist(char *namepart, char dirnames[][MAXLEN+1],
            int maxnames)
{
  char cmd[MAXCMD+1], inline[MAXLEN+2];
  int i;
  FILE *lsf;
```

```
/* first form command */
strcpy(cmd, "ls ");

/* add additional part of command */
if(namepart != NULL)
        strncat(cmd, namepart, MAXCMD - strlen(cmd));

if(( lsf = popen(cmd, "r")) == NULL) /* start up command */
        return (ERROR);

for(i = 0; i < maxnames; i++)
{
        if(fgets(inline, MAXLEN+2, lsf) == NULL)
                break;

        /* remove newline */
        if(inline[strlen(inline)-1] == '\n')
                inline[strlen(inline)-1] = '\0';

        strcpy(&dirnames[i][0], inline);
}

if(i < maxnames)
        dirnames[i][0] = '\0';

pclose(lsf);
return(SUCCESS);
}
```

`getlist` can be used with a call such as:

```
getlist("*.c", namebuf, 100);
```

This will place the name of C programs in the current working directory into
`namebuf`.

The next example solves a common problem for the administrators of UNIX
systems: how to quickly 'unfreeze' a terminal which has been jammed, for example,
by an untested screen-oriented program. `unfreeze` takes a terminal name and a list
of programs as its arguments. It then runs the process status command `ps` via `popen`
to obtain the list of processes associated with the terminal. It searches this list for
any processes running one of the named programs. For all processes that fulfil this
criterion, `unfreeze` asks the user whether or not it should be killed.

`ps` is a highly system-dependent program. This is because it has to examine
the kernel directly (via a special file that represents memory) to get hold of the
system's process table. On the machine we used for this example, the `ps` command
which displays the processes associated with a particular terminal has the general
form:

`$ ps -t ttyname`

where `ttyname` is the name of a terminal special file in the /dev directory, such as tty01, `console`, pts/8 etc. Again referring just to the machine on which we developed the example, this type of `ps` command produces output like:

PID	TTY	TIME	COMMAND
29	co	0:04	sh
39	co	0:49	vi
42	co	0:00	sh
43	co	0:01	ps

Column 1 contains the process-id. Column 2 contains the name of the terminal in question; here `co` stands for console. Column 3 gives the cumulative execution time for the process. Lastly, column 4 gives the name of the program which is running. Notice the first line, which acts as a column header. It will have to be discarded by `unfreeze`, the source for which follows:

```
/* unfreeze -- unfreeze a terminal */

#include <unistd.h>
#include <stdio.h>
#include <signal.h>

#define     LINESZ      50
#define     SUCCESS     0
#define     ERROR       (-1)

main(int argc, char **argv)
{
/* the initialization of these depends on your system */
static char *pspart = "ps -t ";
static char *fmt = "%d %*s %*s %s";

char comline[LINESZ], inbuf[LINESZ], header[LINESZ];
char name[LINESZ];
FILE *f;
int killflag = 0, j;
pid_t pid;

if(argc <= 2)
{
        fprintf(stderr, "usage: %s tty program ...\n", argv[0]);
        exit(1);
}

/* assemble command line */
strcpy(comline, pspart);
strcat(comline, argv[1]);

/* start ps command */
if((f = popen(comline, "r")) == NULL)
{
        fprintf(stderr, "%s:could not run ps program\n", argv[0]);
        exit(2);
}
```

```
/* get and ignore first line from ps */
if( fgets(header, LINESZ, f) == NULL)
{
     fprintf(stderr, "%s:no output from ps?\n", argv[0]);
     exit(3);
}

/* look for program to kill */
while(fgets(inbuf, LINESZ, f) != NULL)
{
     if(sscanf(inbuf, fmt, &pid, name) < 2)
          break;

     for(j = 2; j < argc; j++)
     {
          if(strcmp(name, argv[j]) == 0)
          {
               if(dokill(pid, inbuf, header) == SUCCESS)
                    killflag++;
          }
     }
}

/* this is a warning, not an error */
if(!killflag)
     fprintf(stderr, "%s: no program killed on %s\n", argv[0],
                                                       argv[1]);

exit(0);
}
```

The dokill routine called by unfreeze is implemented as shown below. Notice the use of scanf to read the first non-space character (we could have instead used the yesno function introduced in Section 11.8).

```
/* confirm then kill */
int dokill(pid_t procid, const char *line, const char *hd)
{
 char c;

 printf("\nProcess running named program found :\n");
 printf("\t%s\t%s\n", hd, line);
 printf("Type 'y' to kill process %d\n", procid);
 printf("\nAnswer > ");

 /* get next non-white space character */
 scanf("%1s", &c);

 if(c == 'y' || c == 'Y')
 {
      kill(procid, SIGKILL);
      return(SUCCESS);
 }
 return(ERROR);
}
```

Exercise 11.9 Write your own version of `getcwd`, the routine that returns a string containing the name of the current working directory. Call your version `wdir`. Hint: use the standard command `pwd`.

Exercise 11.10 Write a program called `arrived` that uses the `who` program in conjunction with `popen` to check (at intervals of 60 seconds) whether one or more people from a list of users has logged on. The list of names should be passed to `arrived` via command line arguments. When it detects a user from the list, `arrived` should display a message. Your program must be efficient. Make sure you use `sleep` to suspend execution between checks. The `who` command will be described in your system's user manual.

11.14 Miscellaneous calls

In this section we will briefly describe miscellaneous calls from the Standard I/O Library. For more details consult your system's official documentation.

11.14.1 `freopen` and `fdopen`

Usage
| ```
#include <stdio.h>

FILE * freopen(const char *filename, const char *type,
               FILE *oldstream);

FILE * fdopen(int filedes, const char *type);
``` |

`freopen` closes `oldstream`, then reopens it for input from `filename`. `type` determines the mode of access for the new `FILE` structure and takes the same value as its counterpart for `fopen` (r, w, etc.). It is usually used for reassigning `stdin`, `stdout` or `stderr`. For example:

```
if(freopen("new.input", "r", stdin) == NULL)
  fatal("stdin could not be reassigned");
```

`fdopen` associates a new `FILE` structure with an integer file descriptor `filedes` that has been obtained from a previous call to one of the system calls `creat`, `open`, `pipe` or `dup2`.

Both routines return `NULL` on error.
```

11.14.2 Buffer control: `setbuf` and `setvbuf`

> **Usage**
>
> ```
> #include <stdio.h>
>
> void setbuf(FILE *stream, char *buf1);
>
> int setvbuf(FILE *stream, char *buf2, int type, size_t size);
> ```

Both these routines allow the programmer to control to some extent the buffering associated with a file. They must be used after a file has been opened, but before it is read or written.

`setbuf` is used to substitute `buf1` in place of the buffer normally allocated by the Standard I/O Library. The size required of `buf1` is determined by the constant `BUFSIZ` from `<stdio.h>`.

If `setbuf` is passed a `NULL` character pointer instead, then input or output will be unbuffered. This can be useful during debugging when the program is terminating abnormally, and data held in buffers is being lost.

`setvbuf` allows finer control than `setbuf`. The `buf2` parameter gives the address of an optional new buffer. `size` specifies the size of `buf2`. If `NULL` is passed, instead of an actual address, then default buffering will be used. The `type` parameter to `setvbuf` determines how `stream` is to be buffered. It can be used to tailor the file stream for use with disk files or terminal devices. The three permitted values for `type` are taken from `<stdio.h>`. They are:

_IOFBF   The file stream will be fully buffered. This is the default for all file streams not attached to a terminal. Data will therefore be written, or read, in chunks of `BUFSIZ` bytes to maximize efficiency.

_IOLBF   Output will be line-buffered, and the buffer will be flushed whenever a newline is written. It will also be flushed when the buffer is full, or input is requested. This is the default for terminals, and is designed to aid interactive use.

_IOBNF   This causes input and output to be unbuffered. In this case `buf2` and `size` will be ignored. This is a mode suitable, among other things, for error logging.

Note that if an illegal value for either `type` or `size` is given, `setvbuf` returns a non-zero value. Conversely, zero denotes success.

CHAPTER 12

Miscellaneous system calls and library routines

12.1 Introduction

In this final chapter we examine a handful of system calls and some useful library routines that did not logically fit into previous chapters. The topics we will cover include memory management, time functions, character validation and string manipulation.

12.2 Dynamic memory management

Each of the programs we have examined so far has used data structures which were totally determined by standard C declarations, such as:

```
struct something x, y, *z, a[20];
```

In other words, the layout of the data used by our examples has been determined at compile time. Many computing problems, however, are best approached by creating and destroying data structures dynamically, which means the data layout used by the program is only finally determined during execution. Under UNIX, the `malloc` family of library functions (the name `malloc` stands for memory allocation) allow the C programmer to create objects dynamically on the program 'heap'. `malloc` itself is defined as follows:

Usage

```
#include <stdlib.h>

void *malloc(size_t nbytes);
```

This call normally causes `malloc` to return a pointer to `nbytes` bytes worth of contiguous new storage. In effect, the program has gained an extra array of characters which it can use as it sees fit. If there is insufficient memory available, and `malloc` cannot allocate the requested amount, it returns a null pointer instead.

Perhaps more typically, `malloc` can also be used to create storage to hold one (or more) data structures. For example:

```
struct item *p;

p = (struct item *) malloc(sizeof(struct item));
```

If successful, this `malloc` call creates a new `item` structure, which can be referenced via the pointer p. Notice how the return value from `malloc` is cast into the appropriate pointer type. This will avoid complaints from the compiler or tools such as `lint`. The cast is meaningful because `malloc` is implemented so that the storage it returns can hold any type of object, providing the amount of space requested is big enough. Problems such as word alignment are taken care of internally by the `malloc` algorithm. Note how the size of the `item` structure is obtained with the C operator `sizeof`, which returns a value measured in bytes.

The inverse of `malloc` is `free`, which releases storage previously allocated by the `malloc` algorithm, making it available for reuse. `free` is passed a pointer that was previously obtained from a call to `malloc`:

```
struct item *ptr;
.
.
.

ptr = (struct item *)malloc( sizeof(struct item) );

/* do the work ... */

free( (void *)ptr );
```

After free has been called in this way, the space pointed to by ptr must not be used, since malloc may later reallocate all or part of it. It is very important that free is passed a pointer that really was originally generated by malloc, or one of its two sister functions calloc or realloc (described shortly). If the pointer does not fit this criterion, serious memory errors will almost certainly result, leading to erroneous program behaviour or even a catastrophic core dump. Misuse of free is a very, very common programming error.

Two more functions in the malloc family are directly concerned with memory allocation. The first of these is calloc.

Usage

```
#include <stdlib.h>

void * calloc(size_t nelem, size_t nbytes);
```

---

calloc allocates space for an array of nelem elements each of which is nbytes in size. It is typically used along the following lines:

```
/* allocate array of structures */

struct item *aptr;
 .
 .
 .
aptr = (struct item *) calloc(nitem, sizeof(struct item));
```

Unlike malloc, the storage allocated by calloc is set to zeros, which obviously has an execution time overhead, but can be useful when such initialization is required.

The final allocation function in the malloc family is realloc.

Usage

```
#include <stdlib.h>

void * realloc(void *oldptr, size_t newsize);
```

---

realloc is used to change the size of the memory block pointed to by oldptr, which must have been obtained previously from either malloc, calloc or realloc. realloc may have to move the block within memory, so a pointer is returned to mark its new starting position. The contents of the block are preserved up to the smaller of the new and old sizes.

A `malloc` *example: linked lists*

There are many types of dynamic data structure encountered in computer science. One classical example is the linked list, where a group of identical objects are chained into a single logical entity. In this section we will develop a simple linked list example to demonstrate use of the `malloc` family. We will start by looking at the header file `list.h`:

```
/* list.h -- header file for linked list example */
#include <stdio.h>
#include <stdlib.h>

/* fundamental structure definition */

typedef struct list_member {
 char *m_data;
 struct list_member *m_next;
} MEMBER;

/* function definitions */
MEMBER *new_member(char *);
void add_member(MEMBER **head, MEMBER *newmem);
void free_list(MEMBER **head);
void printlist(MEMBER *);
```

The `typedef` statement introduces a type called MEMBER, which has two fields. The first `m_data` will, in an actual occurrence of a MEMBER, point to some arbitrary string. The second component `m_next` points to another MEMBER. In defining `m_next`, we have to use `struct list_member *m_next` rather than `MEMBER *m_next` for syntactical reasons.

In a linked list of MEMBER-type structures, each `m_next` will point to the next MEMBER in the list; that is, given one element of the list, we can find the next simply by using its `m_next` pointer. Because there is only one pointer for each MEMBER in the list, it can only be scanned in one direction. Such lists are described as being **singly linked**. If we had defined an `m_prev` pointer, the list could also be joined in the reverse direction, and would in this case be **doubly linked**.

The address of the start or head MEMBER of a list is usually recorded in a special pointer declared in a manner similar to:

```
MEMBER *head = (MEMBER *)0;
```

The end of a list is marked by a null value in the `m_next` field of the last actual MEMBER in the list.

A simple three-element list is shown in Figure 12.1. Its start is indicated by a pointer called `head`.

We will now introduce a small set of routines for manipulating these structures. The first function we shall look at is called `new_member`. It uses `malloc` to create enough store for a MEMBER structure. Notice the way we set the `m_next`

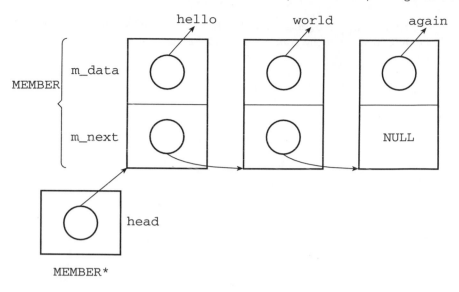

Figure 12.1 *A linked list of* MEMBER*s.*

pointer to a null pointer, here represented as (MEMBER *)0. This is because malloc does not zero the memory it allocates. So, when a MEMBER is created, m_next could well contain a spurious but seemingly plausible address.

```
/* new_member -- allocate memory for new member */

#include <string.h>
#include "list.h"

MEMBER * new_member(char *data)
{
 MEMBER *newmem;

 if((newmem=(MEMBER *)malloc(sizeof(MEMBER)))==(MEMBER *)0)
      fprintf(stderr, "out of memory in new_member\n");
 else
 {
      /* create memory to copy data into */
      newmem->m_data = (char *)malloc(strlen(data)+1);

      /* copy data into structure, assuming it is a string */
      strcpy(newmem->m_data, data);

      /* set the pointer in the structure to null */
      newmem->m_next = (MEMBER *)0;
 }
 return (newmem);
}
```

The next routine `add_member` adds a MEMBER to the list rooted in `*head`. You should be able to see that the routine always adds the new MEMBER to the very start of the list.

```
/* add_member -- add MEMBER to list */

#include "list.h"

void add_member(MEMBER **head, MEMBER *newmem)
{
 /* This simple routine pushes new member
  * onto the start of the list
  */

 newmem->m_next = *head;
 *head = newmem;
}
```

The final utility routine we shall examine is `free_list`. It takes a pointer rooted in `*head` and frees the memory used by all its constituent MEMBER structures. It also sets `*head` to the null pointer, making sure that `*head` does not contain a now meaningless value (if we did not, `*head` might be misused elsewhere).

```
/* free_list -- free entire list */

#include "list.h"

void free_list(MEMBER **head)
{
 MEMBER *curr, *next;

 for(curr = *head; curr != (MEMBER *)0; curr = next)
 {
       next = curr->m_next;
       /* free the memory created for the data */
       free((void *)curr->m_data);
       /* free the memory created for the list structure */
       free((void *)curr);
 }

 /* reset start of list pointer */
 *head = (MEMBER *)0;
}
```

The simple example program that follows puts everything together. It creates the same linked list we saw in Figure 12.1, then frees it. Notice the way the routine `printlist` scans through the list. Its `for` loop is very typical of programs that use linked lists.

```
/* test program for list routines */

#include "list.h"
```

```
char *strings[] = { "again", "world", "Hello"};

main()
{
 MEMBER *head, *newm;
 int j;

 /* initialize list */
 head = (MEMBER *)0;

 /* add members to list */
 for(j = 0; j < 3; j++)
 {
       newm = new_member(strings[j]);
       add_member(&head, newm);
 }

 /* display members of list */
 printlist(head);

 /* free list */
 free_list(&head);

 /* display members of list */
 printlist(head);
}
/* scan list and print */
void printlist(MEMBER *listhead)
{
 MEMBER *m;

 printf("\nList Contents:\n");

 if(listhead == (MEMBER *)0)
       printf("\t(empty)\n");
 else
       for(m = listhead; m != (MEMBER *)0; m = m->m_next)
            printf("\t%s\n", m->m_data);
}
```

Also notice the way we initialize the list at the beginning of the program by setting head to (MEMBER *)0. This is important, otherwise garbage may creep into the list, and again memory errors might result.

The program produces the following output:

```
List Contents:
 Hello
 world
 again

List Contents:
 (empty)
```

The brk *and* sbrk *calls*

For completeness, we should also mention the brk and sbrk calls. They are the primitive calls for dynamic memory allocation provided by UNIX. They work by adjusting the size of the process' data segment, or, to be more precise, the position of the first byte above the process' data segment. brk moves this position to an absolute address, while sbrk makes a relative adjustment. For most situations, you are very strongly advised to use malloc and its relations, not these two primitive calls.

Exercise 12.1   Our example linked list can be used to implement a stack where the member last added is the first used. add_member gives us the **push** operation; write the **pop** operation that removes the first element from the list.

Exercise 12.2   Write a program that uses members of the malloc family to create storage for a single integer, an array of float variables and an array of pointers to char.

12.3 Memory mapped I/O and memory manipulation

Whenever a process has to perform large amounts of disk I/O there is a performance overhead in copying the data from the disk to the kernel's internal buffers and then copying that same data into data structures contained in a user process. Memory mapped I/O increases the speed of file access by 'mapping' the file held on disk into a process' memory space directly. The routines to do this are mmap and munmap. As was seen in the shared memory examples in Section 8.3.4, manipulating data in a process' address space is the most efficient form of access. (However, although providing a speed increase in file access times, the use of memory mapped I/O on a large scale may reduce the amount of memory available to other memory allocation functions.)

   We will examine mmap and munmap shortly. First, let us introduce some simple routines to manipulate chunks of memory.

Usage

```
#include <string.h>

void * memset(void *buf, int character, size_t size);

void * memcpy(void *buf1, const void *buf2, size_t size);
void * memmove(void *buf1, const void *buf2, size_t size);

int memcmp(const void *buf1, const void *buf2, size_t size);

void * memchr(const void *buf, int character, size_t size);
```

For initialization purposes, `memset` can be used to set `size` bytes of `buf` to character.

To make a direct copy of one piece of memory to another you can use either `memcpy` or `memmove`. Both functions move `size` bytes of storage from the region starting at `buf2` to that starting at `buf1`. The difference between the two functions is that `memmove` ensures that if `buf1` and `buf2` overlap there will be no corruption of data during the move. To achieve this `memmove` copies `buf2` into a temporary array and then copies the data in the temporary array into `buf1`.

The function `memcmp` works in the same way as `strcmp`. So, if the first `size` bytes of `buf1` are the same as the first `size` bytes of `buf2` then `memcmp` will return 0.

`memchr` searches the first `size` bytes of `buf` and returns the address of the first occurrence of `character` or `NULL`. In general, the other routines return the value of the first pointer in the relevant parameter list.

The `mmap` and `munmap` system calls

Let us see how to set and unset the initial mapping. Memory mapped I/O is implemented through the `mmap` system call. `mmap` works on pages of memory and the file must be aligned on page boundaries within memory. `mmap` is defined as follows:

Usage

```
#include <sys/mman.h>

void * mmap(void *address, size_t length, int protection,
            int flags, int filedes, off_t offset);
```

The file in question must first be opened with the `open` system call. The file descriptor returned by `open` is then used as the `filedes` argument to `mmap`.

The first `mmap` argument, `address`, allows the programmer to specify where the mapping should start in the process' address space. As we saw with `shmat` in Section 8.3.4, the ability to specify the address means that the programmer needs to know how the process' memory is laid out. It is of course safer and more portable to allow the system to choose the starting address and this is achieved by setting `address` to 0. The return value from `mmap` is then the address of the start of the mapping. `mmap` returns `(void *)-1` if an error occurs.

The `offset` parameter determines where in the file to start mapping from. In most applications the programmer will want to map the whole file to memory, and therefore `offset` will be set to 0 – the beginning of the file. If `offset` is not 0, it must be a multiple of the memory's page size.

The number of bytes of the file to be mapped from the `offset` is specified by `length`. If `length` is not a multiple of the memory's page size, the actual `length` bytes are seen as expected, and the remainder of the page is zero filled.

The `protection` parameter determines whether data can be read, written, executed or accessed within the address space. `protection` can take one or more of the following values, as defined in <sys/mman.h>:

PROT_READ	Memory can be read.
PROT_WRITE	Memory can be written.
PROT_EXEC	Memory can be executed.
PROT_NONE	Memory cannot be accessed.

The value of `protection` must, however, match the way in which the file was opened.

The `flags` parameter affects the way in which a write to the file mapping is viewed by other processes. The following values are the most useful:

MAP_SHARED	Allows any changes to the region to be seen by other processes mapping the file, and modifications are written to the actual file.
MAP_PRIVATE	Modifications to the region are not seen by other processes, and are not written to the actual file.

Once the file has been mapped, it can be accessed via the memory locations directly. When a memory location is read the corresponding bytes of the file become visible.

When the process terminates, the file is unmapped. However, to force the unmapping to happen before program termination the `munmap` call can be used.

Usage

```
#include <sys/mman.h>

int munmap(void *address, size_t length);
```

If `MAP_SHARED` was set, the file is updated with any remaining changes. If `MAP_PRIVATE` was set, any modifications are discarded.

Beware that this function only unmaps the file from memory, it does not close the file. This should still be done with the `close` system call.

The following example is a repeat of the `copyfile` program we last saw in Section 11.4. The program opens both an input and an output file and copies one to the other. We have left out some error-handling for clarity.

```
#include <stdio.h>
#include <sys/mman.h>
#include <fcntl.h>

main(int argc, char **argv)
```

```
{
    int input, output;
    size_t filesize;
    void *source, *target;
    char endchar = '\0';

    /* check that the correct number of parameters have passed */
    if(argc != 3)
    {
        fprintf(stderr, "usage: copyfile source target\n");
        exit(1);
    }

    /* open both the input and output files */
    if((input = open(argv[1], O_RDONLY)) == -1)
    {
        fprintf(stderr, "Error opening file %s\n", argv[1]);
        exit(1);
    }

    if( (output = open(argv[2], O_RDWR | O_CREAT | O_TRUNC, 0666)) == -1)
    {
        close(input);
        fprintf(stderr, "Error opening file %s\n", argv[2]);
        exit(2);
    }

    /* create second file as same size as first file */
    filesize = lseek(input, 0, SEEK_END);
    lseek(output, filesize - 1, SEEK_SET);
    write(output, &endchar, 1);

    /* memory map both input and output files */
    if( (source = mmap(0, filesize, PROT_READ, MAP_SHARED, input,
                    0)) == (void *)-1)
    {
        fprintf(stderr, "Error mapping first file\n");
        exit(1);
    }

    if( (target = mmap(0, filesize, PROT_WRITE, MAP_SHARED, output,
                    0)) == (void *)-1)
    {
        fprintf(stderr, "Error mapping second file\n");
        exit(2);
    }

    /* copy */
    memcpy(target, source, filesize);

    /* unmap both files */
    munmap(source, filesize);
    munmap(target, filesize);
```

```
/* close both files */
close(input);
close(output);

exit(0);

}
```

Of course the files would be unmapped and closed at the natural termination of the program, we have added the lines here for completeness.

12.4 Time

UNIX provides a handful of routines for finding out and setting the system's idea of the time. Time is measured in terms of the number of seconds elapsed since 00:00:00 GMT, 1 January 1970, and this sort of figure must be held in at least a long integer. The system therefore provides a type time_t which is defined in <sys/types.h>.

The most basic call is time, a system call which returns the current time in the standard UNIX form.

Usage
#include <time.h>   time_t time(time_t *now);

After this call, now will contain the system's idea of the time. The time call also returns the current time through its return value, but this is normally ignored.

It is pretty hard for human beings to think in terms of large numbers of seconds, so UNIX provides a series of library routines for producing time information in a more understandable form. The most basic of these is ctime, which generates a 26-character string from the output of the time call. For example:

```
#include <time.h>

main()
{
  time_t timeval;

  time(&timeval);
  printf("The time is %s\n", ctime(&timeval));
  exit(0);
}
```

produces output like:

```
The time is Tue Mar 18 00:17:06 1998
```

and so proves how late some of us work, but not quite as late as the first edition!

Associated with ctime are a series of routines that use struct tm structures. The tm template is defined in the header file <time.h> to include the following members:

```
int    tm_sec;      /* seconds */
int    tm_min;      /* minutes */
int    tm_hour;     /* hours 0 to 24 */
int    tm_mday;     /* day of month 1 to 31 */
int    tm_mon;      /* month 0 to 11 */
int    tm_year;     /* year minus 1900 */
int    tm_wday;     /* weekday Sunday = 0 */
int    tm_yday;     /* day of year 0-365 */
int    tm_isdst;    /* daylight saving flag for USA only */
```

The purpose of each member should be self-explanatory. Some of the routines that use this structure are shown below.

Usage

```
#include <time.h>

struct tm * localtime(const time_t *timeval);

struct tm * gmtime(const time_t *timeval);

char * asctime(const struct tm *tptr);

time_t mktime(struct tm *tptr);

double difftime(time_t time1, time_t time2);
```

Both localtime and gmtime take a value previously obtained from time and convert it into a tm structure, returning local and GMT versions, respectively. For example:

```
/* tm -- tm struct demo */

#include <sys/types.h>
#include <time.h>

main()
{
  time_t t;
  struct tm *tp;

  /* get time from system */
  time(&t);

  /* get tm structure */
  tp = localtime(&t);
```

```
    printf("Time %d:%d:%d\n", tp->tm_hour, tp->tm_min, tp->tm_sec);
    exit(0);
}
```

produces a message like:

```
Time 1:13:23
```

asctime converts a tm structure into a ctime-like string and mktime converts a tm structure into its equivalent number of seconds. difftime returns the difference, in seconds, between two calendar time values.

Exercise 12.3   Write your own version of asctime.

Exercise 12.4   Write a function weekday that returns 1 if the day is a weekday, zero otherwise. Write its inverse weekend. Make this configurable in some way.

Exercise 12.5   Write routines that return the difference in days, months, years and seconds between two dates obtained from time. Remember leap years!

12.5 String and character manipulation

The UNIX libraries are rich in functions that manipulate string or character data. These are useful enough to warrant a brief examination.

12.5.1 The string family

We have already used some of these well-known routines in the text, for example, strcat and strcpy. A more extensive list follows.

Usage

```
#include <string.h>

char * strcat(char *s1, const char *s2);
char * strncat(char *s1, const char *s2, size_t length);

int strcmp(const char *s1, const char *s2);
int strncmp(const char *s1, const char *s2, size_t length);
int strcasecmp(const char *s1, const char *s2);
int strncasecmp(const char *s1, const char *s2, size_t length);

char *strcpy(char *s1, const char *s2);
char *strncpy(char *s1, const char *s2, size_t length);
char *strdup(const char *s1);
```

```
size_t strlen(const char *s1);

char * strchr(const char *s1, int c);
char * strrchr(const char *s1, int c);
char * strstr(const char *s1, const char *s2);

char * strpbrk(const char *s1, const char *s2);

size_t strspn(const char *s1, const char *s2);
size_t strcspn(const char *s1, const char *s2);

char * strtok(char *s1, const char *s2); /* first call */
char * strtok(NULL, const char *s2); /* later calls */
```

strcat concatenates s2 onto the end of s1. strncat does the same, but concatenates only length characters at the most. Both return a pointer to s1. An example usage of strcat is:

```
strcat(fileprefix, ".dat");
```

If fileprefix initially contains "file", it will end up containing "file.dat". An important point to note is that strcat alters the string pointed to by its first argument. This characteristic is shared by strncat, strcpy, strncpy and strtok. Since a C routine cannot find out the size of an array passed to it, a programmer must make sure that the first argument for these routines is large enough to hold the result of the requested operation.

strcmp compares the two strings s1 and s2, returning an indicator variable. If the return value is positive, it means s1 is lexicographically greater then s2 according to the ordering of the ASCII character set. A negative value means that s1 is lexicographically less than s2. If the return value is zero, the strings are identical. strncmp is similar, but compares only length characters at most. The strcasecmp and strncasecmp functions perform exactly the same comparisons but ignore differences in case. An example use of strcmp is:

```
if(strcmp(token, "print") == 0)
{
  /* process print keyword */
}
```

strcpy is a close relation to strcat. It copies the contents of s2 into s1, overwriting the original contents of s1. strncpy copies exactly length characters, truncating or adding nulls as necessary (which can mean that s1 is not null-terminated). strdup returns a pointer to a new duplicate of s1. The returned pointer can be passed to free, since the space comes from malloc.

strlen simply returns the length of s1. In other words, it returns the number of characters in s1, not including the terminating null.

strchr returns a pointer to the first occurrence of character c (actually declared as int) in string s1, or NULL if no match is found. strrchr does the same for the last occurrence of c. strstr returns a pointer to the first occurrence of the string s2 in the string s1. We used strrchr in Chapter 4 to strip off the initial pathname part of a filename:

```
/* strip off pathname part */
filename = strrchr(pathname, '/');
```

strpbrk returns a pointer to the first occurrence in s1 of any character in the string s2. The null pointer is returned if there is no match.

strspn returns the length of that part of the string s1, starting from the first character in s1, which consists entirely of characters from s2. strcspn returns the length of the initial segment of s1 which does not include any character from s2.

Finally, strtok allows a program to split a string s1 into individual lexical tokens. Here the string s2 contains the characters that can separate the tokens (for example: spaces, tabs and/or newlines). The first call, with the first argument set to s1, causes strtok to remember the string. A pointer to the first token will be returned. Subsequent calls, with the first argument set to NULL, will produce further tokens from s1. The null pointer is returned when no tokens remain.

12.5.2 String to numeric conversions

The ANSI C standard provides two sets of functions to convert strings to numbers:

Usage

```
#include <stdlib.h>

/* string to integer */
long int strtol(const char *str, char **endptr, int base);
long int atol(const char *str);
int atoi(const char *str);

/* string to double */
double strtod(const char *str, char **endptr);
double atof(const char *str);
```

The atoi, atol and atof functions take a string constant and convert it to an integer, long and double, respectively. However, these functions have now been superseded by strtol and strtod.

The strtod and strtol functions are far more robust. They both take the string str and strip off any white space at the beginning of the string and any unrecognizable characters at the end of the string (including the null character). They then store the string to be converted in endptr, as long as endptr is not null. The last strtol parameter, base, can be set to any value between 0 and 36 and the string will be converted to this specified base.

12.5.3 Characters: validation and conversion

UNIX provides two useful sets of macros and functions for manipulating characters, both of which are defined in the header file <ctype.h>. The first set, which is grouped under the heading ctype, is intended for validation of single characters. They are all Boolean macros which return 1 (*true*) if a condition is true, 0 (*false*) if it is not. For example, isalpha tests whether a character is a letter, that is, in the range a-z or A-Z, or not:

```
#include <ctype.h>
int c;
.
.
.
/* "isalpha" is a ctype macro */

if( isalpha(c) )
{
 /* process alphabetic character, i.e. a letter */
}
else
 warn("Character is not a letter");
```

Notice the way c is declared as an int. The full list of ctype macros is:

isalpha(c)   Is c a letter?

isupper(c)   Is c an upper-case letter?

islower(c)   Is c a lower-case letter?

isdigit(c)   Is c a digit (0–9)?

isxdigit(c)   Is c a hexadecimal digit?

isalnum(c)   Is c a letter or digit?

isspace(c)   Is c a white-space character; that is, one of space, tab, carriage-return, newline, form-feed or vertical-tab?

ispunct(c)   Is c a punctuation character?

isprint(c)   Is c a printable character? In the ASCII character set, this means any character in the range space (040) to tilde (~ or 0176).

isgraph(c)   Is c a printable character, and not a space?

iscntrl(c)   Is c a control character? ASCII delete is counted as a control character, as well as anything with a numeric value of less than 040.

isascii(c)   Is c in the ASCII character set at all? Note that an integer value passed to any of the other ctype routines must satisfy this test, with the one exception of EOF from <stdio.h> (this exception allows ctype macros to be used with getc, etc.).

The other set of character-based utilities is intended for simple character translation. For example, tolower is a function that translates an upper-case character to its lower-case equivalent, via its return value.

```
#include <ctype.h>
int newc, c;
.
.
.

/* translate upper case to lower case */
/* eg: map 'A' to 'a' */

newc = tolower(c);
```

If c is an upper-case letter, it is converted to lower case. Otherwise, it is left alone. The other routines and macros (which may be under the heading conv in your manual) are:

toupper(c)   A function that converts c to upper case, if it is a lower-case character. Otherwise it leaves c alone.

toascii(c)   A macro that converts a non-ASCII integer value to ASCII by stripping off non-ASCII bits.

_toupper(c)   A fast macro version of toupper that does no checking, and so must be passed a lower-case character.

_tolower(c)   A fast macro version of tolower, with similar limitations to _toupper.

12.6 Additional facilities

We have focused in this book on those calls and routines which we think give a useful grounding in UNIX system programming. If you have got this far, you will have the tools to solve a very large number of problems. UNIX is of course a rich system, and there are quite a few other routines which offer specialized functionality. This last section simply brings some of these to your attention. Try navigating your local manual for further details.

12.6.1 More about sockets

Sockets are a very powerful and popular way of communicating between processes and machines; Chapter 10 gave a brief introduction. If you want to know more, you should get a specialized text. As a first further step, you could investigate the following routines, which get information about the network environment:

```
gethostent        getservbyname
gethostbyaddr      getservbyport
gethostbyname      getservent
```

12.6.2 Threads

Threads are a lightweight version of a process – and systems supporting them allow you to run multiple threads within an existing process, all accessing data within the process. They can be very valuable for getting optimal performance for certain very special classes of problem – but they are generally complex to use. The UNIX process model is usually what is needed. Many versions of UNIX have supported various approaches for threads, but now standard models are included in *POSIX* and Version 5 of the *XSI* documentation. Try looking for routines in your manual with the prefix pthread_.

12.6.3 Real-time extensions

Recent POSIX work has added certain optional real-time extensions. Again, this is specialized and complex territory, and 'core' UNIX has sufficient power for most types of problem. Specific features for real time include:

- queuing for signals and additional signal features. (See sigwaitinfo, sigtimedwait, sigqueue.)

- priority/scheduling control. (Look for routines beginning with sched_.)

- more features on timers, asynchronous i/o and synchronous i/o.

- alternatives to the message passing, semaphone and shared memory interfaces we have covered. (Try looking for routines beginning with mq_, sem_ and shm_.)

12.6.4 Interrogating the local system

We have already covered many useful routines for this (such as pathconf). Other available facilities include:

sysconf	Gives access to system limits and configuration parameters held in <limits.h> and <unistd.h>.
uname	Returns a pointer to a utsname structure which contains a system name, a node name that might be used by the system on a communications network, and release and version data for UNIX itself.

`getpwent`	This family of routines allows access to data from the password file, `/etc/passwd`. All of the following calls return a pointer to a `passwd` structure which is defined in `<pwd.h>`. The calls which can be made are:

```
getpwnam(const char *username);
getpwuid(uid_t uid);
getpwent(void);
```

`getgrent`	This family of routines is concerned with accessing the group file, `/etc/group`.
`getrlimit`	Gives access to limits concerning system resources, such as memory or file space.
`getlogin,` `cuserid`	Gets login name for current process.

12.6.5 Internationalization

Many versions of UNIX will support various international flavours – allowing for differences in language, collation sequences, monetary symbols, numeric formats etc. Try looking for routines such as `setlocale`, or `catopen`. Your local manual may have details on relevant environment parameters under the heading `environ`.

12.6.6 Mathematical routines

UNIX provides a largish library of mathematical routines for the scientific or technical programmer. Some of these routines should be used in conjunction with the header file `<math.h>`, which includes function definitions, definitions for some important constants (such as e and π), and structure definitions to do with error handling. To use the majority of the routines we will touch on below, you will also need to link your programs against the UNIX maths library with a command like

cc -o mathprog mathprog.c -lm

The routines appear in UNIX manuals and the *XSI* under the following headings:

`abs`	Returns the absolute value of an integer. Part of the standard C library, so you do not need to link against the maths library.
`cbrt`	Finds the cube root of a number.
`div`	Computes the quotient and remainder of an integer division.
`drand48`	A set of functions to generate pseudo-random numbers. (See also `rand` – a simpler version.)

erf	The mathematical error function (which is not to be confused with error handling in the programming sense).
exp/log	A set of exponential and logarithmic functions.
floor	Routines for truncating or obtaining the absolute value of floating-point expressions. (See also ceil.)
frexp	Routines for manipulating parts of floating-part numbers.
gamma	A version of the log gamma function.
hypot	The Euclidean distance function. Useful for proving to your children that computers are really quite useful.
sinh	This heading covers sinh, cosh and tanh functions.
sqrt	Finds the square root of a number.
trig	Denotes a group of trigonometric functions: sin, cos, tan, asin, acos, atan and atan2. They may have their own individual manual entries.

APPENDIX A

errno error codes and associated messages

A.1 Introduction

As we saw first in Chapter 2, UNIX provides a set of standard error codes and messages that describe the errors that can be returned by system calls. More specifically, each system call error has an error number, a mnemonic code and a message string. These can be used by including the errno.h header file.

errno is set by a system call whenever an error occurs. In almost all cases, the system call will also return −1 to the calling process to tell it an error has arisen. errno can then be tested against the mnemonic codes defined in errno.h. For example:

```
#include <unistd.h>
#include <stdio.h>
#include <errno.h>

pid_t pid;
    .
    .
    .

if((pid = fork()) == -1)
{
 if(errno == EAGAIN)
        fprintf(stderr, "process limit reached, try again\n");
 else
        fprintf(stderr, "other error\n");
}
```

The external array `sys_errlist` is a table of the error messages printed by the `perror` routine. `errno` can be used as an index into the array when the message appropriate to an error situation is required. The external integer `sys_nerr` gives the current size of the `sys_errlist` table. `errno` should always be checked against `sys_nerr` if you want to index into `sys_errlist`, since new error numbers may be added before the string table is extended.

A.2 A list of error codes and messages

A list of the system call error messages follows. It is based on information from Issue 4.2 of the X/Open System Interfaces Standard. Each entry gives the mnemonic code from `errno.h`, the system error message contained in `sys_errlist` and a short description. Note that the text of the error messages may vary depending on the setting of the LC_MESSAGES category in the current **locale** (which is concerned with international use of UNIX).

E2BIG	*Argument list too long.* This often means that an over-long argument list (in terms of total number of bytes) has been passed to an `exec` call.
EACCES	*Permission denied.* A file permission error occurred. Can occur with `open`, `link`, `creat` and similar system calls. It can also be generated with `exec` if execution permission is not set.
EADDRINUSE	*Address in use.* This means that an address requested by a programmer is already in use.
EADDRNOTAVAIL	*Address not available.* This can occur if the programmer requests an address that is already in use by the process.
EAFNOSUPPORT	*Address family not supported.* When using the socket call interface an address family was specified that is not supported by this system.
EAGAIN	*Resource temporarily unavailable, try again later.* This usually means a particular system table is full. It can be generated by `fork` (too many processes) and the IPC calls (too many of a particular IPC object type).
EALREADY	*Connection already in progress.* This means that the connection, which is being attempted on a socket, has been rejected because the socket is already dealing with such a request.
EBADF	*Bad file descriptor.* This means that either a file descriptor does not represent an opened file, or that the access mode,

that is, read-only, write-only, does not allow the requested operation. Generated by a great many calls, including read and write.

EBADMSG

Bad message. This will be generated if a system call receives a message that it cannot read. For example, it would be generated if a read was made on the head of a STREAM and it received a STREAM control message rather than a data message.

EBUSY

Device or resource busy. Can be generated, for example, when a process tries to rmdir a directory which is being used by another process.

ECHILD

No child processes. wait or waitpid was called, but no suitable child processes existed.

ECONNABORTED

Connection aborted. The network connection has been aborted for some unspecified reason.

ECONNREFUSED

Connection refused. The queue of requests is full or no process is listening.

ECONNRESET

Connection reset. The connection has been closed by the other process.

EDEADLK

Resource deadlock would occur. This means that, if successful, the call would have produced a deadlock (in other words, a situation where two processes were sleeping, each awaiting an action from the other). This error can be set by fcntl and lockf.

EDESTADDRREQ

Destination request required. A required address was omitted from a socket operation.

EDOM

Domain error. A mathematics package error, it means that the argument of a function is outside the domain of that function. It can be set by the trig, exp and gamma functions, among others.

EDQUOT

Reserved.

EEXIST

File exists. This indicates that a file exists which prevents an operation from being carried out. Can be set by link, mkdir, mkfifo, shmget and open.

EFAULT

Bad address. Generated by the system after a memory protection hardware fault. Usually means an absurd address had been specified. The ability of systems to generate this error will vary considerably.

EFBIG	*File too large.* An attempt was made to extend a file beyond the process' file size limit (as set by ulimit) or the system's maximum file size.
EHOSTUNREACH	*Host is unreachable.* This will be generated by the network if the host is down or is unreachable by the router.
EIDRM	*Identifier removed.* This indicates that an IPC identifier, for example, a shared memory id, has been removed by the use of the ipcrm command.
EILSEQ	*Illegal byte sequence.* The character does not correspond to anything valid. Can be generated by calls to fprintf, and fscanf.
EINPROGRESS	*Connection in progress.* This means that a connect call will block until the socket is ready to accept it. In order for this to happen the O_NONBLOCK flag has to be set on the socket.
EINTR	*Interrupted function call.* Returned when a signal is caught while a program is executing a system call. (Only certain calls are affected – see local documentation.)
EINVAL	*Invalid argument.* Simply means an invalid parameter or set of parameters was passed to a system call. Can be generated by fcntl, sigaction and some of the IPC routines. Can also be set by mathematical routines.
EIO	*I/O error.* A physical error has occurred during I/O.
EISCONN	*Socket is connected.* The required socket already has a connection.
EISDIR	*Is a directory.* An attempt was made to open a directory file for writing. This error is generated by open, read or rename.
ELOOP	*Too many levels of symbolic links.* This is returned when the system has to follow too many symbolic links when trying to find a file or directory. This can be generated by any system call which has a pathname parameter.
EMFILE	*Too many open files in a process.* Occurs when a file is being opened; it means the per-process limit on open file descriptors has been reached. Limit specified by OPEN_MAX in <limits.h>.
EMLINK	*Too many links.* Generated by link when the maximum number of links associated with a single physical file has already been reached. Limit specified by LINK_MAX in <limits.h>.

EMSGSIZE   *Message too large.*   Generated on a network if the message sent is too large to store in the internal buffer of the receiver.

EMULTIHOP   *Reserved.*

ENAMETOOLONG   *Filename too long.*   This can either mean that an individual filename is longer than NAME_MAX or a pathname exceeds PATH_MAX. This can be returned for any system call which uses a pathname or filename as a parameter.

ENETDOWN   *Network is down.*

ENETUNREACH   *Network unreachable.*   No route is available to reach the required network.

ENFILE   *File table overflow.*   Generated by calls which return an open file descriptor (such as creat, open and pipe). It means that the internal file table within the kernel is full, and no more file descriptors can be opened.

ENOBUFS   *No buffer space is available.*   This call is pertinent to sockets. The error message is returned if no buffer space is available for any of the socket calls.

ENODATA   *No message available.*   Returned by a call to read when no message is waiting at the STREAM head.

ENODEV   *No such device.*   An attempt was made to perform an invalid system call on a device (such as reading a write-only device).

ENOENT   *No such file or directory.*   This occurs when no actual file corresponds to a pathname (for example, with open), or one of the directories in a pathname does not exist.

ENOEXEC   *Exec format error.*   The program file to be executed is not recognized as being in a valid executable format. Produced by exec.

ENOLCK   *No locks available.*   There are no more record locks available for an fcntl lock.

ENOLINK   *Reserved.*

ENOMEM   *Not enough space.*   A general memory error, occurring when a process asks for more space than the system can supply. Can be generated by exec, fork and the routines brk and sbrk, which are concerned with memory allocation.

ENOMSG   *No message of the desired type.* Returned when `msgrcv` cannot find a message or a message of the desired type on the message queue.

ENOPROTOOPT   *Protocol not available.* The desired protocol is not available to the socket system call.

ENOSPC   *No space left on device.* The device in question is full, and a file cannot be extended or a directory entry created. Can be generated by `write`, `creat`, `open`, `mknod` and `link`.

ENOSR   *No streams resources.* A temporary condition which is reported when a STREAMs memory resource is not available.

ENOSTR   *Not a STREAM.* Returned if a STREAMs function such as an `ioctl` 'push' is called on a non-STREAM device.

ENOSYS   *Function not implemented.* This means that a call was made to a system call which is not available in the current implementation.

ENOTCONN   *Socket not connected.* If a `sendmsg` or `rcvmsg` call is made on a socket which has no connection then this error is generated.

ENOTDIR   *Not a directory.* This occurs when a pathname does not represent a directory when the context demands it. Can be set by `chdir`, `mkdir`, `link` and many other calls.

ENOTEMPTY   *Directory not empty.* For example returned by `rmdir` if an attempt has been made to remove a directory which is not empty.

ENOTSOCK   *Not a socket.* A file descriptor used by a network call, such as `connect`, was not a socket descriptor.

ENOTTY   *Not a character device.* A call was made to `ioctl` on an open file that is not a special character device.

ENXIO   *No such device or address.* Occurs when an attempt is made to access a device, or device address, which does not exist. Offline devices can cause this error.

EOPNOTSUPP   *Operation not supported on a socket.* The address family associated with the socket does not support the function call.

EOVERFLOW	*Value too large to be stored in the data type.*
EPERM	*Operation not permitted.* This indicates that a process tried to manipulate a file in a manner allowed only to the file owner or superuser (root). It can also mean that an attempt was made to perform an operation allowed only to superuser.
EPIPE	*Broken pipe.* Set by write, to signify that an attempt was made to write on a pipe which is not open for reading by any process; in fact, this condition would normally cause the writing process to be interrupted by the signal SIGPIPE. EPIPE is only set if SIGPIPE is caught and the process does not terminate.
EPROTO	*Protocol error.* This error is device specific and indicates that a protocol error was received.
EPROTONOSUPPORT	*Protocol not supported.* This is returned by the socket system call if the address family is not supported by the system.
EPROTOTYPE	*Socket type not supported.* This is also returned by the socket call if the protocol type, such as SOCK_DGRAM, is not supported by the system.
ERANGE	*Result too large or too small.* A maths error, it means that the return value of a function cannot be represented on the host processor.
EROFS	*Read-only file system.* An attempt to write to, or modify, a directory entry, was made on a file system that has been mounted read-only for protection purposes.
ESPIPE	*Illegal seek.* A meaningless call to lseek was made on a pipe.
ESRCH	*No such process.* Non-existent process specified. Generated by kill.
ESTALE	*Reserved.*
ETIME	*ioctl timeout on a STREAM.* A timeout can be set on an ioctl call on a STREAM, this indicates that the timeout has failed. It could indicate that the timeout should be lengthened.
ETIMEDOUT	*Connection timed out.* When a process attempts to connect to another system it can be timed out if that system is down, or there are too many requests waiting for that particular connection.

ETXTBSY *Text file busy.* When generated by exec calls, it means that an attempt was made to run a shared-text program which is currently open for writing. When generated by calls which return a file descriptor, it means that an attempt was made to open for writing a shared-text program that is being executed.

EWOULDBLOCK *Operation would block.* If a socket has been opened as non-blocking and an operation such as read or write would normally block, then this error will be returned. EWOULDBLOCK should have the same value as EAGAIN in an *XSI* conformant system.

EXDEV *Cross-device link.* Occurs when link is called to link files across file systems.

APPENDIX B

Major standards

B.1 History

UNIX has had a long history since Ken Thomson, Dennis Ritchie and others started work on a 'little-used PDP-7 in a corner' in 1969. UNIX has appeared in a variety of guises since then, as a commercial offering, academic variant or the basis for standardization efforts.

Selected landmark versions or events include.

- *Sixth Edition* or *Version 6* (1975)   First widely available offering, at least in the technical community, and the basis for the first Berkeley UNIX.

- *Xenix* (1980)   A version from Microsoft – one of a number of oddly named commercial variants in the early eighties.

- *System V* (1983–92)   One of the most influential versions of UNIX from AT&T, the originators of UNIX. Descendant of Version 7 and the later System III.

- *Berkeley UNIX* (4.2 in 1984, 4.4 in 1993)   Arising out of work at Berkeley University, this again was one of the most important versions of UNIX, with many additional features.

- *POSIX* (1988 onwards)   A landmark set of standards from the IEEE (see below).

- *X/Open Portability Guides* (XPG3 in 1990, XPG4.2 in 1994)   A practical specification, unifying a number of base standards and industry practices. X/Open eventually acquired the UNIX trademark.

There have also been many commercial interactions, such as the movement of the UNIX brand from AT&T to Novell and then to X/Open, and the merger of

X/Open and the Open Software Foundation. This is a much simplified view of the past and a true family tree is very complex.

B.2 Key standards

The current standards relevant to this text include:

SVID

The *SVID* is at the AT&T *System V Interface Definition*. It was originally produced in the spring of 1985 to clarify a standard interface for the System V version of UNIX. The *SVID* had a number of releases, culminating in the third edition in 1989. The first edition of this book was based on the *SVID*.

ANSI C

The ANSI committee specifies standards for all manner of programming-related issues. The particular standard of interest to the UNIX systems programmer is ANSI C.

IEEE/POSIX

The Institute of Electrical and Electronics Engineers (IEEE) produces, among other things, the standard for a *Portable Operating Systems Interface* (*POSIX*) which is directly derived from UNIX. This standard was first published in 1988 and has had several updates since. The two most relevant baselines to this text are:

1. IEEE Std 1003.1-1990, which is identical to ISO POSIX-1 – ISO/IEC 9945-1: 1990, Information Technology – Portable Operating System Interface (POSIX) – Part 1: System Application Program Interface (API) [C Language].

2. IEEE Std 1003.2-1992, which is identical to ISO POSIX-2 – ISO/IEC 9945-2: 1993, Information Technology – Portable Operating System Interface (POSIX) – Part 2: Shell and Utilities.

Extensions and additions to these include: 1003.1b-1993, 1003.1c-1995, 1003.1i-1995 covering topics such as real time features and threads.

X/Open (now the Open Group)

The X/Open Group combined the standards mentioned above, and others, into one whole called the Common Applications Environment (*CAE*) Specification. The *CAE* covers both system interfaces and networking interfaces.

There have been a number of revisions since the first publication in July 1985. The most relevant text for this book is *Issue 4 Version 2 X/Open CAE Specification*, August 1994, System Interface and Headers. This represents a stable baseline, but note that Issue 5 of the CAE Specifications (1997) includes some of the more recent POSIX features for real time and threads, and other extensions from industry practice. This update is also included in the Open Group's *Version 2 of the Single UNIX Specification* and their *UNIX98* brand.

Bibliography and further reading

Bach, M.J. (1986) *The Design of the UNIX Operating System*. Prentice-Hall.

Curry, D.A. (1996) *UNIX System Programming for SVR4*. Sebastopol, CA: O'Reilly & Associates, Inc.

Dijkstra, E.W. (1968) 'Co-operating Sequential Processes' in Genugs, F. (ed.) *Programming Languages*. Academic Press.

Galimeister. B.O. (1995) *POSIX.4: Programming for the Real World*. Sebastopol, CA: O'Reilly & Associates, Inc.

Kernighan, B.W. and Pike, R. (1984) *The UNIX Programming Environment*. Prentice-Hall.

Kernighan, B.W. and Ritchie, D. (1978) *The C Programming Language*. Prentice-Hall.

Northrup, C.J. (1996) *Programming with UNIX Threads*. New York, NY: Wiley.

Stevens, W.R. (1992) *Advanced Programming in the UNIX Environment*. Reading, MA: Addison-Wesley.

Various. (1978) *The Bell System Technical Journal (Computer Science and Systems)*. AT&T Bell Laboratories. July–August.

Various. (1984) *AT&T Bell Laboratories Technical Journal (Computer Science and Systems), The UNIX System*. AT&T Bell Laboratories. July–August.

Index